TWO
AGAINST
THE NORTH

TWO AGAINST THE NORTH

by
ADA WHITE SHARPLES

 335843

THE DIAL PRESS   1961   NEW YORK

$4.50

DESIGNED BY WILLIAM R. MEINHARDT
MANUFACTURED IN THE UNITED STATES OF AMERICA
BY THE HADDON CRAFTSMEN, SCRANTON, PA.

TWO
AGAINST
THE NORTH

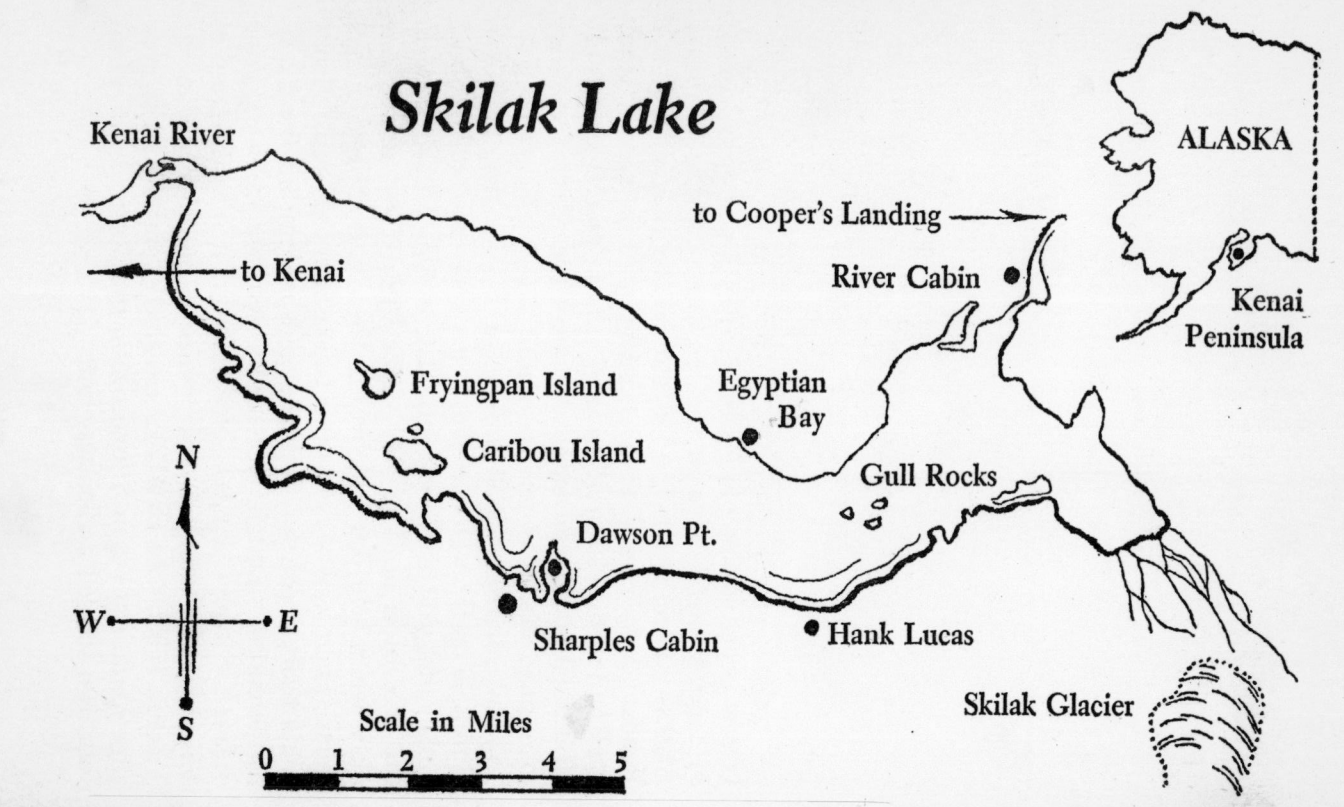

Skilak Lake

Kenai River

to Kenai

to Cooper's Landing

River Cabin

Fryingpan Island

Egyptian Bay

Caribou Island

Gull Rocks

N

Dawson Pt.

W   E

Sharples Cabin   Hank Lucas

S

Skilak Glacier

Scale in Miles

0   1   2   3   4   5

ALASKA

Kenai
Peninsula

CHAPTER 1

It was a cold morning in February, 1938. I sat apprehensively in a government office in the territorial capital of Juneau, Alaska, waiting to see the Director of the Bureau of Public Roads. Clerks smiled at me fleetingly as they passed busily back and forth. Half a dozen men were waiting there as well, all dressed in the conventional garb of the Alaskan working-man, plaid mackinaw and shoepacs.

Two of them stood looking at a large map of Kenai Peninsula on the wall near me; in low tones they talked about a road that was to be built one day, to Skilak Lake, deep in the wilderness heart of this virgin land. "Now there's one place where you can still live off the country," said one of them. There was a note of enthusiasm in his voice that I could well appreciate. To homestead, to "live off the land," in the enormous virgin areas of the territory was a recurring dream for many Alaskans. Not only did it offer the lure of adventure and complete independence, but to many in the Thirties, when jobs in Alaska remained painfully short even after conditions began to improve in the States, to go off on your own seemed a good way out.

3

I tried to shut out these voices. Their enthusiasm struck a responsive chord, but I had my own problems and this sort of dream did not seem to be the answer to them. My husband, Jack, had an appointment to apply for a job at the same hour as mine. What we really needed was for him to become established again. He had not had a permanent and secure job for almost seven years. It was a long time, and while he never mentioned it, I knew he feared that jobs would be even scarcer now that he had reached the age of fifty.

And even if he got the job he was after, there was a frightening stack of unpaid bills. Our tangled financial affairs could not be redeemed at one stroke. It would take time and I simply had to have this job.

Just then a clerk appeared and beckoned. "Mr. Williams will see you now," she said.

I jumped up eagerly. The door closed behind me and I was ready for a warm welcome. Mr. Williams was an old and dear friend; Jack and I had known him well ever since coming to Juneau. We were close neighbors and I had done occasional office work for him before, although it had never been a regular position.

To my surprise, however, he didn't get up at once. "Hello, there," he said. "Excuse me just a minute till I've signed these letters." His voice sounded oddly cold.

I felt a strange twinge of premonition, but sat down and tried to appear calm and poised. The large office, with its wide windows overlooking Gastineau Channel and the mountain peaks beyond, seemed curiously serene, far from the troubles that beset people like us.

"I'm surprised to find you applying for this position," he said frowning. "You know how I feel about married women working . . ."

"I'm applying for the job because I need it," I interrupted. If I hadn't needed the job so badly I would have told him he was old-fashioned. "I thought you might have changed your attitude by this time," I said tactfully. "So many married women work nowadays."

"No, I haven't changed," he said stubbornly. "You know as well as I do that it's the policy in government offices in Alaska not to hire married women. And I feel that in your case especially it would not be good."

"But why me? I need the salary and I'm competent . . ."

"I know that, honey, but Jack should make a living for you. You wouldn't be helping him by working."

"Jack is investigating a job this morning," I said, "as manager of a new store. He's sure to get it, but won't be established for some time. I just want to help."

"You can help Jack best by making him see it's his duty to support you," Mr. Williams said kindly but firmly. "He won't get anywhere until he stops drinking."

I trembled with shock at his words. It was agonizing to discuss this subject with anyone. No one had ever mentioned Jack's drinking to me before; no one had dared. But now through my agitation I felt suddenly grateful that someone cared enough to come out with it. "He's trying," I said, grateful that my voice was steady, "and I'm trying to help him. I believe a job is all he needs. He has just become discouraged."

"I'm very interested in both you and Jack," Williams said gently, "and I'd like to help you. But I can't believe this is the right course for you, Ada." He paused, then went on, "Actually the position you're applying for has already been filled. We hired a girl just out of high school."

The last vestige of my assurance vanished. Could it be he thought I was too old? I was forty-six and my hair was gray, but never before had I thought of being old. For a moment the thought was more overwhelming than the realization that I had failed to get the job.

"She'll have nothing to unlearn," he added, "and we can train her. I hope she'll be with us for many years."

"I hope she gets married next week." I laughed gaily, and made a face at him as I pulled on my gloves. He laughed too and came to the door with me.

It was a long walk home. I was scarcely aware of my surroundings until I turned into the steep road that wound

upward along the side of the mountain toward home. The
sharp air and vigorous climbing awakened me from the numb-
ness within. There were patches of snow along the sides of
the road, and the mountains on all sides were still white, but
spring was in the air. I could smell it.

As I walked I argued myself out of the prickly sense of
self. What had occurred was not important. Mr. Williams
had meant to be kind. It was his privilege to think as he
chose, and perhaps he was right.

It was true that Jack had been drinking a good deal
lately; I could not deny it. My heart ached for him, and I
could not blame him for being discouraged. Who wouldn't
be? The vicious circle had begun when he started his own
store in Washington, an ill-timed venture at the beginning
of the depression. Jack was bitterly disappointed when the
store did not go well, and finally sold out at a loss to return
to Alaska. He had always been successful here, but he soon
found that conditions had changed here too. His first job, in
a shoe store, ended after a few months when the owner
decided to move to California. Several temporary jobs had
followed, becoming fewer and less desirable as time passed.
Gradually his drinking became a problem. There had been
periods of joblessness, drink, more joblessness, more drink,
that led in an ever-widening spiral to this low point. We really
had our backs to the wall and had to find some way out.

I was sure he would stop drinking if only he had a good
job. I had almost despaired of his finding one until yesterday
when he came home whistling, to tell me about his appointment for this morning.

I was glad I hadn't told him of my own plans; now it
would not be necessary for me to tell him at all. My job was
to have been only an extra dividend.

The house was very quiet when I arrived. I called but there
was no answer. Jack could not have returned. I thought I
would have lunch ready when he came, but got no further
than the kitchen door. Jack stood leaning back against the
sink, his hands gripping the drainboard on each side, his chin

on his chest. He did not look up when I came in, and his face had a strange gray look that frightened me. Unk, our little black dog, sat at his feet, gazing into his face with troubled, anxious eyes. I looked for the signs I knew so well of an attempt to escape from reality. Not this time: the hurt was too deep.

"Darling, it doesn't matter," I said. "Don't care like that."

When he raised his eyes I saw absolute despair in their depths. Still holding onto the drainboard as if for support, he said dully, "Erickson told me he couldn't risk hiring an unstable manager."

"Oh, Jack!"

"I asked him to give me a minor job until I proved myself, but—" Jack swallowed, and went on with difficulty "—he said every other job had been filled."

I had no words to comfort him. Blindly I turned on the range and filled the teakettle. Dear God, what could I do? Suddenly the thought of the men looking at the map of Kenai Peninsula came to me. I heard the words again, "One place where you can live off the country . . ."

Suddenly I remembered that someone I knew actually lived on Kenai Peninsula, on an island in Skilak Lake, and had homesteaded there successfully for many years. Why shouldn't Jack and I go to some remote place like that and begin life over again?

The thought did not bring me peace: I knew we should be able to find a solution at home. Yet, I thought, the streams had dried up for us as they had for Elijah—and Elijah had accepted this as a sign to move on. Perhaps we should do the same.

From the window over the sink I looked across white fields to the Channel, where the black waters were dotted with fishing boats. In the background wooded mountains, wearing aloof white crowns, rose from the shore of Douglas Island. Worry about jobs and money was out of harmony with this beautiful land. I longed to be free.

I did not stop to consider; it was as if I dived blindly into icy water, my eyes shut tight. "Jack," I said, "would you be willing to leave Juneau? Would you be willing to go live on a homestead on Skilak Lake?" Even then a plan was taking shape in my mind.

Not a muscle of his gray face relaxed. I put my arms around him, but he was rigid as a statue. "Skilak?" he said tonelessly. "I never heard of Skilak Lake."

"Yes, you have," I said. "Mrs. Anderson—you know, the woman I write to about wildflowers—lives with her husband and son on an island there." The Andersons have lived there for years," I went on hurriedly. "They have very little money, she tells me, but they live a satisfactory life and are happy. She's described the country to me. It must be very beautiful."

I had started corresponding with Mrs. Anderson about five years earlier, when I was writing a book about Alaska wildflowers and was told she could give me information about the flowers in her area. Through our letters we had become friends. Mrs. Anderson seemed a fine, cultured woman, and she was a talented artist, as I knew from her exquisite watercolors of native flowers that she had sent me.

"I remember," Jack answered indifferently. "But why should *we* go out there?" He still would not look up.

I considered my words carefully. Why, indeed, should we give up what we had for an uncertain future? I had to have better reasons than my inner hunch that it was the right thing to do. "I was reminded of Skilak this morning," I said. "I heard some men in Mr. Williams's office talking about it. One of them said it was one place where you could still live off the country, and that kind of idea of a homestead has always appealed to me. We could be free there, and make our own way. It would be a fresh start for both of us. We both love that kind of life, and I know we could stand the hardships. We can do anything," I said forcefully, "if we work together."

Jack made no response. "It occurred to me," I went on

nervously, "that if we did decide to take up a homestead, Skilak would be a good place to go. The Andersons would be good neighbors and could give us any information we need."

Jack turned from me and shrugged coldly. "We haven't enough money for that kind of nonsense."

"We have a house."

"We have a house with a mortgage on it."

My determination was rising despite his opposition.

"I know there's a mortgage on our home," I agreed, "but it's only a small one." "Besides, the Holdens have told us they will buy the house any time we want to give it up. There'd be at least a few thousand left when our debts are paid—enough to make the move and get settled."

"I'd never sell the house," Jack protested. "It means too much to you."

Suddenly my throat seemed to close. He was right. Selling the house would be like cutting off my right arm. But I pushed on doggedly.

"It doesn't mean anything at all," I said cheerfully. "We'll have a home wherever we are."

"But we're too old to make a fresh start," he objected. "We aren't kids any more."

"No," I replied. "We're old enough to be careful and young enough for adventure. We're just the right age: kids wouldn't be interested."

I could see the idea working its spell on Jack now. He loved the rough, primitive wilderness as I did, and I knew that striking out on his own appealed to him deeply. "But, hon," he said doubtfully, "can we just drop everything and run off to something we know nothing about?"

"No dear," I said. "But we must do *something*. We just don't seem to have much of a future here."

"But we can't be irresponsible," Jack said with a frown.

"Why not?" I asked recklessly. "What difference does it make to anyone but ourselves? It isn't as if we had children or anyone dependent on us. We're not tied here in any way.

We're free to do anything we dare." I tried to arouse him with one final appeal. "It must be an inner urgency, Jack," I said. "It's something like—" I hesitated and searched my brain for an example "—something like the urge that makes the birds migrate." I began to laugh, realizing how ridiculous my words sounded. Jack looked up at me, startled. "Would the birds believe it," I went on, "if they were told that they wouldn't find enough to eat on the way—or that they might get tired flying, or lose their way? They just know they want to."

"We're not birds," Jack said. "That's silly." But he managed a tired little grin. His head did not droop again.

And so, sitting in our kitchen as the short Alaska day ended, we continued for hours to discuss the idea. We admitted it was a slap-happy notion, but neither of us could find a better one. I felt encouraged that Jack at last took enough interest to give his attention fully to the idea. Even if he did raise objections, I thought, he was considering it as a concrete possibility.

Jack became full of practical questions. "What does Mr. Anderson do for a living?" he asked.

"Well, he's licensed to guide hunters and there's considerable trapping around there." By this time I could see only the rosy side of the plan.

"I couldn't qualify as a guide," Jack said dubiously, "and I don't know how to trap."

"Oh, you can learn to trap," I said. "Besides, that's only one possibility. Others will come up as we go along."

I had kept a thick file of letters that Mrs. Anderson had written me. They were long letters that an isolated woman who was very lonely would write, although she made their life sound very interesting. She had given me a great deal of information not only about wildflowers, but also about their own way of life.

That night we got out her letters and reread them together. They gave birth to a new thought. "Ever since I finished my book," I told Jack, "I've wanted to start a business of selling wildflower seeds by mail. I could do that on Skilak, where the climate is drier. In Juneau it rains too much for the seeds to mature."

"The climate *would* be different, I suppose," Jack said. "Much drier, and colder in winter."

"That's right," I replied, "but the growing season ought to be long enough in that area for wildflowers. It seems to me a seed business would be a real possibility for future income. I intend to go right on with my study of wildflowers, and I'd like to continue writing about them. There's a market for articles in horticultural magazines and books. We won't have much time at first, but once we're settled . . ."

"And perhaps I *could* learn to trap," Jack interrupted, "and there may be some chance of my getting work in summer."

"We'll have a lot of questions for the Andersons."

We included a long list of questions in a letter to Mrs. Anderson we sent off next day. Would they like to have us for neighbors? How would supplies be delivered, and at what cost? Were there other islands besides theirs in the lake? Did they produce most of their food? How far would we have to travel for mail? Should we dispose of our household goods or bring them with us? We also took pains to make our position very plain, saying that we had very little money, and eventually would have to depend on what little we could earn.

After a maddening delay Mrs. Anderson's reply arrived. I flew home from the post office to open it.

They would be delighted to have us for neighbors, she said. She suggested that if we came that year we should not wait longer than absolutely necessary as the summers were very short. She also very kindly offered us lodging over the winter, saying that we would need several months to pick a homestead and clear and prepare it before we would want to start building a house.

We would go by boat to Seward; then by train thirty
miles to Moose Pass. From there a truck would haul our
goods to Cooper's Landing, another thirty miles, where Mr.
Anderson would meet us in his boat and transport us down
the Kenai River to the lake. He would not charge us much,
since they would be so glad to have us.

Mail was delivered at Cooper's Landing every two weeks.
There were no other islands in the lake suitable for homesteading and we would have to settle on the mainland. A
trip for mail would include crossing the lake by boat, a ten-
mile hike, and seven miles by car if you were lucky enough to
get a ride. This sounded formidable, but it was a comfort
to remember that they had lived there for eighteen years and
liked it.

Their garden produced an abundance of vegetables, but
there was no market for produce for lack of transportation. It
was the only place in Alaska where I heard that string beans
could be raised. Mrs. Anderson said that tomatoes would
sometimes ripen. The climate was evidently very different
from that of Juneau, colder in winter, but with a light rainfall and much sunshine.

Our hopes that Jack might earn a little extra money at a
job were dashed. Mr. Anderson, we were told, had not been
earning much as a guide lately, since the use of airplanes had
changed hunting in the area. His main source of income came
from trapping coyotes in winter, for the Territory paid a
bounty of twenty dollars each and he sold the skins as well.

However, we could live very cheaply, Mrs. Anderson
wrote. Game and fish were plentiful, and they bought only
warm clothes, and such necessities as flour, sugar, and gasoline for the outboard motor. As for household goods, Mrs.
Anderson advised bringing everything with us. We would
need furniture, and her husband was equipped to haul our
freight down the difficult and dangerous river and across the
lake.

In spite of her cheerful instructions, my heart sank when

I thought of our furniture, including heirlooms from my family home in South Carolina. We finally decided to store the furniture and send for it later when we had a house built for it.

Another problem would be to uproot Unk from the only home he had ever known. Unk was not just a dog; he was one of us. His mother was a small black cocker spaniel. He had inherited her size and her short bowed legs, but his coat was smooth and shining. This was because his other parent was a big black Labrador retriever. This also accounted for his long hound's tail and the shape of his head. Unk was far from handsome; in fact, he was built like a flatcar. But he possessed the dignity of a British butler, and a heart full of loyalty and dog wisdom.

He was only a pup when Jack brought him home in his overcoat pocket one cold midwinter night. I loved dogs but this one seemed a little mongrel with no charm, and I had never liked black dogs. That he proved to be unhousebroken was just too much, and I demanded that Jack take him back in the morning. But somehow he was never taken back. He learned quickly and made a place for himself in our hearts. We named him "Unk" for Jack's favorite uncle in Illinois. People would say, "What's that you call your dog? Unk? Oh, an Indian name!"

Already one blessing had come as a result of our plans: Jack and I were drawn closer together than we had been for a long time. We spent long hours figuring and exchanging ideas. We avoided our friends; we would explain later. I know now that many of our hopes were based on wishful thinking, but in those days we walked by faith.

One day, while our bridges were burning merrily behind us, Jack swept into the house on a blast of April wind.

"Well," he said with feigned calmness, "I've got a job."

"A job?" I gasped.

"Yes. The Alaska Construction Company has a contract to build two bridges on the highway beyond Moose Pass, and a friend of mine is hiring. There was only one job in the camp that required no special skill, and I accepted it before I knew what it was." He was chuckling happily. "He offered me the job of assistant to the cook."

"What kind of a job is that?"

"Well, I'll wait on table and help the cook at such things as peeling potatoes and washing dishes. In other words, I'll be the cookhouse flunky."

Was that anything to be so radiant about? I was sick with disappointment. "You didn't take it!" I exclaimed. "You'd hate it! You've never done work like that."

Quietly he took hold of my hands. "I decided a long time ago," he said, "that I would take the first job I could get, no matter what it was. It's only for a few months." His grin was easy and confident. It had taken only this small morsel of success to bring about a magical change in him.

"It isn't worth changing our plans for," I argued weakly.

"Well," he said hesitantly, "I was wondering if we would have to change our plans. What if you went on alone? The Andersons have offered to put us up, and you could pick a spot for our home and I could come in the fall to work on it when the construction job is done."

My heart ached at the thought of being separated from Jack. "Do you think it's really necessary?" I said.

"Yes, I'm afraid so," he replied. "We just don't know how long it will take to become self-sufficient, and we'll need every cent to tide us over."

I knew he was right, and in my heart was overjoyed at his renewed confidence and initiative. Besides, I saw some consolation in the news. "Well, at least Moose Pass is on the way to Skilak Lake," I said. "This will be the first step. It must be an omen." I had always been able to recognize an omen. Why not? Wasn't I the thirteenth child in my family and born on Friday?"

Jack had to leave at once, so it fell to me to sell the house that had been our home for most of our married life. Instead of returning to his home in Chicago at the end of World War I, Jack had come to Juneau when he was released from the Army. We met there a year later when I came to work as a newspaper reporter.

Jack's concern grew as he realized what a task he was leaving me. "Can you do all this alone, hon?" he asked anxiously. "Maybe I should wait for a later boat and help you sell the house and finish up the details."

"No, that isn't necessary," I insisted. "I can get a lawyer, and a man to help with the packing. You must go on to your work. Don't worry about me."

At this point I discovered I had a faculty I had not known I possessed: I could close my mind to fears and unpleasantness, to the wrench of leaving the old house and the worries about the new life, and not think about them. This might not have worked, when I told Jack a tearful good-bye, if I had not had so much work to do. I was more calm than Jack was.

Selling our home and packing our possessions was not nearly so difficult as telling our incredulous friends and listening to their pity and discouragement. "How will you make a living?" they wanted to know. "Terrible things could happen to you. Suppose you have to have an emergency operation?" Many of their questions I could not answer. They were exactly like the arguments against leaving my home in the South years before. I had gained courage from the fact that this had not been disastrous. Besides, I had Jack now.

Unk convinced me that he had ideas of his own about these unusual preparations. We had never used a leash for him but one would be necessary for the trip. Something told me he would rebel at a collar, so I bought a leather harness that would be more comfortable. I buckled it on him so that he would become used to it, and rushed off to do an errand downtown. On my return, Unk was sitting in the middle of the living room floor, surrounded by tiny bits of chewed leather. His tail did not wag and his unrepentant eyes said very plainly, "It won't be necessary for you to lead me. Just let me show you where to go." I didn't entirely trust him though, and thereupon got a stout collar and leash.

The half-hour whistle blew hoarsely. The smiling faces that looked up at me from the dock were so kind. More than one voice called out, "You'll be back." But I knew that our life in Juneau was ended.

The figures on the dock were dimmed for a moment by tears, and soon they began to grow smaller as the ship began to move. It was as if a cable that connected me with the old life was being stretched thinner and thinner until at last it parted.

I watched until I could not distinguish one figure on the dock from another. Then I turned to go and see about Unk. I had left him wildly struggling to follow me, as a steward grasped his leash with both hands. I had to bid him a temporary farewell, for he was to be quartered down in the hold.

Even if I had been allowed to visit him there, which I was not, I could not have lifted my head from the pillow while the boat cavorted across the open waters of the Gulf of Alaska. But at Cordova, two nights and a day later, Unk and I were reunited. The steward, unprepared for his enthusiasm at the sight of me, allowed the leash to zip from his hand, and Unk tripped and scattered disembarking passengers right and left.

When he had decided that I was really me, he let me lead him ashore for exercise. He was as pleased as I to land on a surface that did not rise and fall.

A tourist gushed, "What a cute dachshund!" and I was afraid Unk would resent it. But he had something else on his mind. At the bottom of the gangplank he dragged me helplessly toward a piling, where I turned my back to the crowd and stared into space while he relieved himself of his accumulated frustrations. There was no use pulling on the leash until what seemed an hour had passed, and Unk lowered his leg and glared disdainfully at the tittering spectators.

Out of Seward he loathed the baggage coach of the train as much as he had detested the boat. As we traveled, when the conductor opened the car door faint outraged howls were wafted through with the smell of coal smoke.

When we got in the car at Moose Pass for the next leg of our journey to Cooper's Landing, I held Unk in my arms. His troubled eyes never left my face.

CHAPTER 2

"I HEAR ANDY'S MOTOR!" Charlie Lean called out to me late one afternoon from the door of my cabin. For three days I had been a guest of the Leans while awaiting the arrival of Mr. Anderson to take me in his boat to Skilak Lake. We were only sixty miles from Seward, but so isolated and remote was this small settlement of Cooper's Landing, spread along the banks of the Kenai River in the hollow of tall mountains, that it seemed more like six hundred. Jack Lean, Charlie's brother, kept the little store. The Andersons lived about twenty-five miles farther on. I had expected Mr. Anderson to be at the Landing to meet me, but Charlie explained that a north wind was blowing that would prevent him from crossing the lake, hence the delay.

I hurried out just in time to see a sturdy outboard-motor-boat pull up to the dock. Two men sprang out nimbly and strode up to greet us, and Charlie made the introductions. The dark thin man with the small graying mustache was Mr. Anderson. His first name was Hjalmar but everybody called him Andy. The young man with the sun-bleached blond hair and twin cowlicks was Cliff, Mrs. Anderson's nephew, who had come from Seattle several years before to live with them and help with the work. I wondered if they were as interested in our meeting as I was.

Mr. Anderson was about Jack's age and Cliff possibly twenty-five. They both wore their hair quite long—probably because they never saw a barber and home haircuts were a bother. Mr. Anderson spoke with a very slight accent, and I remembered his wife had told me he had come to America from Sweden when he was twelve. I had thought all Swedes were blond, but Andy was dark, his complexion tanned by sun and wind. His figure was spare and agile, and there was an air of competence and quiet strength about him that inspired immediate trust.

Cliff looked hardly more than a boy. He smiled when our eyes met, and there was something very gentle and appealing about him. I liked both of them at once, and my spirits, which had been drooping during my wait, rose sharply once more.

It was too late to start out that day, so we all stayed over with the Leans. At dinner that night Charlie Lean told one story that made me think I might be letting myself in for more than I'd bargained for.

"A couple of weeks ago Nick here," he nodded at his fourteen-year-old son, "gave us an awful scare. He and I were huntin' over there on that mountain." He pointed through the window at one of the great peaks that rose abruptly on the other side of the river. "We came on a big brown bear. I shot it but only wounded it. Nick was nearer to it than I was, and it charged him. It happened so quick it was on him before I could pull the trigger again. I shot carefully that time. Nick was wearing a heavy packsack on his back and that saved him. Even so, his back was badly torn."

"It's almost healed now," Mrs. Lean added. "I still can't bear to think about it. I haven't slept soundly since."

"Yes," Charlie went on, "that was a close call. You can never tell what a brownie will do. Most of them run, but once in a while one will charge."

At the thought of charging bears my heart quailed within

me. I'd hoped I'd never run into *any* bears, of whatever disposition.

"There's a law against shootin' game from a plane, but
they often spot it from the air, and land on some lake or
river, get it quick, and rush back to the city with their tro-
phies. The old fellows around—Dunc Little, Frank Towle,
and the others—won't give up. They expect the old days to
come back, but they're gone forever."

After supper, Charlie took me to the woodshed and
brought out a grinning death's head. "This is the skull of that
bear," he said. "See what a big one it was?" To me it looked
like the skull of a hippopotamus. "I didn't keep the hide,"
Charlie went on. "Wasn't any good—had been rubbed too
badly."

I could not avoid a violent shudder, and asked in a small
voice, "Are there any bears around Skilak Lake?"

"The biggest in the world," he answered with a teasing
smile. "Mr. Sharples will have to practice shootin'."

Next day at noon, Andy carefully settled Unk and me in
the very center of his boat, with my luggage stowed around us.
"The boat must be balanced well," he explained. "We'll pass
through some rough water."

Cliff sat silently in the bow with the oars and Andy seated
himself in the stern, with an alert hand on the steering rod
of the outboard motor. He started the motor as soon as Cliff
had guided the boat into the current of the river, and with a
loud sputter we quickly lost sight of the knot of people who
waved good-bye from the dock. When we were moving along
rapidly, Andy shut off the motor, and we drifted in the current.

The two men appeared confident but wary. Andy wore
a red bandanna as a turban, and Cliff's blond hair was held by
a band around his head, Indian fashion. Evidently they did
not wish to be distracted by their long hair falling into their
eyes.

"This is the mouth of Russian River," Andy explained, as
we were swept past the place where the two rivers met in a

turbulent froth. Two men who were fly-casting from the bank waved at us. In a flash they had disappeared.

Afterward I was very grateful that I had that ride down the Kenai at the very beginning of my experience, before I had been influenced by many tales of danger and narrow escapes and before I had learned of its treachery. As it was, I enjoyed myself immensely; I had absolute confidence in my navigators.

From Seward on there had been a gradual change in the vegetation. Since Seward was on the ocean it was much like the part of southeastern Alaska I knew so well. The vegetation was lush and jungle-like in the abundant rains. Here it was much thinner. Along the hillsides columns of white spruce were intermingled with birch, both brown and paper-white. Small alders and willows grew along the river banks, with an occasional clump of tall cottonwoods.

"We have to keep a sharp lookout for 'sweepers,'" Andy warned.

"Sweepers?" I asked. "What are they?"

He pointed to a huge spruce on the bank with the soil washed from its feet. It leaned out over the rushing water, earthbound by only a few roots, its great evergreen top bowing and dipping in the current, beating the water into spume. "We could easily be swept into one like that and be overturned." By the time Andy had finished the sentence we had left the "sweeper" far behind. The current then quickened and became troubled. "Now it's the rocks below the surface you've got to look out for," he went on. "You have to read the water here."

Andy and Cliff became even more watchful as the water boiled and eddied around the tops of rocks that were barely visible above the surface. The boat leaped and lurched, but Andy grimly held it in its course through the maze of boulders. Cliff's work was to fend the boat off the rocks with the oars. At times a crash appeared to be inevitable but he would thrust out an oar like a fencer's rapier just in time.

"This is what's called 'white water,' isn't it?" I asked,

not in the least afraid. Andy nodded, too busy to speak. "What do you mean by 'reading' water?" I questioned, when we hit a stretch of quieter water.

Andy smiled. "Well, you see a little riffle and that tells you there's a boulder underneath. Then you've got to judge from the riffle how far down the boulder lies." He started the motor again, and we could not talk for the noise.

Ahead the stream ran head on into an island with big trees growing on it, and divided in two. Along one branch were several sweepers, so we followed the other. Soon the two flowed together again, and the river went hurrying on to keep its appointment with Skilak Lake. The white water ended. Andy shut off the motor and the boat drifted smoothly once more.

"Look!" Andy called, pointing to a mother duck swimming near the shore with a flock of babies. She became frightened upon seeing us and began to swim frantically. Her babies could not keep up with her, and she suddenly submerged beneath them and came up with the ducklings clinging to her back. Away she went, yellow feet paddling madly. We passed close enough for me to see the fear and triumph in her eyes. "That's a merganser," Andy explained. "See the crest on its head?"

The smooth water soon ended, and Andy started the motor again. "Canyon's just ahead," he said.

Andy and Cliff seemed to be prepared for what happened next, but I was not. The boat was caught in a whirlpool and spun dizzily around, so that for one tense moment we traveled stern first. All of Andy's strength was needed to hold the motor steady and Cliff dug in with the oars to help him. Slowly the boat swung back to equilibrium.

In a matter of seconds the swirling water swept us through the opening of the canyon. A channel had been cut by the river through solid rock and the walls were compressed into a narrow passage. Dark, smooth palisades, twenty feet high, towered on each side. Andy used the entire power of the motor to retain control and prevent the boat from being dashed against the walls. This force, added to that of the racing water, carried the boat at breath-taking speed. I noticed, however, that small plants, shining with moisture, clung tenaciously to the rocks above my head. They seemed to be glued to the impervious stone, but I knew that their roots had found tiny cracks through which they grew, nurtured by the spray from the turbulent river.

When we had emerged between low banks again, I found it impossible to reckon the length of the canyon. My impression had been only of a few moments of madly flowing water and the echo of the motor against the rock walls. I was surprised to find that I was wet from the spray.

Once more we drifted, but there was nothing slow or lazy about it. A heavy, dark spruce forest whipped by us on both sides. "We're almost to the lake," Andy said, and my heart quickened its beat. I leaned forward eagerly.

Abruptly the forest parted in front of us and opened into space filled with glassy water, sky, and light. The water of the river, clear against the milkiness of glacier-fed Skilak Lake, entered it with such force that the current continued far out into the lake, carrying the boat with it.

Suddenly there was no longer any momentum, and the boat slowed to a stop. Cliff rowed to the beach, and he and Andy pulled the boat up on the gravel and filled the tank with gasoline. Evidently I was not expected to get out, so I swung around in my seat and looked back, receiving for the first time the full impact of the lake spread out before me. I was meeting it face to face.

There appeared to be no limit to the blank, impersonal vastness of water that stretched endlessly toward the west. I could not believe that the lake was only twenty miles long, as Mrs. Anderson had told me. I could not explain my reaction to the lake; I only knew that I was repelled, vaguely frightened, and painfully disappointed.

Strange that I should have been so wrong about what it

would be like! Mrs. Anderson had described it vividly in her letters, but my wishful thinking had pictured it tucked away among mountain peaks, so intimate that I could grasp it all at once. I knew it would be big, and I had expected it to be wild and lonely and rugged—all Alaska was like that, which was why I loved it so. But in a flash of intuition I knew that I would never understand the lake and would always have to fight it. Unk leaned against me and I could feel him trembling.

How on earth could I have been so sure that this was the right move for us? I had made a terrible mistake. I had persuaded Jack and been unfair to him. He would hate the lake and blame me. Doubt and panic tore at me.

The men must not see, I thought; they would never understand. The motor needed adjustment, and they conferred together, talking in low tones.

I turned around and looked away from the lake, back to the mouth of the river from which we had been ejected. I had a wild desire to jump out of the boat and go running through the woods, back to Juneau, back to some place where I belonged. But there was nothing for me in Juneau now; someone else was living in our home. I could not possibly go back. Only Jack remained to me, and he was out of my reach. I could not visualize him in a strange work camp, washing dishes. I felt that I had wrecked our lives. Tears began to roll down my cheeks.

Andy and Cliff had removed the motor and were working on it. Fortunately it took them a long time, and while they worked I was able to think more calmly. Gradually I saw that I had been acting childishly. There was nothing about the lake that I should not have realized before. The Andersons had lived there alone for years, and Jack and I would have the advantage of these kind neighbors. There was no sense in my being bowled over because the lake was bigger than I had expected it to be.

The thought of Jessie Anderson waiting for me at the

end of the journey brought me back to complete normality. In Jessie's welcome my fears would only be something for us to laugh at together. I would learn to see this country through her wholesome eyes.

Andy pulled the starting cord and the motor coughed and burst into little explosions. He turned to me with a smile. "We had to fix the wiring," he explained. "Sorry you had to wait." Surrendering the steering rod to Cliff, he balanced himself with the movement of the boat and came to sit near me.

We traveled down the middle of the lake, the boat a tiny speck on the immense sheet of water. I could not make out objects on the faraway shore, but there were tall cliffs of rock at the water's edge, and mountains rising harshly from the beach.

"The place where the old dead glacier empties into the lake is on the other side of that mountain," he pointed out. "The Kenai River drains the lake into the ocean to the west, but the mouth is too far away from here to see."

Soon we passed a cluster of rocky islands. Andy pointed to a great multitude of screaming gulls that took flight at the approach of the boat. "They nest here," he shouted above the strident cackling and the sputter of the motor; "hatching's just finished."

The water was perfectly calm. Sky and water reflected soft buff and blue, becoming orange where the sun was about to set behind islands far in the distance.

As we traveled and the lake widened, the scenery changed. The mountains no longer thrust up from the water's edge, but there was a flat foreground between them and the shore. The islands in the distance were growing steadily bigger.

I sensed that Andy loved his home deeply and wanted me to see the beauty he saw there. "We came to Caribou Island eighteen years ago, just after we were married," he said. "We've homesteaded it, and now it belongs to us. The island contains just one hundred and sixty acres, the number that one is allowed to homestead." I nodded and smiled. My spirits were soaring again. "The little island close to Caribou we call Little Caribou. There's Fryingpan Island," he continued, pointing to an island almost as large as Caribou, with dark spruce-covered slopes, outlined against the salmon-colored sky. "It's shaped like a frying pan; there's a long spit on the other side that looks like a handle. Art Frisbie has homesteaded that. He works on the Yukon River in summer and will be down this winter."

We were rapidly approaching a wharf on a large island. There was a log house among the trees, with a column of smoke rising into the still air. The Anderson homestead appeared under the most favorable circumstances in that June sunset.

A large dark-haired woman hurried through the gate and down to the wharf. Andy leaped into the water, shallow enough now so that it did not reach the top of his rubber boots, and left the landing to Cliff. He quickly kissed the woman and, turning to me with an old-world bow, introduced his wife with very evident pride.

I was so surprised I could not remove my eyes from her. What astonished me most was that she was so large. I afterward learned that she weighed around three hundred pounds, but she was not grossly fat. She was wide-shouldered and well proportioned and wore a becoming yellow silk afternoon dress. She was, I thought, probably between thirty-five and forty. I had understood that her health was poor, but she looked the picture of vitality. Her abundant black hair was elaborately curled. I found later that this meant hours of heating old-fashioned curling irons in the chimney of a kerosene lamp. The curls were drawn low over her face, covering her forehead and ears so that she looked like a star of the silent movies.

She offered me a soft and well-kept hand. This was no hard-bitten pioneer woman. From her letters I had gathered that she was serenely content in helping her husband conquer the wilderness, but this woman looked far from serene. I found something disturbing about her in spite of her laughing welcome and hearty voice. I had expected our friendship to be as it had been in our letters, but she seemed an entire stranger. I shook off my disappointment; we would soon become acquainted.

She was dressed with evident care and elaborately made up. Her small, even white teeth were in sharp contrast to precisely reddened lips. From her black eyes little sparks of light darted constantly.

A tall boy came running and leaping, and I remembered that there was a twelve-year-old son named Valdemar, or Val. His long straight hair flopped about as he ran, so that I thought at first he was a girl dressed in jeans. He was at the gawky age and somewhat resembled his father, and I thought that he must look like a young Swedish boy. When I saw him come close to his mother and surreptitiously hold on to a fold of her skirt, I realized how painfully shy he was. He did not look at me but laughed loudly, and when I moved in his direction, Val backed away like an unbroken colt.

We walked along a flagstone path to the door. The log house, with its sheltering birches and smooth emerald green lawn, was lovely. The roof was covered with thick hand-split shakes, warped by sun and wind, giving the appearance of an old-world thatched roof. Swallows twittered from their nests in boxes placed wherever there was a place for them in the trees and under the eaves. Beds on every side were planted in flowers. Delphiniums and lilacs were in bloom against a weathered rustic fence.

I paused at the door of the kitchen, with its large wood-burning range, and decided that nothing was to be as I had expected it. Log houses in Alaska were commonplace, and often crude and ugly, but this log cabin showed good taste in every detail. There were rows of neatly painted cupboards, and on every foot of available wall space were painted palm

trees that looked so real I could almost hear the leaves rustle
in the trade winds. I remembered Mrs. Anderson's watercolors of flowers. Her work was exquisite.

"What an attractive home you have!" I exclaimed. On
every side I saw evidence of love of the same things I loved,
and my heart sang.

"We built it for a temporary home only," Andy said.
"I'm glad that we can soon replace it now that we have a
sawmill. We're planning to build on top of the bluff at the
head of the Island."

"A stone house with purple shutters and a circular stair-
case!" Mrs. Anderson added triumphantly, and then her voice
took on a petulant note. "From there I can watch for him to
come home when he goes away."

"I had to whipsaw all the lumber," Andy said.

"Whipsaw?" I said. "That's new to me."

"It's slow work. A log is stood on end and braced and I
saw the boards downward with a crosscut saw. I've a wind-
driven sawmill now that I have just finished, so we won't
have to work so hard any more." I wondered if Jack could
learn how to whipsaw.

It was impossible for me to curb my curiosity and interest. I was like a tourist in a museum and the Andersons did
not seem to mind my looking about. "You must be very
proud of having made such a charming home, and so much
of it your own work," I said.

"We have to make everything ourselves since we have
no money," Mrs. Anderson answered. "It probably looks very
crude to you."

"Oh, no! I've never seen such an interesting place. I
only hope Jack and I can do half as well." That pleased her
and her black eyes sparkled.

Yellow ruffled curtains hung at small-paned windows in
the living room, and there were many watercolor paintings
on the walls. In one corner was a rock fireplace. The furniture
was homemade with good lines and nicely painted. I noticed

what I thought at first was a spider web covering one of the window panes, with a fat spider in the center. But I found that a small hole had been broken in the glass, with cracks radiating out of it, and this had been used as the basis for the painted spider web. "That's what I mean," I said. "Money can't buy taste and originality."

I stood looking at rows of books that covered one wall from floor to ceiling. They were all good solid reading. Several shelves held books dealing only with the tropics, and there were many volumes of travel and adventure—as well as rows of reference books. I was extremely happy to see them.

Andy came in, dressed all in white—shirt, trousers, and shoes. I suddenly realized that they were dressed up for the occasion while I was in sweater and slacks. I hurried into the bedroom, where the men had taken my luggage, and quickly put on a somewhat travel-wrinkled dress.

Mrs. Anderson opened up the table and set it with attractive linen, silver, and china. She must have had much of the dinner prepared beforehand, for very soon there appeared on the table a green salad, hot rolls, a delicious casserole made of canned moose meat, and a dessert of baked rhubarb with whipped cream. Mrs. Anderson announced that all the food had been produced on the Island. I decided after my first taste of goat's milk that it was enough like cow's milk to make no difference.

When the meal was finished, Cliff began gathering up the dishes and I got up to help him. "You learn quickly," he said, handing me a dishtowel. He laughed softly in a characteristic way, as if trying to suppress his amusement. After that, it became customary for Cliff and me to wash the dishes.

I watched Cliff milk the half-dozen goats, and felt that I could hardly wait until we had goats of our own. The Andersons evidently set much store by goats, and Val remarked that they could not get along without them.

"We certainly couldn't," his father agreed. "Goat milk

saved your life when you were a baby, and we could find no
other food to agree with you." Val flushed crimson, as always
when attention was drawn to him.

"Goats are comparatively safe from bears and coyotes
on the Island," Andy said.

Mrs. Anderson had joined the rest of us in the yard.
"I've never seen but one black bear and, at another time, a
brown bear on the Island," she said. "We presume they swam
over from the mainland, but bears don't often swim so far."

"Are there many bears on the mainland?" I asked fearfully. The thought of bears still terrified me, after hearing
Charlie Lean's grisly story.

"Yes. A good many of both kinds. We often see them
on the beach over there across the strip of water." Andy spoke
so matter-of-factly I was somewhat reassured. "Have you seen
a moose yet?" he asked.

"No, but I almost did at Cooper's Landing," I answered.
"There were tracks one morning just outside the window
where I slept. A cow and her calf had jumped over the fence
in the night."

"If you'll come with me a little beyond the barn," said
Andy, "I think we'll see one with her calf. She stays around
here much of the time. Every spring several cows bear their
calves on the Island. They must sense that they're safe
with us."

The great shaggy cow moose stood awkwardly, staring at
us, sober and aloof but not in the least afraid. There was an
expression in her eyes of contempt and defiance and none of
the soulful beauty of a deer's eyes. The long-legged baby that
nuzzled her side was a miniature copy of his mother.

When Andy and I slowly drew near, the cow moose
shielded her little one by shoving it with her nose, and with
an almost imperceptible movement withdrew to a safer distance.

The family slept under a spruce tree in the yard. I was
glad to have the information that there were no mosquitoes
borne out by this proof.

Cliff occupied a little cabin behind the house, and I had the only bedroom, my pile of luggage crowding it to the limit. I retired early. Unk lay on a handmade braided rug by the bed. I wondered if I had been mistaken when I thought some cold looks had been directed at Unk, and determined to keep close watch and not let him disturb anyone. I reached down to give him a good-night pat and he licked my hand.

My last thought before falling asleep was wonder. First, there had been the shock of seeing the lake so unlike what I had expected, and then Jessie—simply incredible. Well, I thought sleepily, anything I can't understand now I can figure out in the morning. The beach was only a few yards from the open window and, listening to the waves slapping softly on the rocks, I drifted off.

CHAPTER 3

I WAS UP and about next morning as soon as I heard someone rattling the lids of the kitchen range. Andy was wearing a chef's cap and beating batter in a bowl. Whistling softly to himself, he swung between the table and stove as if in rhythm with music. Here, I felt, was a man who was inwardly happy.

"Good morning!" I said. "Isn't this a grand day?"

"It would be grander if it were raining," he answered good-humoredly. "The garden needs rain badly."

Mrs. Anderson came in, followed by Val. She brought a bouquet of dewy lilacs and arranged them artistically for the table.

"Have you ever tasted Swedish pancakes?" Andy asked me.

"No, I haven't," I answered, watching him spread with butter and roll with two forks a very thin pancake that covered the entire pan.

"Powdered sugar or lingonberry sauce?" he asked, smiling.

"Powdered sugar, please." I didn't know how the lingonberries might taste, but for the next one I chose the sauce and found it delicious. Andy explained that the low-bush cranberries that grew all over the Island were the same as those that grew in Sweden, where they were called lingonberries.

After an initial "Good morning!" Mrs. Anderson hardly spoke during the meal. Whenever she thought I wasn't looking, her eyes bored into me. I knew she was sizing me up, and it made me uncomfortable, for beneath her surface politeness lay something else—disappointment, perhaps, or even envy. She certainly struck me very differently than the impression made in her letters; perhaps she found me different from what she expected too. I was determined to try to make friends, and not to be sensitive.

After breakfast, when Cliff and I had washed the dishes, I found Mrs. Anderson sitting on the rock-paved terrace in front of the doorway. Her fingers flew as she knitted a mitten in an intricate Scandinavian pattern requiring two sets of needles. I sat down on the steps. She frowningly concentrated as she counted stitches, so we did not talk. Her enormous arms tapered to shapely plump hands, dimpled like a baby's. I was fascinated to watch them flash among the bright strands of wool.

It was very pleasant there in the sun. I had never seen the atmosphere in Alaska so clear and bright. The lake sparkled, the sky was forget-me-not blue, the snow-capped mountains dazzling. This is a beautiful place, I thought; I'm going to like it here and I'll soon get used to Mrs. Anderson.

Mrs. Anderson dropped her knitting in her lap and looked out across the lawn and the strip of water to the mainland, with its background of snowy peaks. "I thought it was beautiful too when I first saw it," she said grimly.

"But you are so artistic!" I said in astonishment. "Can't you see beauty in this now?"

She laughed harshly. "I don't mind it this time of year. But I've seen too many mountains. It's not so bad when my flowers are blooming, and there are young animals. I hate goats except when they are very young kids. The baby ducks, geese, and chickens are interesting. They're happy in the summer time." Her voice turned hard. "But winters here are horrible. Don't imagine it's always like this."

"I judged from your letters that you loved living here," I said, really puzzled, for she had written with such seeming satisfaction.

"I would rather live here than any place else in Alaska," she said. "It would kill me to live in Seward with all those smirking women. Besides, Hjalmar's crazy about living here. He lived on an island in Sweden." She dropped a ball of yarn and I retrieved it for her. "Some years ago," she continued flatly, "when Hjalmar was having good success as a guide, I hoped we might carry out my dream of going to the South Sea islands in our own boat. But that was like all my other dreams and plans—we never did."

I remembered the rows of books dealing with the tropics, the delicately painted palm trees, and there were fig and avocado shrubs in tubs at the edge of the terrace. I felt I was beginning to understand, and pitied her deeply. She had been very young when she came to the Island as a bride.

She picked up her knitting and went on bitterly, "Now that I have high blood pressure, I can't walk the trail, and the motor's not heavy enough to take me up the river. I'll be here the rest of my life."

Suddenly in imagination I saw the lake as it must have appeared to Mrs. Anderson. The sunshine, which before had seemed so bright and warm, became thin and pallid; the sparkling blue waters of the lake changed to a bleak gray, an impassable, forbidding separation from the outside world; the Island was a prison. What would it be like, I thought, to be compelled to stay there the rest of one's life? I realized that this wilderness retreat could be a very lonely and unfriendly place to anyone who did not truly love it, and in the midst of the warm sunshine I felt a sudden chill. I was filled with pity for Mrs. Anderson and longed to help her.

Neither of us spoke for some time. She was absorbed in

her knitting, and I was lost in thought. Where, I wondered, was the placid pioneer woman whose portrait she had painted in her letters? Her letters, I thought, must have been an outpouring of imagination when she was lonely and dissatisfied. But why had she invited me to stay with them and seemed sincerely to want us to come? It was too much for me.

I decided to go ahead and ask questions and not reveal my inner disturbance. "Am I the kind of person you expected?" I asked bluntly.

"Yes," she answered, slowly and thoughtfully, "in a way. . . . But I thought you would be younger and better-looking." I could see she was trying to be completely honest. "You probably were not so homely when you were young." She went on knitting and did not look at me, for which I was grateful. I wanted to jump up and run away, but I sat on as if hypnotized. After all, I had asked for it. After a pause she went on, "Hjalmar was very anxious for you to come here when he heard that you were interested. He thinks I need companionship. The doctor told us that my condition was caused mostly from being alone too much."

"I suppose this is Val's vacation from school," I said, trying to change the subject. This should be safe ground. She had written me that she taught Val.

"Yes," she said proudly. "I follow the schedule of the territorial schools. He has nine months of school and three of vacation. He took the tests and is ready for the eighth grade in September. I get books from the Board of Education in Juneau. He's very bright."

"He must be. Are you going to send him away for more schooling when he's older?"

"Oh, no. I can teach him enough. He reads a great deal. Hjalmar and I couldn't let him go away—we would miss him too much. In fact, we couldn't make him go. My sister in Seattle, Cliff's mother, urges us to let Val stay with her and go through high school, but it would never do. He doesn't like people."

I dared not comment on that, but got up and examined the plants in the windowboxes. I talked about the flowers until I was able to slip away gracefully, with the excuse that I must put the bedroom in order. It disturbed me to realize that my belongings were occupying such a large share of the house.

Unk was not accustomed to being tied up, and we both wanted to explore. I was eager also to escape the pitiful and unhappy Mrs. Anderson. Unk and I went for a walk along the beach and through a green meadow where three horses grazed. Goats raised their heads from feeding and looked at us, their bells tinkling. I kept a tight hold on Unk's leash. How he would have loved to chase them! I saw many lovely and familiar wildflowers.

Behind the house was a tent that seemed to have but little in it, and an idea was born. I searched out Andy in his log workshop and put my proposal to him.

"I wanted to ask you, Andy, if you could spare that tent," I said. "Couldn't I rent it from you and live there? I'm afraid I take up too much room in the house."

Andy looked up from his work, and answered, "There's plenty of room for you in the house. But would you like to live in a tent?"

"Oh, I certainly would," I said, thinking of the sharp looks his wife had given me, "if you can spare it. I have bedding."

"Well, I'll put up a stove. I think I can make you comfortable, but you must take your meals with us."

"Probably that would be better than trying to prepare my own," I admitted. "Perhaps I can help with the cooking."

There was nothing I could do until he prepared the tent. I went to tell Mrs. Anderson. "That's a good idea," she said pleasantly. We again sat, she in her chair knitting and I on the steps.

Val was down on the beach, wading barefoot in the shallow water. "Ma, tell her to let her dog come and play with me," he called. Unk dashed away as soon as I had unfastened his leash. He loved the water, and was soon splashing about in it.

"Val's an interesting child," I remarked, to make conversation.

"He has ideas of his own," his mother answered, frowning over her knitting.

Soon Val called, "Ma, tell her to call her dog away; I'm tired of playing with him. I don't like him." Val had evidently never had a dog of his own to play with.

"Come, Unk!" I called quickly. Unk was not being any more successful than I with these strange people.

"Val's honest like I am," Mrs. Anderson remarked calmly. "We both say what we think." She looked at me appraisingly. "You're very deceitful."

This was really too much, and I was absolutely speechless. The situation was saved by Andy appearing to tell me he was ready to carry my things into the tent.

He had set up a small campstove and left a stack of wood outside the tent entrance. My bed was a pen of boards in one corner, filled with sweet-smelling hay. With a piece of canvas to cover the hay and my blankets spread over that, it made a comfortable, fragrant resting place. At least, I thought, I had a place of my own and need not risk incurring Mrs. Anderson's further ill-will by usurping the only bedroom.

When I came to breakfast a few mornings later, I found my hosts all bustling about. Mrs. Anderson was happy and excited as a child.

"Eat your cereal, Val," Andy said. "We must hurry."

"This is the Fourth of July, you know," Mrs. Anderson said. "We always have a picnic on the Fourth."

"We want to show you all the good homesites on the lake," Andy added. "You'll want to consider them so you can make your selection."

"That would be very kind," I said. "I'd love to go." It

would be a good chance to explore—already I had gone over every foot of the Island.

"Do you intend to wait until your husband comes before deciding?" Andy asked.

"Oh, no. Jack knows I couldn't wait patiently until he comes; he agreed to leave it to me."

Mrs. Anderson was in a very friendly mood, and we had a good time preparing lunch together. I began to hope that we might become friends after all.

"We'll stop at Dawson Bay first," Andy said, as we approached the shore about a mile and a half from the Island. "This is a possible site, but we think you'll select Egyptian Bay. We'll go there too."

"Egyptian Bay is the most beautiful place on the lake," Mrs. Anderson added. "That's the place for you. From Dawson Bay the setting sun is cut off by those rocky cliffs, and you wouldn't want that."

Their words meant little to me. I wanted to see for myself and sat forward eagerly in the boat.

Dawson Point was a long wooded peninsula, with steep rocky hills ending in cliffs along the shore, which pushed out into the lake to form Dawson Bay.

"The Point contains about seventy-five acres," Andy explained. "That's where I get logs for my buildings—we have only birch on the Island."

"Now that you're sawing boards on the sawmill, you'll need many more logs, Hjalmar," Mrs. Anderson said sharply. Evidently her mind was fixed on the house Andy had promised to build her.

Cliff guided the boat expertly into the bay. There was really nothing for me to be so excited about; this was only our first stop, and the Andersons had brushed it aside. But it was so beautiful! There was a rim of white mountains in the distance, then a line of foothills, with a soft covering of pale green birch and scattered, pointing black fingers of spruce, set back a little way from the shore.

We landed in a little cove. Tall rock cliffs rose from the shore. My eyes strained to see what the blue flowers and the fuzzy-leaved yellow ones were that grew in the cracks of the rocks. One large rock had broken off from the cliff and formed a little island. A gnarled spruce that looked like a dwarf Japanese tree, with a ground cover of juniper, kinni-kinnick, and low-bush cranberry, grew on top of it. Jack can make a bridge across that space, I thought, and I'll have the island for my own. I was taking possession. Minute by minute the conviction grew, but I was determined to keep quiet. It was foolish to be so sure; the Andersons would think I had been carried away by the first place I had seen. So I assumed what I hoped was a poker face and curbed my enthusiasm.

We walked up an incline to the top of a promontory, about half an acre in extent. The ground was carpeted with lovely low shrubs—cranberry, kinnikinnick, trailing dogwood, and Labrador tea blooming together. Their perfume was released by the warm sun, and there was no heavy, oppressive undergrowth. I had a strange feeling of having been there before—everything looked just the way I expected.

"This whole country was burned over about thirty-five years ago," Andy explained. "That's why the growth isn't any higher. The Point escaped the forest fire, and the water protected those big spruces near the beach."

There were scattered clumps of prim little spruces, none more than twenty feet tall, as well as many beautiful birches, large and small. Scores of deformed dead stubs, however, marred the beauty of the scene.

"What made them die?" I asked Andy.

"Some of them can't stand being bitten off by the moose year after year," he explained. "But when they get tall enough so the moose can't reach the top, they grow up in a hurry and soon look like this." He caressed the glistening bark of one of the tall birches, and I knew he loved trees just as I did.

The level top of the plateau was a perfect house site, with walls of bedrock forming terraces. My thoughts raced ahead; I could see rockgardens and fields of wildflowers. In spite of my efforts not to show how thrilled I was, my feelings must have been transmitted to the others.

"The Point protects the bay from the wind," Andy said. "Your boats would have shelter. Even if you don't homestead the Point, you would have that advantage. I don't think it would be worthwhile to homestead the Point itself, though."

"You should homestead the Point by all means," Cliff disagreed. "You'll need it as pasture for your goats. You'd only have to fence the neck; goats won't cross ice." Mrs. Anderson gave Cliff a stern look; it was plain she didn't want her timber supply jeopardized.

I longed to tell Jack all about it, and hated to leave before I had preserved it all in memory, but it was past noon and much more had been planned for the day. Cliff guided the boat close to shore around Dawson Point.

Andy pointed to the spruce trees growing in abundance above the cliffs. "Just the right size for cabin timber," he said, smiling at me.

We landed on a sandy beach at the very end of the Point and climbed over the rocks to the top, where the men made a fire and we had our picnic. There was a glorious view out over the lake.

After lunch we continued our journey, keeping close to the south shore of the lake. Some two miles beyond Dawson Bay we passed the homestead of Hank Lucas and George Nelson, but did not stop, as Andy explained that the owners had gone to live at Cooper's Landing. We then crossed the lake and headed for Egyptian Bay.

"How did the bay get its name," I asked, as we approached.

"See those two big rocks at the entrance of the bay?" Andy answered. "We thought they looked like the Pyramids. This is a good site, and it's open for homesteading."

"A couple came here about four years ago, filed on it, and built a cabin," Mrs. Anderson added contemptuously.

"But they didn't stay. They were afraid of hardships and soon got tired of it."

If I am ever afraid, I thought, I must not let her know.

There appeared to be no opening in the rugged coast line until the boat passed between the pyramids and entered the calm water of a completely landlocked bay. Someone with an eye for beauty had selected the location for the little log cabin that sat high above the water on the edge of the cliff. A stream meandered down from the hills and the soil seemed fertile. There were many advantages to this sheltered place, but my mind was made up. I had given my heart to Dawson Bay.

It was growing late and dark clouds had gathered. Andy seemed concerned about the wind that had sprung up—my first taste of Skilak wind.

"I think we should go on home now," he decided. "But we'll bring you back any time. There are several other places that might interest you. Take your time about deciding."

We had scarcely pulled away from the beach when we were surrounded by whitecaps tossing spray into the boat. Cliff controlled the motor firmly and we were carried sturdily toward the Island, but I began to be fearful.

It must be dangerous, I thought as we lurched and dipped, but I must not scream or make a scene. I must not be the first to cry out. I looked at the others apprehensively but, huddled in wraps against the cold wind, they all seemed quite calm.

To hide my fright I pulled up my coat collar and turned away, looking out over the flying waves. In the dim twilight they looked like a great herd of white horses, with high-flung manes and tails, stampeding on and on into the distance.

My anxiety lessened as we neared the Island, and soon we pulled up to the wharf. My hands were numb from holding tightly to the seat.

Next morning at breakfast I asked Mrs. Anderson, "Do you often have such storms as we had yesterday?"

She seemed surprised, and answered, "Oh, that wasn't a storm. We never have them this time of year, but in the fall and also in spring we are sure to have some terrific ones. At those seasons we don't travel on the Lake unless we have to."

The noises and smells of animal life around the premises roused Unk's hunting instincts to the breaking point. More than anything, he trembled at the peeping of the chickens, ducks, and geese. I kept him tied securely in the tent at night and never let him off the leash.

Some ten days had passed, and it appeared to me that his interest in the birds was waning. Also, he was not getting enough exercise. I decided to unfasten his leash for just a little while. He ran around joyously sniffing, until he found a bone, and lay down to gnaw it.

Gulls mewed and cackled around the wharf and Arctic terns sailed gracefully overhead, diving swiftly for fish. Sandpipers and yellowlegs ran through the shallow water. It was another of those blue and gold days which had followed each other since I had come. Diamonds winked on the water. I watched a tern dive and fly up with a fish in its mouth, and all its friends and relatives came screaming at the top of their voices and tried to take it away.

I was walking along the shore and turned to call Unk. My mouth was open to speak his name, but Unk wasn't there.

A terrible premonition of disaster turned my knees to water. Without knowing how I got there I was through the gate back of the house that led to where the fowls were kept. I caught a glimpse of Unk, his head held high, a gosling in his mouth, racing through the grass. I screamed and Unk stopped, looking at me questioningly, still holding the gosling in his mouth. I felt sick and dizzy.

Mrs. Anderson and Val had followed me. "How many were there?" I choked. We counted them. Two additional small geese, making three with the one I had taken from Unk, and one baby duck lay dead. One duck was missing and was never found. Three geese and two ducks! The old gander, of which Unk was deeply afraid, was not there to protect them.

I was holding my head on each side; it felt as if it was about to burst. I knew by this time how precious the little fowls were to Mrs. Anderson. I had seen her sit for hours watching and delighting in them, and I was in terror of what she might say or do, but she gave me the surprise of my life. "Don't feel so badly, dear," she comforted me, putting her arms around me. "Something's always happening to them." I was deeply touched by her magnanimity.

When Andy came to the house, Val announced, "Her dog killed three little geese and two ducks, Pa."

"Oh, Andy, I'm terribly sorry," I sobbed.

"You couldn't help it. You mind much more than we do." He smiled at me kindly. "I've heard that a dog could be broken of the habit of killing chickens by tying a dead chicken around his neck until he's sick of it."

"I don't believe I could stand that myself," I answered. "I'll have to keep him near me."

The Andersons were very kind, but they weren't dog lovers, and I knew they would never tolerate Unk after this. No punishment would have any effect unless I could make Unk understand, and I doubted I could. He knew nothing of barnyard fowls, and had been born a hunting dog. If Jack were only there! The only thing I could do was to leave at once. Of course I would leave rather than have Unk shot, but I wanted to stay on Skilak Lake. I couldn't bear to leave.

I had to be alone so I could think. I walked blindly through the gate back of the house, and there I came face to face with Cliff. He had just heard of the trouble.

"I know how you feel," he said. "Once my dog killed the neighbors' chickens; I worked all summer to pay for them." He sat down on the grass and I sat with him.

"Cliff, I'm desperate," I sobbed. "What on earth can I do?"

He thought for some time and then offered: "I've

thought of this—I'm planning a trip to the Landing anyway, and I can go on to Seward—I've got to see a dentist. I can go by the camp where your husband works. Couldn't I take Unk to him?"

"Would you do that, Cliff?" I clutched at this hope like a drowning person. "I'm not sure that Jack would be able to keep him, but perhaps he could manage. I don't like to send him without knowing more about the conditions, though."

"Men in work camps usually like to have dogs around," Cliff said. "Anyway, the problem's too much for you. Let him figure it out."

"I'm so grateful to you, Cliff," I whispered.

"Never mind that," he grinned and shook his hair back from his eyes as he jumped to his feet. "Just protect me when Jack finds out it was my bright idea."

Next morning the boat carried Unk away, his howls sounding faintly above the noise of the motor.

I was wakeful that night in my lonely tent. Weird cries like those of a howling dog came over the water. Sick at heart, I wondered if Unk might have gotten away from Cliff and made his way back along the shore. I didn't fall asleep until just before dawn, and woke suddenly. The sun was shining brightly through the roof of the tent, the leaves of a birch tree making a pattern of shadows above me. I was much less depressed. When I confided my fears to the family at breakfast, they all laughed.

Val laughed loudest. "A howling dog," he jeered. "Gee, that's a good one! A howling dog!"

"Those were loons you heard," Andy explained kindly. "They swim around in the lake and holler all night this time of year."

I never was quite at peace until a week later when I heard Cliff's little motor chugging home. I ran down to the wharf and, as he guided the boat through the rocks, I peered anxiously to see if Unk was in the boat.

Cliff understood. He didn't even make me to wait until

he landed. Grinning widely, he called, "Everything's just fine. It was the right thing to do." He didn't stop to pull the boat up but jumped into the shallow water and began searching through his pockets. "Unk ran on ahead of me when we got out of the car," he went on, chuckling as he talked. "Must have smelled Jack. Jack's eyes bugged out but I couldn't stop to explain as Charlie was in a hurry. I just handed him your note and said, 'Killed ducks,' and ran back to the car. Jack came running after me. He took a piece of paper out of his pocket and rested it against the car and wrote this note. Here it is."

Disregarding wet feet I ran into the icy water. I had to see what was in that note! Here was my first message from Jack since leaving Juneau. I snatched the scrap of paper from Cliff's hand, hastily unfolded it and read the words, "My poor little girl. He can sleep under my bunk and lie near me as I work. My love." The very brevity of the note, the very lack of further information, made me happy. It was so like Jack. I felt that my contact with him had been restored, and drew new reassurance from his love. I was no longer adrift.

I began checking off each day as it passed, living only for Jack's coming. When I was not roaming about the Island, I remained in the tent much of the time. The tent had become my sanctuary. Mrs. Anderson seemed to grow increasingly unfriendly. Hour after hour she sat in her wicker chair and looked listlessly out of the window, her black eyes smoldering.

"Have you finished your knitting?" I asked innocently.

"I have no money to buy wool," she answered without expression, not removing her eyes from a faraway point.

She took no apparent interest in her home. Andy did the laundry and baked the bread and gradually I had taken over the task of preparing dinner, the one important meal of the day. Occasionally Val went with me on my walks, but it was just as impossible to reach a comfortable footing with Val as it was with his mother.

Many an hour did I spend sitting near the top of the tall bluff on that portion of the Island that commanded a view of Dawson Bay across the water. There wasn't enough to fill the hours; I was not accomplishing anything. How I wished that Jack could come! Mrs. Anderson's depression was contagious; one felt secure on an island only if the island was one's happy home; otherwise it was a prison. Often I would walk entirely around the shore trying to dispel this helpless feeling, but this only intensified it. The lake seemed to mock me.

The daylight hours grew noticeably less. Gone were the lazy summer days, and the entire atmosphere was pervaded with the urge to prepare for winter. The family rose earlier in the morning, and Cliff and Andy hustled with harvesting, hauling wood, and haying.

One day I found them nailing the last split shakes on the roof of a tiny log cabin which they had built near the beach in a clump of birches.

"What are you going to use the cabin for, Andy?" I asked.

"We need more room, and I want to have it ready for next summer. Government officials often stop with us."

"If you can spare it this winter, couldn't Jack and I rent it from you? It'll be awfully cold in the tent in winter."

"We just made a fire in the fireplace," Cliff said, with a grin. "At the moment the cabin would make a good smoke-house."

"I think you would be comfortable," Andy said stiffly. "I can put in a stove."

I longed for the privacy of a home of my own, and was happy because the cabin was some distance from the house, with its back turned to it.

Letters came from Jack only at long intervals; the men were too busy emulating squirrels to go for mail. The nights had become very cold. I went to bed in my tent chilled to the bone and dreaded getting up in the morning. Wood for the stove was scarce. I gathered all the dry pieces I could find along the beach, but most of it was water-soaked.

The men were away several days, hauling hay in the horse scow towed by the boat, when I decided to move into the cabin. Val surprised me by offering to help me move my things. He had never been in my tent. He would not even look in when he brought a message, but would stand some distance away and deliver it. I saw his present friendliness was only childish curiosity, but I accepted it gratefully as a chance to win his confidence. He asked for the hammer when I was nailing up a shelf, and proved to be remarkably skillful.

Like that of his mother, Val's attitude toward me was very disconcerting at times, but I could not blame him. Val had never played marbles or baseball with other little boys; he played alone. Because he was so often in his mother's company, he naturally reflected her loneliness and frustration. My heart went out to Val; I had been a shy child myself.

I had very little with which to make the cabin homelike. I would not have a lamp until Andy brought more of my freight, but I had a whole box of candles and used bottles for candlesticks. Over the mantel I hung a brightly striped Turkish towel.

Val laughed loudly. "Whoever heard of hanging a towel on the wall?" he jeered.

All the food that freezing would not injure went into a small tent Andy had erected outside my door. I placed on the floor a box spring and mattress and covered my bed with a red blanket. When Jack came he would have to make some bunk beds of poles. I had a nice table with an oilcloth cover and three wooden boxes for seats. Cooking utensils hung on the wall. It began to look like a home, but I remembered achingly that it would be at least six weeks before Jack could come.

There had been no need for a fire while the sun shone in the window, but when it sank behind the mountain an icy chill crept into the cabin.

"Gosh! It's getting late," Val said suddenly. "I must help

Ma milk the goats." He dashed out the door, pulling on his parka as he ran.

"You've been a wonderful help, Val," I called after him, but he was running too fast to hear. I closed the door he had left open.

I started a very small fire in the fireplace, at the edge of the hearth so it would not smoke too much. I boiled water in a pan over the fire and made tea, and opened a can of tuna fish which I ate with crackers. Light from the candles on the mantel cast a warm glow over the room. I wished that Mrs. Anderson would come so that we could talk, but when it had been dark for a long time I knew no one was coming.

For a week I was too busy moving to take my favorite walk up the hill toward the far side of the Island, where the pale trunks of white birch trees, uniform in size, stretched on and on over several acres. There was no undergrowth except the close ground cover of low-bush cranberry. I could stand in the midst of the grove and see nothing else in any direction. In September, almost overnight, the birch leaves had turned to pure gold.

By the time I visited the grove again the leaves had begun to fall. Enough leaves had dropped to cover the ground completely, but they could not be missed from the branches overhead. So there was a canopy of clear yellow above, the pinkish cream boles of the trees beneath, and a golden carpet on the ground. The beauty of the birch grove was very helpful to me while I waited for Jack.

Andy brought me an armful of wood. "I've never seen the lake so high," he said. "It's past the gate now and covers part of the lawn."

"Why does the water rise?" I asked. "There's been no rain."

"Just before winter sets in we usually have a flood. It's caused by the snow melting on the mountains. We're worried about the vegetables. We leave them in the ground to grow as long as possible."

"Will the water ruin them?"

"It will if it lasts long enough," Andy answered, looking harassed. "I guess we should harvest them."

"I'll come over and help," I offered. I had not seen Mrs. Anderson since I had moved two weeks before.

I was shocked at what I found. The water was creeping over the lawn toward the house and would probably rise higher. No one but me seemed to be alarmed. Andy knew all the caprices of the lake and said there was no danger of the water reaching the house.

All hands set to work busily harvesting vegetables, and cabbage, celery, peas, and beans soon filled boxes and baskets, ready to be taken to the root cellar. There was another garden on the hill where the root vegetables grew. These were safe.

I offered to help Mrs. Anderson can some of the peas and beans. They had a pressure cooker and sealed them in tin cans. She very generously insisted that I take with me some cans for our winter store. We finished the last of the canning by lamplight.

Down from the head of the lake a savage wind lashed the swollen lake into fury. Mountainous waves pounded over the little wharf Andy had built with patient painstaking labor. Parts of it were torn away until the whole structure was a wreck. There was no safe place for the boats anywhere on the Island. Andy moved them and the horse scow many times. One small boat was broken in two and damaged beyond repair. The water rose halfway up the tall stack of hay and there was no way to move it, so most of this valuable winter food for horses and goats was ruined.

I watched, frightened and fascinated by the power of the lake. It seemed wicked and malicious.

Once again I thought of the white horses. Now they were frenzied—berserk. During the three nights that the storm lasted the sound of their whinnying and snorting was borne on the wind.

On the first day after the storm cleared Andy and Cliff left for the Landing. There must have been tons of freight waiting to be brought—ours and Andy's and some for Art Frisbie, soon to arrive at his homestead on Fryingpan Island. It was growing very cold and the work of hauling would be difficult. My own list was a long one. All the Andersons had taken a lively interest in my choice and gave me advice. Because they insisted, I ordered some things I wasn't sure we would need.

Val's ears could pick up the beat of a motor long before anyone else could hear it, and he ran to tell me that they were coming, but that it was Cliff's little motor. They had taken the big one as well, but I could not tell the difference in the sound. The motor must have broken down but I was thinking only of hearing from Jack. I thought he should know by now when he would come.

I always tried to remember, no matter how impatient I was for the mail, not to intrude on these homecomings, so I waited until they had time to unload. Before I reached the door I sensed trouble. The usual bustle, talk and laughter were missing. Mrs. Anderson sat crying dejectedly. The men stood holding steaming cups of coffee, their hands blue and stiff with cold. I stared from Andy to Cliff and back again. Something terrible had happened that they couldn't tell me. "What is it, Andy?" I whispered. "Is it Jack?"

Both of them smiled reassuringly. "Oh, no. He's all right," Andy said. "A man at the Landing said he had just seen your husband and he told him he would be here soon. But we had an accident in the river. I think the boat was not balanced well and it struck a sweeper and overturned. We both managed to swim ashore, but I'm sorry to say I lost some of your freight, Mrs. Sharples."

"It's wonderful that you're both safe," I answered. I was so relieved that it was not bad news of Jack I didn't care about freight.

Mrs. Anderson made no effort to control the tears that

streamed down her cheeks and spoiled her careful make-up.
She had dressed for possible visitors when she heard the
motor. It was time for Art Frisbie to come, and Cliff's brother
John was expected to spend the winter. "Nobody will trust
you now," she sniffed. "We can't make any more money that
way."

Andy winced. "Of course, Mrs. Sharples, I will repay you
for every cent of your loss."

"But who'll pay you for the loss of your motor?" his wife
demanded.

Andy went on speaking to me. "We saved the boat but
the motor sank in deep water where the river's very swift. If I
can't get another motor, I promise you I'll bring your supplies down the trail with the horses." I felt perfect confidence
in him.

Mrs. Anderson's tears redoubled. "Now that you have no
motor, I can never leave here."

I watched the tears course down her cheeks uncurbed
and realized that she was once more overcome by the desolate
fear of being trapped and imprisoned by the lake. I sensed
her deep unhappiness and was released from my resentment
of her difficult ways.

"Don't worry, Jess," Andy said soothingly. "I'll get another motor, and I can always take you with the horses."

CHAPTER 4

A WEEK LATER another furious storm lashed the water, filling my cabin with its roar. Suddenly, above the noise of the wind and surf, I heard the sound of a powerful motor, coming from the lower end of the lake. As I watched from the window, a large boat approached and landed. I counted five men pulling it up on the beach. In the early darkness I could make out only that they were Indians. No doubt, I thought, they were from Kenai, the Indian village on the coast.

Next morning, as I dug wood from under the snow that had fallen the night before, Val came running to the cabin. "The Indians loaned Pa their motor!" he panted. "They said everyone at Kenai has heard that Pa's an honest man so he can keep it till spring!"

I didn't believe it. "How can they get home without their motor?"

"Oh, they had two motors with them," he answered triumphantly.

At the house, Val's announcement was confirmed; the Indians had gone and left their high-powered motor. It was a miracle! I was deeply touched by their generosity, but did not realize until long afterward just how wonderful it had been.

The Andersons passed by my window one bright, sunny morning in the middle of the month. At my first glimpse of them I sensed that Jack's message had come.

"We've got news for you," Andy called, before I could get the door open. "Just came in over the radio."

I tried to grasp the marvellous fact that Jack was almost there, but I was speechless, just staring at them.

"I know just how you feel," Mrs. Anderson said warmly. "I can remember every word. It said, 'Please meet me at Cooper's Landing. Will wait for you. Love to my wife.' We were glad he said 'Please,' " she said primly. "That shows he's considerate."

She handed me a plate covered with a napkin. I uncovered two luscious cream puffs and winked back tears at her kindness—perhaps she liked me after all. This was the first time since I moved that she had come to my cabin. I hoped that from now on, now the initial strangeness had worn off, we would get along better. In this remote world, I could see, friendship meant a great deal.

Two days later I was on the beach, straining for a glimpse of the boat while it was nothing more than a faint throb. A biting wind whipped the ends of my wool scarf; it was already painful to go out with my ears uncovered.

After what seemed an eternity, the boat was close enough for me to pick out the figures in it. Was Jack that strange figure in the brown parka? Because of the extreme cold the fur-edged hood was pulled closely over his face and I could only make out the eyes, but I knew deep in my heart that it was he.

Unk was the first to land, splashing through the shallow water. He gave me a sidelong look, but he did not come to me, instead running off and sniffing logs of the wharf. Evidently he wasn't sure I could be trusted.

Andy jumped out of the boat, grinning and beating his arms around his body to warm his hands. "Well, here he is," he announced, "safe and sound."

Without a word, Jack reached out and hugged my shoulders. Then he helped Andy with the boat. The water was low, and it had to be pulled some distance over the rocks. When Cliff came running, Jack was no longer needed. I beckoned and he followed me toward the little cabin, our first home together in the wilderness.

Inside, Jack pushed back his parka hood and opened wide his arms. I rushed into them, feeling safer and happier than I had since our parting. How good it was to have him back!

Unk, however, was strangely indifferent to my welcome. He suffered my caresses without so much as a wag of his tail. "Doesn't he act funny, Jack?" I said. "I believe he holds a grudge against me for sending him away. Here, Unk, here's a nice moose bone I've saved for you."

Unk looked at me questioningly. The floor was made of half logs with the smooth side up. It was rough and uneven, with wide cracks, and I had long since given up trying to keep it clean beyond sweeping it. Unk laid the bone down and brought a piece of paper from the pile I kept near the stove for starting fires. He placed the bone on the paper and lay down contentedly to gnaw. I felt my cheeks burn. In our old home we had always placed his bones on paper to protect the floor. Unk's manner plainly indicated that, even though I had lowered my standards, he hadn't forgotten the proprieties.

The little cabin was snug and comfortable, and we sat for hours by the stove talking. Jack had gained weight. He looked splendid—contented and relaxed. I searched his face for the dreaded signs, but obviously he had not been bothered by alcohol during the summer. My heart sang. This was a good omen for the future.

"Andy's a wonderful fellow," Jack said. "You should have seen him taking care of me on the way."

"He's been wonderfully kind."

"Do you like Mrs. Anderson as much as you expected to, hon? I thought you wrote sometimes as if you were disappointed."

"She's a strange woman," I answered, "really fine in many ways. I admire her but we haven't quite become friends."

"What's wrong?"

"At first I thought she hated me."

"Isn't that strange after she wrote you those letters?"

"I understand her better now. She's terribly lonely and I guess she has had a good many disappointments out here. It's inevitable, I'm afraid, that she takes out some of her troubles on the people around her. I think we're getting used to each other, though. Lately she's been very kind."

"Well," Jack said, munching a piece of the fudge I had made in his honor, "having a place of our own will probably help."

"All the same," I said, "I'm convinced Mrs. Anderson's problems come from isolation, and it frightens me. If you see me getting like that, you must send me away, even if I don't want to go."

"Don't worry, hon!" Jack grinned at me and reached for another piece of candy. "You could never be antisocial. I never believed those stories about the effect of isolation anyway."

The Anderson home was filled with youthful laughter and pranks. By this time Art Frisbie had arrived to take up his homestead on Fryingpan Island. He brought with him a young cousin, George Johan, who was to spend the winter with him. Cliff's brother John had arrived too.

Art and George were staying there while they made livable a little cabin on Fryingpan Island; wind had taken its roof off since the year before. They were going to live in the cabin while they finished Art's elaborate house with a stone basement. Cliff and John, who was as dark as Cliff was fair, were getting together their traps and supplies to camp at Egyptian Bay for the winter. Val followed the young men everywhere, and their gay, wholesome company did him noticeable good.

We were especially interested in Art. The other new arrivals only intended to spend the winter, but Art was to be our permanent neighbor. He was tall, dark, and handsome, a little older than the other boys, with a forceful personality. All the Andersons seemed to adore him and we liked him too.

Andy had killed a young bull moose on the Island, and Mrs. Anderson had canned a large portion of it, but with the arrival of these additional young appetites the meat disappeared rapidly. The men all had hunting licenses and were entitled to one moose each for the season. Jack and Cliff crossed to the mainland and got two at the "Lick," a mysterious swamp where moose came at certain seasons to lick the mud. Andy said it had minerals in it they craved. Only a part of each beast could be carried in the boat at one time, and the other boys went back for the rest of it next day. Soon such quantities of meat as I had never seen before were hanging, frozen solid, from a stout rack outside the kitchen door. Mrs. Anderson knew endless ways of cooking it, and I watched and imitated her. The meat was very like good quality beef and we never tired of it. I borrowed the canning outfit and preserved some for the next summer.

Andy told Jack to take some pieces of board at the mill to make shelves, and in a little while one wall looked like a grocery store with the cans neatly arranged. Jack also built sturdy double-deck bunks out of poles, and when we had done all we could to make the cabin comfortable I did not feel cramped by its smallness. I no longer felt restricted by the Island and the lake either after Jack came. We took walks over the Island and gathered driftwood on the beach, hauling it home on Andy's sled for Jack to saw up for the stove.

My impatience for Jack to see Dawson Bay had almost consumed me when Andy offered to take us across in his boat. No one mentioned the other house sites on the lake. I was so confident that I had found the right one that everyone accepted Dawson Bay as our future home.

A few inches of snow had fallen, changing the scene. The slanting noonday sun shone down unobstructed, and there was a feeling of space and freedom. I sometimes felt crowded in by the tall Alaskan mountains which overshadowed us, but this raised land gave the illusion of one's being on a mountain top oneself, high above the lake, with the encircling hills some distance behind. My little alpine plants would have the sun and wind they needed. It was not Jack's nature to be excited, but he accepted it all serenely—just as if it had been preordained.

"Mrs. Anderson has invited us for Christmas morning breakfast, and for dinner in the evening," Jack reported one morning.

"Did she?" I said. "It's nice of them to include us."

"She wants you to come and talk over the plans," he added.

We were each to draw the name of one of the others to give a gift to. The presents had to be homemade; we couldn't have bought anything anyway. Mine was easy—I had drawn John's name, and I knew that the most acceptable thing I could make for him was cookies. When he came to tea he never stopped until the cookie jar was empty. I made several kinds of my most successful ones and wrapped them in tinfoil to keep them fresh, so that John could take them to Egyptian Bay after Christmas.

"What on earth can I make for Val?" Jack grumbled. "I haven't anything to work with. Can't I just give him some of my socks? I have some I've never worn."

"No, that won't do," I answered. "It's against the rules."

For days I tried to think of something to help Jack. When I
found a piece of smooth board, I remembered once seeing a
wooden raccoon with dangling legs that danced on a board
when you tapped the board in time to music.

Jack was not at first enthusiastic; he felt that it wouldn't
be a success.

"Andy said we could help ourselves to paint and nails
and anything we could find in his workshop," I said, ignoring
his pessimism. "See if you can find some wire to fasten on the
legs and arms."

The result of our combined efforts was not bad. The
coon danced acceptably, and his white teeth shone out of his
painted black face.

The day before Christmas dawned on a scene of unearthly beauty. The thermometer stood just at zero, and the
fog had frozen in the night, leaving frost crystals an inch
thick over every exposed surface. The sun was dazzling, and
the frost so delicate and ethereal that the slightest zephyr
would have sent it flying, but at the end of the day there had
not been a breath of wind.

Mrs. Anderson refused my offer to help with the cooking.
"No, please stay away," she said, frowning over a cookbook.
"You'll only make me nervous."

"I have some olives," I offered, "and a can of pickled
peaches and a few other things I'd like to bring."

"That would be nice," she said, with sudden interest.
"I'll tell you something we need even more. Have you by any
chance a can of pumpkin?"

"Oh, yes," I answered, happy to be of use. "I'll bring
two cans."

I brought my contributions to the feast and then was
free. On those cold, frosty days the evening sky was lovely to
behold. I knew that the birch grove would be a place of en-
chantment and felt a little hurt when Jack refused to go with
me to see it at twilight. Still, I understood his deep interest
in the fleshing of a coyote skin that was in progress. Andy

and Cliff were showing the others how it was done. One day this might be our chief means of livelihood.

I went alone to the birch grove, walking quickly to the top of the knoll. Here I stopped and turned slowly in all directions. The hoarfrost covered the ground as completely as if there had been a light snow. Every tiny oval leaf of cranberry, every dried leaf on the ground, was outlined and enlarged with a furry white coat. Every twig and limb of the graceful bare birch trees shimmered, emitting little sparks of light.

There was nothing in any direction except the birches. I walked on to where the trees thinned a little nearer the water. Individual trees were outlined against the rosy sky. I stood there drinking in the beauty for a long time. No one has been up here but me, I thought; this is a Christmas present just for me.

As I watched, the rose of the sky became first mauve and then intense blue. The frosted trees were even lovelier against the blue than they had been before. The sky became more luminous as a glow behind the eastern peaks promised the rising of the moon. I walked to the beach on the far side of the Island.

At last the lake was freezing; it had resisted the ice for days. I always thought of it as a personality, whose mood changed from fierce anger to gloating triumph. It never seemed to have a peaceful blessing for me. The lake was wicked; its glacier-fed waters were ice-cold even on the warmest summer days, and its strength was pitted against the puny humans who ventured upon its surface. Now it groaned hideously and cracked with a sound like cannon, as if it was protesting against the paralysis fast overcoming it.

The call to breakfast on Christmas morning was a peal from Andy's trumpet. We all gathered in the living room, which was unusually warm and comfortable. Birch logs standing on end in the fireplace blazed and crackled cheerily. Breakfast was served buffet style, with bowls of several kinds of fruit, Mrs. Anderson's Swedish rolls filled with nuts and raisins, and quantities of coffee.

The tall decorated tree was alight with candles, the gifts piled underneath. Some of them were wrapped in plain brown paper, others in newspaper, and a few were gay with ribbon and tinsel.

George had drawn my name and delighted me with a pair of authentic Eskimo sunglasses. Two wooden discs, with a thin slit across the middle of each, were held by wire frames. Only a limited amount of light could come through the slits, cutting down the glare, yet I could see amazingly well through them. As an added refinement, bear hair was glued at the top to catch perspiration, so that it didn't run down into the eyes.

Mrs. Anderson gave Jack knitted ear muffs and, in addition, a fruitcake. Art was given an artistic swinging sign for the boat landing on his island. Among the other gifts was a packboard that brought forth much praise from the men as it fitted the back so well; a copper ash tray shaped like a Viking ship; an ingenious mousetrap made of a five-gallon gasoline can. Mrs. Anderson received a mirror in a hand-carved wooden frame. I was touched to receive from her an exquisite life-size water-color painting of Bohemian waxwings. I knew she must have worked hard at painting it and I was deeply grateful. My cookies for John and the coon for Val were a big success. Also, I knew how the Andersons loved books and had ordered some for them. The candles were guttering in their sockets before all the presents had been distributed and admired. Cliff kept a watchful eye on the candles and occasionally snuffed out one that threatened to set fire to the tree.

When we dressed for the evening meal, I searched through my wardrobe for something festive. For a long time I had dressed only in rough outdoor clothes. I looked at the few dresses I had brought and would probably never wear again. It made me shiver to think of wearing any of them, for

I was used to a heavy wool ski suit. I finally decided on a dark knitted wool, with long sleeves and high collar, that looked warmer than the rest. I wore my felt boots and carried high-heeled pumps to put on when I arrived. "What are you going to wear, Jack?" I asked.

"My new plaid wool shirt, I guess," he answered judiciously. "The others will be dressed that way."

Christmas dinner was a revelation of Mrs. Anderson's talent. At Art's request she had prepared what they called "krup krokas," a Swedish delicacy, made by surrounding chopped salt pork, onions, and a herb seasoning with mashed potatoes, and boiling the resulting balls like dumplings. The table was loaded with vegetables and salads and several kinds of Scandinavian rolls and bread. Andy, in high good humor, stood at the head of the table and carved two summer-fattened geese. The feast ended with pumpkin pie and whipped cream.

Mrs. Anderson wore a red dress, and had a red velvet poinsettia in her black curls. Her eyes were feverishly bright and she laughed much of the time.

Radio reception was unusually good, and we listened to some outside stations as well as the usual station KFQD at Anchorage. While some of us played games the boys sang together. The little house must have been experiencing the merriest Christmas it had ever known.

I was deeply happy as Jack and I walked home in the moonlight, the frost crackling under our feet. It seemed natural for us to be there, and this beautiful world promised us freedom and satisfaction beyond anything I had ever dreamed of.

Next morning Jack got out of bed in the frigid dawn and, pulling on the new bathrobe I had given him for Christmas, went to look out the window.

"What are they shouting about?" I asked sleepily.

"The boys are out there skating."

"Do you suppose the ice is safe?"

"Oh, yes, with this cold." And he added eagerly, "It's smooth as glass—I must try my new skates."

Jack did not wait for breakfast. I watched through the window as he sat down on a log and put on his skates. Then he went skimming like a swallow to where the boys were skating some distance from the shore, and a cheer went up from them. Cliff and Val were fine skaters, but George and John were trying, not at first very successfully, to adapt a knowledge of roller skating to this new sport.

They were chasing each other, shouting and laughing, when I arrived at the beach later and sat down on the log to watch. There was a little bit of envy in my heart. In South Carolina the ice was never thick enough for skating and I had never learned properly. It soon became too cold to sit still, so I ran back to the cabin and put on my creepers— metal plates with spikes, strapped to the ball of the foot. I now felt secure on the ice and it was fun to run far out on the lake; for the lake was in chains now and helpless. The bears were asleep too. Jack left the others and came to skate around me in circles.

Andy brought down a sleigh he had made for his wife's Christmas present, and she was tucked in among the blankets. Andy pushed from behind and they came swiftly, as if on wings, to join the crowd. Mrs. Anderson took her mittened hands from the covers and clapped them, laughing like a child. Andy skated alone among the group for a few minutes, then whisked his wife away in her chariot.

"We can walk across to our place now," Jack said that night as we prepared for bed. "I'd like to examine it without all the Anderson eyes watching my reactions."

I laughed happily. "Let's leave in the morning before any of them are about."

We stole away like conspirators, our creepers crunching into the hard ice. The sun had not yet appeared but the east was rosy in anticipation of another fine day. Jack took long strides, and I jogged along at his side, the tassel of my red hood bobbing.

We had provided ourselves with plenty of warm clothes. Jack's drill parka was standard equipment in interior Alaska. It slipped over the head so there was no front opening for the cold to enter. Any number of warm sweaters could be worn under it, and it acted as a windbreaker. We both wore leather mittens, with wool inner mittens. I give up all pretence of wearing skirts and lived in a wool ski suit. Our felt boots were the most sensible footwear in the dry cold. I was ready to dash out of doors at any time after slipping on a coat and hood, and Jack did the same. This way we didn't need to keep our cabin so warm, and the change in temperature when stepping outside was not so painful. Housekeeping in the tiny cabin was soon disposed of. Never had I enjoyed winter so much.

The cold increased with the first days of 1939. Briefly at midday, when the sun shone, the temperature rose a few degrees, but each night was a little colder than the night before. Several times the thermometer reached thirty below zero.

When the moon was full it was almost as bright as day and the great expanse of lake was an invitation. Often Jack and I walked the mile to Fryingpan in the moonlight and looked in on Art and George. Their little cabin had been built partly underground for warmth.

Andy made an ice tester for me, a long pole with a sharpened nail in the end, which I was to jab into the ice ahead of me as I walked. "You must take it with you wherever you go," he admonished, "and use it often. If the ice tester goes through, stay away."

There was very little snow after the first fall at the beginning of winter. Showshoes were not necessary, but Andy and the boys often used skis. We had several soft spells that winter, with blowing rain and water standing several inches deep all over the lake. At forty above it seemed really warm in contrast to the dry cold. I could see that the winters would take some getting used to.

The soft spells were always followed by severe cold. Sometimes the water on top of the ice froze with a glassy surface, and then no one worked for it was such fun to skate. But when the wind blew the ice froze in jagged humps, and the skaters had to wait for another soft spell to polish it.

Moose appeared close by; one could be seen crossing the ice at almost any time. It was hard to distinguish the bulls from the cows after the horns had been dropped. They scrupulously avoided smooth ice, and often tracks could be seen where they had come down to the shore, taken a step or two on the ice, and then turned back. Andy told how a friend had once shot one he found helplessly spreadeagled on the ice. He said that at such times the moose were the prey of coyotes, who often devoured the poor animal alive.

Several moose remained on the Island all the time, browsing on the small birches that covered the hillside behind the house. One would occasionally jump the fence and hang around the barn, but they were not looking for food. They ate only twigs and branches of trees within their reach. "Why do they act so differently now, Andy?" I asked. "Last summer we wouldn't see one for months."

"They're like that every year at this time," he answered. "The cows seem to get lazy just before the calves are born. They feel safe here and don't move about much."

There was much that I had to learn about taking care of food. Almost a whole case of eggs spoiled, and it was the last time I ever bought eggs by the case. Andy showed me how to cover butter with brine, and I learned to wash slabs of bacon in diluted vinegar to remove the mold. At Andy's kindly insistence, we all shared in the contents of the Andersons' root cellar. Fortunately, there seemed to be an abundance for everyone.

The days lengthened fast. About the middle of February Jack started cutting logs for our house, and he and I walked to Dawson Bay every day. Unk would never go with us if the ice was slippery. He didn't mind wallowing in deep snow, but it frightened him when his feet slipped. That was funny. I told him he shouldn't mind when he had such a little way to fall, but it made no impression on him.

The horses also enjoyed crossing to the mainland every day. They found some sparse grazing along the shore and at this time there was an inch of snow on the ice so it was not slippery.

One afternoon Jack and I had just returned from the mainland, and he was bringing water from a hole in the ice. Andy came out on the terrace and I could hear his trumpet calling the horses to the barn. The horses were a long time responding to the call, but at length I could see from the window that they were coming at full gallop across the ice.

The sound of the trumpet stopped suddenly, and I heard excited shouts. Jack dropped the pail he was carrying and raced toward the Andersons' landing. He was shouting too. When I ran outside I saw the three stampeding horses getting close to a large thin spot on the ice that we had been carefully avoiding. Andy had warned us about it; he said a spring probably bubbled up from beneath.

Andy ran out on the ice, shouting and waving his arms, and Jack was not far behind. Buster, the youngest and most lively of the horses, was some distance in the lead. The other two succeeded in stopping, but Buster reared on his hind legs, struggling frantically and unable to turn in time. For an instant he stood upright; then his hind legs broke through, and the thin ice broke in all directions. He immediately sank out of sight.

"Let Andy save him," I prayed. But Buster's head did not reappear. I knew by the way Andy and Jack stood there quietly that it was all over. Always there was a definite current in the lake, drawing the water toward the swift river that ran to the sea. Buster did not have a chance to swim. Before he could come to the surface he had been drawn under the ice.

Andy lent me an instrument which he called a "spud" with which to peel logs for our house. It was fashioned from a doublebitted axe, one blade of which was driven straight into the end of a stout pole. The bark was frozen when I began work early in the mornings, and I had to wait an hour or two until the sun had begun to thaw it before I could make much progress. At lunch time each day Jack made a fire in the fragrant forest, and we had hot tea with our sandwiches. By now the sun gave real warmth in the middle of the day. Spring was at hand, and I awoke each morning with a surge of well-being.

I was far behind Jack, and there remained logs still un-peeled when Art came with the horses to help haul them across the ice from the Point to our homesite. Already the ice was becoming soft and honeycombed on the surface; it would not bear such a load much longer. Jack had carefully cut trees close to the shore so that the logs could be pushed over the cliffs to the ice below. There they were bound with chains on a homemade sled, and the horses drew them easily, half a dozen at a time, across the ice and up the knoll.

Here my log-peeling became easier as the days grew longer and warmer, and Jack began digging holes for the foundation posts of the house. He made fires in the holes to thaw the iron-hard frozen ground, digging out a little more of the soil every day.

The sun was just sinking behind the hills one afternoon when Jack and I walked back to the Island across the ice. Jack always seemed to get ahead of me: I found it far too easy to lag behind, there was so much to be seen and enjoyed.

Suddenly I saw something that caught me up short. "Jack!" I cried. "Look at the beach on the other side! What on earth is it?"

Jack stopped still and looked intently, then answered slowly, "Can't be anything but a mirage."

The beach looked familiar. It could, in fact, have been that of many sections of the lake, but it looked much nearer than it should have been, and tall breakers, with the last of the setting sun glinting on their foaming white crests, had no right to be where the water was solid ice. We knew positively that the ice was intact to the very shore, and there was no wind. How real it looked, even though good sense insisted it was but an illusion!

There was no certainty as to when the ice would begin to break up, but already it was finding it hard to resist April's smiles. We became more and more impatient; the spongy, slushy cover was increasingly a burden, and we wanted to see the last of it.

The trapping season was over. Cliff and John had done very well snaring coyotes. John planned to come back in the fall to take up a homestead, as did George. Since Art's work on the Yukon River boat would start soon, the three of them headed out, picking their way carefully over the dangerous ice.

Art offered to sell us his little skiff and his rubber-tired wheelbarrow. Andy had promised to build us a boat, but he still had to saw the boards on his sawmill and season them. Meanwhile, our need was great. Art's boat had very little free-board and so would be extremely dangerous in rough weather, but we were delighted to have it.

At long last an ever-widening channel gradually formed from the head of the lake to the end of the Island; only in the bays did the ice remain firm. We anxiously watched the condition of the ice as we went back and forth. Andy warned us that it was no longer safe to walk on, and advised us to wait until we could use a boat. The waiting was especially hard, since there was so much to be done, but it was very interesting to watch the coming of the "breakup."

From the top of the bluff at the head of the Island we could see the upper part of the lake was entirely free. All around the island the ice was dark, lying dead and rotting in the sun. If a heavy stone was dropped on it, the stone would break through, yet the ice was still almost as thick as it had been. Its composition had completely changed.

One day in early May a strong wind sprang up from the north and the ice broke into large cakes which shifted and ground together. One morning the ice was all gone, but that afternoon the wind shifted to the south and brought it back again. The cakes ground and pounded into bits. Then the wind shifted again to the north and carried it away forever.

I was surprised to see how well Jack could handle a boat. He certainly had never had much experience, but rowing seemed to come naturally to him. I myself was anxious to learn to row, but he discouraged me. "I'm afraid you'd drown yourself," he said.

We were so eager to start housekeeping on our own place that we set up a tent near the house site and got ready to move from the Island. We still could not sleep comfortably in the tent, however, as the water was too rough to bring the unwieldy beds across. So we were kept from moving for ten days. More frustrated chafing. It seemed to me the lake was, as usual, just being spiteful. We commuted back and forth to our work in the boat, but we were still attached to the Island by an invisible thread of necessity. The time had come for us to take off independently and we were impatiently flapping our wings on the edge of the nest.

Jack laid a floor of poles in the tent and built double-deck beds. The tent was only eight by ten feet, so it was necessary to conserve every inch of space. He used driftboards I had found along the beach for a comparatively smooth floor around the stove. More poles made rough shelves for supplies.

On the seventeenth of May Andy brought the rest of our household furnishings, such as they were, in his motorboat, and we settled in. Mrs. Anderson and Val came too, and I served hot coffee and bread and jam in the tiny tent, still fragrant with pitch from the green poles. It may have been small and cramped, but it was our very own home.

CHAPTER 5

WE ROSE EARLY after the first night on our property. I was still dressing when Jack ducked out of the tent. "Come and look!" he called excitedly. I threw on the rest of my clothes and hastened after him.

Up the hill, a short distance away, stood the biggest bull moose I had ever seen. His horns were in the velvet, only partly grown, but they plainly indicated how huge they would be by October, when the rutting season commences. He stood staring at us without fear, motionless except for the flapping of one ear and then the other to dislodge mosquitoes. Looked at head on, a moose looks strange as if he were only an elongated sad face.

"He looks so philosophical," I decided, "we ought to call him Socrates."

Jack chuckled and threw a stone at him. It landed very close, but Socrates stood his ground, scorning to withdraw. He seemed to be saying, as Socrates himself is reported to have said in the Apology, "I would have you know that if you kill such a one as I am you will injure yourself more than you will injure me."

After breakfast I looked again. Socrates had moved farther up the hill and was unconcernedly browsing on a small birch. Silently I asked his forgiveness for invading the domain that had been his for so long.

Later we came to know Socrates well; but we never saw him with others of his kind. Andy explained that he had probably been conquered in a fight with a younger bull. Usually such a battle meant death for one or the other, but if the old bull admitted defeat he was an outcast ever after. Andy showed us two sets of horns which told the story of such a fight, except that in this case both had lost; the horns were tangled together so that they could not be separated.

"Did the mosquitoes bother you last night?" Jack asked.

"A little," I answered. I had slept with a sheet over my face.

"The first thing I'll do is try to make the tent proof against them." He caught a mosquito in midair and examined it. "I never saw such big ones," he said.

"The swallows probably won't find us this year," I remarked. "We must certainly have boxes for them next time."

But the swallows did find us. They may have instinctively sought out human habitation, or perhaps their path went over our place, but next morning we heard them before we had gotten up. When we hurried out the air was filled with a fluttering, twittering cloud of them, tree swallows and violet-green swallows. Unk ran around barking hysterically, jumping off the ground to snap at them. When they all suddenly took their departure, his expression was comically self-satisfied; but the whole vast colony soon came wheeling back.

"Oh!" I wailed. "Why didn't we have some boxes ready?" My voice was almost drowned by the excited twittering.

Andy had showed us the kind of nesting boxes the swallows preferred—made of a sheet of birch bark about eighteen inches square. This was formed into a long cylinder enclosed at each end with a thin section of log. A small opening was made in the center of the cylinder for an entrance. The nest could be built far back from the opening, and cannibal butcher birds and Canada jays could not reach in and steal the eggs and nestlings.

"Jack, please help me," I panted. "We can make a couple of boxes from the bark of this old log." The bark was in good condition, while the wood was entirely decayed. I hastily pulled off a section and shook out the rotted wood; it needed only the end pieces. "Please, Jack, help me! Saw some pieces from the end of a log."

Jack was far too deliberate to suit me, as he carefully measured the thickness of the rounds before sawing them off, but it was he who nailed in the ends after I had dropped the nails from my fumbling fingers.

When our first box was finished, we both looked up at the sky, and then at each other. There was not a swallow to be seen. We had been too busy to notice when they left.

"Let's make another box anyway," I said, almost crying. "There may be some stragglers later." If we had been forehanded enough to have the boxes ready our mosquito problem would have been solved. But not another swallow visited us that summer. Evidently the whole flock had traveled together.

So we learned all about mosquitoes that year. After Jack closed the cracks in the tent we could keep them out at night fairly well, and during the day a stiff breeze would waft them away. But at other times we had to use quantities of mosquito repellant. Fortunately, the season for these pests lasted only about a month each summer, just at the time when swallows needed quantities of insects to fill the gaping mouths of their offspring.

Jack had placed his foundation posts so that the house would stand between two birch trees, each looking as if it had received several coats of white enamel. It backed up against a perpendicular wall of bedrock, and we planned to have an attic that could be reached from the top of this wall.

Andy and Cliff promised to help with the actual construction. "I don't like to take money for helping our neighbors," Andy protested when we discussed terms.

"You must," Jack assured him. "This will be keeping you from doing your own work."

The house was to be sixteen by twenty-four feet in size. This was considered a large house by everyone but Jack and me. It lacked three feet of being as long as the living room in our Juneau home.

"Do you intend to make log partitions inside?" Andy asked.

"No," I answered. "Just one big room. We'll have a heating stove in one end and the range in the other, and use our beds for couches." I was determined that the cabin should not be divided up, although Jack was not sure it could be effectively heated.

The attic, to be used for storage, was to be six feet high at the peak.

We expected Andy's sawmill to provide the necessary lumber, but the wind proved very unreliable. A medium wind was required for best results; if it was too mild, the saw spun fitfully, with many pauses; if it was too strong, the machine had to be shut off to prevent accidents. Our stockpile of lumber remained small.

It was maddening to be a woman when so much of our work could be done only by men. When I would set about some arduous project or other, Jack would often stop me. "Wait, now," he would say. "I'll do that when I have time." So I had to look around for an outlet for my energy. I dragged away the whitened skeletons of trees, left by the long-ago forest fire, which improved the landscape wonderfully. Most of them had rotted away, but the tough wood of the overturned roots was more lasting. I dragged them into huge piles; they made a fiercely hot fire. I also knocked down and piled up the stubs of dead birch saplings. Jack asked me to put aside any wood that could be chopped into stove lengths, so I felt that I was being really useful for a change.

An old moose trail led down the slope from the house site to the beach. I widened and graded it, carried gravel from the beach, and put in log steps for a good foot trail from the boat landing to the house.

Andy and Cliff had much work of their own at home, and it was June before they came to start the house. Spring, with all its duties, had exploded suddenly as it always did. Their garden had to be left to the care of Mrs. Anderson and Val.

Round by round the walls went up, and the solid little building began to emerge.

Andy, with years of experience, knew exactly how to proceed with the building. The heavy logs were notched and fitted together with great care at the corners. After each log was placed, holes an inch and a half in diameter were bored through it with a long auger into the log below, and pins inserted to hold both logs firmly together. Jack did the boring and other comparatively menial jobs while the technical construction was left to the others. We were endlessly grateful for all the invaluable help and advice these experts gave us. We might have managed somehow, but it would have taken far longer and the results wouldn't have been so sturdy and secure.

Andy constantly used a level and plumb-bob to keep the walls true as they were raised, and we were careful to use straight, well-peeled logs. Just the same, the cracks had to be chinked. Jack and I planned to do this with sphagnum moss after the building was finished.

This was to be only the first unit of the house, and would later become the living room. I could see very plainly the completed house, with a wing on the north for a bedroom and two big closets, and an extension in front containing a kitchen, bath, and stone-floored entrance hall. I began to collect smooth cobblestones of many colors from the beaches for the fireplace in the rear. The sun would pour in through the south windows. The whole would be smothered and submerged in flowers—annuals we would start in a little greenhouse.

I sat on a hump of bedrock near Jack as he worked, and went over my plans. "See here, Jack," I said. "I've drawn the plan to scale."

"That'll make it easier to follow," he replied, a little absently. But as he stopped work and wiped his face and the bald spot on the top of his head with a large blue handkerchief, there was such deep contentment in his eyes as I had never seen before.

"It's easy enough for me to dream up plans," I said, "but you have to do the work."

"Dreams are important too," he replied, "and you're a good dreamer." His smile shone white in sharp contrast to his sun-browned face. How healthy and fit he looked! He seemed in tune with his surroundings, and his personal problems had vanished. He simply did not have time for them. I was far less apprehensive that some disaster might sweep away his new confidence and self-reliance. We would have to work hard, but we were traveling in the right direction.

Certain essentials of living which I had always taken for granted also had to be taken care of. I was far ahead of the present in my dreaming, when Jack called me back to earth. "We've got to have some sort of sanitary system at once."

"Do you mean a bathroom?"

"I mean a privy," he said bluntly.

"I suppose we have to," I agreed, my vision of a neat, well-heated bath vanishing. "Of course, it will be just temporary. Let's at least build it behind the little knoll so it won't be so obvious from the house." I later wished I had been less fussy and built it closer to the door.

Jack built the little house of logs with a tar-paper roof. He had no boards or hinges for making the door, so I sewed together a couple of burlap sacks for a curtain. A galvanized wash tub served us for bathing, the water of the lake being too cold, whatever the season.

The weather was perfect. The men came to work early every morning and I served them lunch on a card table out of doors. My experience with cooking on the small camp-stove was disheartening at first but, after the lifeline between us and the Island had been cut, I learned from sheer necessity. I found after a couple of indigestible experiments that I could make bread that was edible, by baking one loaf at a time. I devoted an entire afternoon each week to the task, and sat reading while carefully feeding fine-cut wood into the stove. If I turned my back, the fire went out or the bread burned on one side, but with fairly constant watching it turned out quite well.

On one of these afternoons a young junco flew in through the flap of the tent and lit on my book. I was probably the first human being he had ever seen, and there was no fear in the beady little eye he cocked at me. I talked to him in a low tone, but my conversation seemed to bore him, for he stretched one leg and yawned before flying away.

The walls were completed, the shorter logs in the gable ends hewed and fitted, the rafters and ridgepole raised. This was as far as Andy and Cliff's help went, and Jack carried on alone.

Over the winter Jack had laboriously made sashes for the windows, following Andy's directions and using his tools. Jack allowed me to put in the glass and putty it, and although I found it was not as easy as it looked, I somehow managed to make them passably weathertight. When the windows were fitted into the openings, I polished them with housewifely zeal until they shone.

Jack made a heavy door, with cross boards for reinforcement. We had to think of some way of stopping the cracks that would appear when the green boards shrank. We carefully took some boxes apart and, after covering the door with several thicknesses of paper, designed the box material in a pattern over it. Then we took some narrow strips left over from making the window sash, and covered the cracks where the box boards joined. The nail holes were neatly hidden.

"No cold can come through that," Jack said approvingly. "I hope I can hang it so there'll be no opening around it." He fitted it very carefully and hung it with big barn door hinges. It was a handsome door, true and heavy. I painted it green.

"Let's put on a wooden latch," I suggested, "with the latchstring hanging out."

"A manufactured one will be better," Jack said prudently. "You can depend on it not to come open some cold night."

He carried out my design for the windowboxes, making them from sections of log. I set in them some nasturtiums I had planted in a box some time earlier. Transplanted, they looked very anemic. I knew Andy would gladly give me some rich soil and fertilizer from the barn, but I didn't want to ask any more favors.

The long days inspired us to work harder and accomplish more than I had thought possible. We never ceased to marvel at the amount of sunshine; the weather was really hot during the day. The sunsets behind Caribou Island were followed by an afterglow of greenish opalescent light that hardly faded before dawn began to flush the sky over Dawson Point, soon after midnight. We were very close to the land of the midnight sun. I begrudged the hours that must be given to sleeping, and often when I slipped into the tent to go to bed I could hear Jack already breathing deeply in restful sleep.

After our evening meal—when work for the day was finished and before I was compelled to go to bed—was the time I liked best. Jack threw a log across the narrow strip of water to the little rock island as a temporary bridge, and Unk and I would cross gingerly and sit in the last rays of the setting sun. It was cool, then, with enough breeze across the water to discourage the mosquitoes.

The bay was the favorite hunting ground for many water birds, especially at dusk. Graceful Arctic terns flew low, searching for a glimpse of fish in the water. Often a tern would suspend itself in midair, wings vibrating like those of a hummingbird, then drop like a stone and rise with a small fish wriggling in its beak. Then the other terns would swoop in, and there would be a screaming struggle for the prize. On the beach were many tern nests, consisting simply of a hollow in the gravel where three eggs were laid. When Unk came near, the parent birds dove down at him with snapping beaks.

Black, ungainly cormorants, as we approached, half-swam, half-flew along the water, with a great splashing and flapping of wings. When the gulls finished nesting on the rocky islands down the lake, they brought their young to Dawson Bay for the salmon run.

Of all the birds I found the loons most interesting. Day and night their strange, unearthly cries rang out across the water. I had heard this cry described as laughter, but to me it never remotely resembled anything so light-hearted. Sometimes a number of them would swim and dive in circles, grunting like hogs. More often, their cry was a wail or howl, and I had heard them give a sharp yelp like that of an injured dog. I was also impressed by their ability to swim under water for an incredible length of time when frightened.

The lake was now full of salmon on their way to the spawning grounds in the streams. They could often be seen jumping clear of the water as they passed.

There had been so much to do that it was only gradually I realized that we were getting low on many food staples. I trusted Andy, but at times felt a little fearful. "Jack," I wailed, "we have no baking powder, and our flour and sugar are almost gone. What are we going to do?"

"I've decided to have a little talk with Andy," Jack answered. "Come on, let's get the boat."

"And I want to see if they'll sell me some fresh eggs," I added, hurrying to keep up with him. "I've been suspicious of gull eggs ever since the little gull gasped at me when I opened one."

Andy had seen us coming and was at the landing to meet us. As we walked up the path to the house, Jack asked him, "Have you any plans for hauling our freight soon, old man? Our cupboard's almost as bare as Mother Hubbard's."

"You don't need to worry," Andy answered easily. "The Road Commission sent me some money for fixing the trail, and in a month we'll have it in fine shape to bring your freight with the horses."

My anxiety was quieted. A month was a long time, but I knew we could manage on what we had. "We should be living in our house by the Fourth of July, shouldn't we, Andy?" I asked, changing the subject. The Fourth was only a week away, but I was always optimistic.

"Oh, yes. It won't take long to get the roof on and the floor in. I'll soon have the lumber sawed."

"I'd like so much for us to give the annual picnic!" I exclaimed. "Won't it be fun! The first anniversary of the day I discovered Dawson Bay."

"Is there anything I can bring?" Mrs. Anderson asked. "Not that we have anything," she said fretfully, "but we're supposed to take food to a picnic, aren't we?"

"Oh, no," I assured her. "We want you as real guests." Then I thought it might make her happier after all to bring something. "Well," I added, "if your celery is high enough, it would be wonderful to have some for the salad."

I bought some eggs, and they generously gave us lettuce, onions, and radishes from the garden, and a gallon of goat's milk.

"Why hasn't he told us before about fixing the trail?" Jack muttered, when we had shoved off in the boat. "I know it's in bad shape, and I've been worrying. Even with a good trail, it will be an awful job to bring a year's supply of groceries, with all the other things we all need."

"Andy does a lot for us, Jack. We must be fair to him." I was thinking of all the welcome food they had just given us.

"Oh, I know it," Jack replied. "It's not his fault. It's just that I have to depend on other people so. We came out here to be on our own—I don't like to be beholden, or to worry what would happen if the Andersons weren't around to look after us."

Unfortunately, the day of the picnic was chilly, with dashes of rain. We had a flag flying bravely from the peak of the gable, but as yet no roof.

Our guests waved gaily from the boat. Cliff, in his rubber boots, jumped into the water close to shore and pulled the boat up on the gravel, so that the others could step out on dry land.

Andy was jauntily dressed in his white suit and a blue sweater. Cliff and Val had on blue shirts, and all three wore red ties. When Mrs. Anderson was helped ashore I saw that she wore a blue linen dress with white collar and cuffs and a red bow at her throat.

"Look, Jack!" I cried. "They're all wearing red, white and blue. I wish we had thought of that. How nice of you!"

Jack made them all comfortable on logs and boxes around a big bonfire he had made of my bleached stumps. We drew up close, for although the rain had stopped the wind was cold.

"Jessie hasn't been well for several days," Andy confided, "but I made her come. I thought it would be good for her to get out of the house."

I then noticed that she really did look sick. There were dark circles under her eyes, and her shoulders drooped listlessly. She seemed preoccupied and far away, hardly paying attention to the rest of us or saying a word.

The day before I had spent many hours baking buns, three at a time, something I had never before attempted in the little campstove. We roasted on sticks over the fire some canned wieners I had saved for months. With mustard they tasted almost like the usual kind. Mrs. Anderson's tender celery gave zest to the potato salad, as did the wild cress I had found in the woods. I also used a little wild onion, but very little, as it was strong as garlic.

Since dawn, beans had been baking in a tin can in a hole in the ground, lined with rock. "Are you sure they'll get done?" Jack asked doubtfully.

"Well, the Girl Scouts cook beans that way," I answered, "and I'm giving them plenty of time." It worked surprisingly well, although the heat caused the rocks to crumble.

Andy was very much interested. "I've cooked beans that way, too," he said. "Next time try using granite rocks and they won't break."

Mrs. Anderson was still very quiet and scarcely touched her food. I had looked forward to showing her all we had done, but she wasn't interested. After some urging, she consented to enter the roofless house.

"See how much light we'll have from the windows!" I pointed out enthusiastically. She did not answer, so I went on to explain, "Jack says he can build a balcony of poles over the rear of the room, until we get lumber for a ceiling. We'll have a ladder and keep our supplies up there. The kitchen will be under the balcony."

But she had returned to the doorway and, with her wide back turned, stood looking out over the lake. "Nonsense!" she said over her shoulder. "If you're depending on getting lumber from Hjalmar, you might as well forget it. That's one of the dreams that will never come true." Her black eyes were desolate. "Here no dreams ever come true."

"Oh, no!" I answered, trying with all my might to sound gay and reassuring. "I'll never believe that, even if I'm beaten to my knees. Our dreams will all come true, and we'll have a beautiful home. You already have one—I'll be happy when we have as much as you have. And look! From this window I can see the place where your new stone house will stand on top of the bluff."

"My new stone house!" she jeered, her voice bitter. "It would take a lot of lumber and materials that we haven't the money to buy, and never will have. Instead of doing our work at home, Hjalmar's fixing the trail to bring your freight."

"He'd have to fix the trail anyway so he can bring your own freight, wouldn't he?" I said quietly. I felt that whatever I said would probably infuriate her. "Besides, we will pay him for the work."

Mrs. Anderson heaved her shoulders around as she often did when angry. She brushed past me and returned to the fire. "I'm cold, Hjalmar," she said. "We should start home."

I was not so vulnerable now that we had our own place, and Mrs. Anderson's mercurial moods affected me much less. My thoughts were occupied with my own plans, and my hands with hard, satisfying work.

Jack leveled and graded a wide trail from the beach to the proposed location for the vegetable garden. Meanwhile, I gradually cleared a good-sized area in front of the house, digging up low-bush cranberry and shaking the soil from its roots. I burned the bushes and spread the ashes over the soil. The earth was very poor, but just relieving the ground of its smothering blanket of cranberry, digging over the surface, and letting in sunshine and air improved it.

We decided to have a lawn—the Andersons' lawn was very attractive and neat. I prepared the ground, with occasional help from Jack, in the space immediately in front of the house and also on the north side, expecting to seed it next spring. The wildflower section was to surround the lawn, dividing it from the woods.

As soon as we moved we had brought raspberry plants from the Island for a large patch. The Andersons said it had to be fenced, otherwise the moose would destroy the plants in winter; so during the summer Jack built a mooseproof fence of poles around it. We buried surplus fish around the plants, and they grew well from the beginning.

I studied the native flora and made notes about seeding. To gather seeds from the wildflowers required the utmost alertness. Even after I knew just where the plants could be found and the approximate time of seed maturity, it was often impossible to reach them before a storm blew the seeds away or the birds gobbled them up. Many of the plants I was particularly interested in grew along the beach, and the seeds matured just at the time when the late summer high water would ruin them. There were problems aplenty. I resolved to make a place near the house for plants whose seeds were the most elusive.

The fragrance of wildflowers was noticeably stronger than that of the same flowers growing in southeastern Alaska. No doubt this was because of the lighter rainfall. In damp places in the shade hundreds of the dwarf *Pyrola uniflora* grew, their delicate perfume spreading over a great distance.

Especially at the end of a warm day at twilight, I caught whiffs of the most enchanting perfume. At first I thought it came from the blossoms of the low-bush cranberry which covered the ground in all directions; but long after its pink bells had faded, I continued to be haunted by those whiffs of sweetness, until I discovered one day that it was the distinctive scent of the trailing Twin-flower that covered large areas around us.

Two weeks had passed since Andy and Cliff left to work on the trail. We hoped they would soon return with our freight; we had ordered a good many things we needed badly for the house.

One morning Jack went to the beach with the water pail. "I believe I hear a motor," he called. "Come listen and see if you can hear it." The water carried sound clearly, and, sure enough, I could hear from far away the low hum of an approaching motorboat. As the hum grew louder we could tell it was not Cliff's little "eggbeater," but a powerful motor. As the boat rounded the end of the Point we saw that it carried two men, and soon I recognized Andy's red turban.

When the boat touched the gravel, Andy leaped ashore.

I saw a number of things that must be ours protruding from beneath a tarpaulin. The other man, thin and frail looking, climbed out stiffly, and Andy introduced Hank Lucas, who owned a homestead farther down the shore, but now lived at the Landing.

"While I was so near the Landing I decided to go in yesterday and get Hank to help bring down the heaviest pieces of your freight," Andy explained.

We were cheered to see the heating stove, kitchen range, outboard motor, and roofing paper we needed so desperately. They had also brought the radio, battery, and pieces of the windcharger which we had ordered after a good deal of soul-searching. We had placed our orders with great care, after much poring over catalogs and counting our pennies. So far our expenses were not alarming. Of course a day of reckoning would come when we must earn a living, but I felt a strange lack of concern over money since we did not handle it regularly. At any rate, our only real luxury thus far was the radio, with its battery and the propeller-driven windcharger to recharge the battery. Since it was our only source of outside news, it was a luxury that came close to being a necessity.

Andy and Jack tried to dissuade Hank, who looked as if the slightest strain might be the end of him, from helping to unload the cumbersome range from the boat, but he insisted on doing his share. "Christ! It's a heavy brute!" he panted. Hank began every sentence with "Christ!" Christ, he was glad to meet us. Christ, it was a fine day. Finally the heavy crate was out of the boat and resting on the gravel.

Andy sat down on the bow of the boat to roll a cigarette. He appeared to intend leaving the freight on the beach, and I could see it embarrassed Jack to ask him, "Could you help me get the range up to the house? We can handle the other things ourselves."

"Oh, of course!" Andy answered indulgently, and with

much straining and puffing the crate was desposited in front
of the door.

"Don't do any more," I begged. "Let's have lunch.
Water's hot for coffee."

"Coffee's tempting," Andy replied, "but Jess and Val are
waiting for us." Jack gave him a check for the freight, and
they were off.

It was hard to decide whether to try out the outboard
motor or the radio first. Jack tested the battery and found it
fully charged. But, after all, a motor was the most important
thing in our lives just then; so, after a few minutes, Jack called
to me to come on. The sputter was music to my ears.

Jack, Unk and I had a lovely ride around the end of the
Point, circling far out into the lake. I think Unk enjoyed it
most. He loved to be taken out in the boat, and would always sit upright in the bow, his nose pointed into the wind.

The motor was small, only five horsepower, and it was
just right for our little fourteen-foot skiff. "I'm afraid we
made a mistake in getting one so small," Jack said apologetically when he had shut off the motor and we were drifting
onto the beach. "We'll have to have a bigger boat soon."

He then hooked up the radio and the sound came
through without interference. We had never heard such good
reception in Alaska; and all the rest of the day we listened to
the news and to music on the dial and heard Big Ben strike
the hour. All of Europe was preparing for war. We felt far
away from it indeed in our wilderness home.

CHAPTER 6

THERE WAS A STORM with high wind for several days, and we didn't see Andy again until the morning after it cleared, when we saw him coming around the Point, standing upright as he rowed his heavy boat.

He let the boat drift close to shore, but made no effort to beach it. He looked tired and worried. "I'm on my way to work on the trail," he said. "Jessie was very sick when I got home. She's some better now but I hate to be away any more than I have to."

"Won't the trail soon be finished," I asked, "so you can stay at home?"

"I hope it'll take only a few more days." Andy turned toward Jack with a wry smile. "I'm certainly sorry to bring you bad news. I tried to saw some lumber on the mill yesterday, but the wind was too strong and I couldn't control the propeller. It began going too fast and broke badly. I'll have to do a lot of work on it before we can cut any more."

Jack and I looked at each other in dismay. What about our roof?

"You can probably find enough boards around the sawmill to go under your roof," Andy added, as if he could read our minds. "Some of them will not be good—too thick or too thin on one side—but you can have them cheap."

"Well, since I have a motor now," Jack said slowly, "I guess I can get them over here."

"I wish I could help you haul them," Andy said apologetically, "but I think we should finish working on the trail before bad weather comes. It's important to get all our freight hauled." He was in a hurry to be gone and bent to the oars once more. "Take anything at the mill that you can use," he called.

"Well, isn't that a fine note!" Jack said gloomily. "We can get along without a floor for a while, but we can't get along without a roof. We'll just have to go to the Island and see what there is."

"Jack, that pile of boards he's cut was for the new house. She won't want us to have them."

"We can't help it," Jack answered firmly. "We've got to have a roof, and this late we can't get the lumber from anybody else. We depended on Andy instead of ordering it elsewhere, and we'll just have to make do with what there is." He began busily loading rope, a hammer, and nails in the boat.

We found Mrs. Anderson in bed. She was very ill-looking, her black eyes sunken and dark-circled.

I felt awkward and tongue-tied. "I wish you didn't have to stay alone so much with no one but Val," I said. "Would you like for me to stay with you while Andy is away?" We were very busy, but if she needed help I was willing to stay.

"No, I'd rather be alone—I'm used to it." A tear trickled down her cheek. "It was the same when he was a guide. Regardless of how sick I was he would leave me and take care of other people."

"Did Andy tell you he was letting us have the lumber at the mill so we can get our roof on?" I asked. I could think of no way to lead up to the subject diplomatically.

"Take it," she said dully. "I don't care any more. I never believed I would get a house."

I had to go help Jack make a raft of the boards so we

could tow them home. Val stood by and watched, glaring at us silently, and I felt like a thief. Two trips were required to tow the boards, but still there would be barely enough for the roof. We made a third trip to gather odds and ends and any small pieces that we could find. Val never said a word to us —just stood silent and forlorn on the beach.

Andy had cut the logs twelve feet long, so the boards were uniform in length. A few of them were uniformly one inch thick. We carried them up from the beach two at a time, Jack at one end and I at the other.

"The surface will have to be smooth under the paper," he said, "or it won't wear well and will leak." He planed the thick edges down, and built up the thin ones with strips underneath. All this took more than a week. It was uncomfortable work, for the weather had turned dark and cold, but at last the roof was ready for the tar paper. I held one end of each strip to keep the wind from whipping and tearing it, while Jack applied tar and nailed it down. We finally had a weatherproof roof over our heads even though we ended up looking like tar babies.

Jack leveled the floor, and together we shoveled clean gravel from the beach a foot deep over the earth. Jack tamped it down flat with a heavy log. "I wish I had something to make a sprinkling can out of," he said thoughtfully.

"Oh, I know," I said, and hurried out to the tent. "Here's this five-gallon gasoline can I found on the beach. Of course," I apologized, "it's very rusty."

Jack smiled. "It'll do in a pinch." He punched holes in the bottom and filled it with water again and again, until there was no sign of dust or sand left, and the gravel was clean and fresh.

We later noticed that dust found its way up through the stones, but a good sprinkling was all that was necessary to keep it clean and fresh. This became a regular part of our housekeeping.

We admired our work when we had finished. I suddenly leaned on Jack's arm, giggling.

"What's the matter now?"

"Don't you like our floor covering? Wall-to-wall gravel!" He pretended he thought I was very silly, but he could not hide the affectionate amusement in his eyes.

We put up the heating stove and made a crackling fire, basking in its welcome warmth and grinning at each other triumphantly. Unk crowded close too. He demanded his comforts and with one reproachful glance could make me feel very inefficient.

Jack had used tin to protect the roof where the stovepipe pierced it. "It's awfully dangerous," he said, "but it'll have to do temporarily. I would hate to lose all we had worked for in a fire."

"Oh, Jack! That would be terrible. We must be very careful."

"We'll just have to keep our eye on it," Jack answered, watching intently as smoke and heat were sucked upward through the stovepipe, and adjusting the flow gently with the damper. "Maybe someday we can manage something better. Jack Lean, I know, recommends concrete sewer pipe. We ought to get some as soon as we can."

Soon a succession of heavy frosts laid low the summer vegetation, and one morning a thin coating of crisp snow covered the ground, only to vanish under the noonday sun. Almost overnight the hills turned pure gold. When the sun shone brightly the color was almost painfully dazzling to the eye. It was the birches, which grew thick on the hillsides, that gave them their bright hue, with occasional spruces looking almost black by contrast.

One day at twilight we saw Cliff's little boat chug toward the Island, towing the scow with the two horses. We planned to go over early next morning to see if they had brought any mail but even before it was quite day we heard the sound of their motor approaching.

Andy was haggard, and his hand shook as I handed him

a usual cup of coffee. It was strong, the way he liked it. "I found Jessie very sick when I got home," he said tensely. "This can't go on. I'm going to Seward to see if I can get a doctor to come. If I can't do that, I'll arrange for a plane to take her to the hospital."

"I'm so sorry, Andy," I said awkwardly.

Jack added, "Gosh, yes! We'll do anything we possibly can to help."

"I came to borrow your motor as it's heavier than Cliff's," he said tersely. "I must make every moment count. I'll be back tonight." Andy put his hands over his face and groaned. "I shouldn't have left her so long." He swallowed his coffee hastily and hurried out.

I called to him when he was halfway down the trail, "We'll go over to the Island right away, Andy—I'll stay until you get back."

"I'd appreciate it," he answered, without turning, and waved his arm.

Jack took me over at once to do what I could. As I got into the boat, Unk leaped aboard and established himself firmly in his usual place in the bow. No amount of threats or persuasion could dislodge him. "Unk may be a nuisance to you," Jack said as we approached the Island, "but he'll stew all the time if he isn't with you." He gave Unk a friendly whack on the rear and picked him up and tossed him on the beach. He then held out his hand to steady me as I jumped out and, without leaving the boat, turned back toward his numerous duties at home.

Mrs. Anderson was in bed, but I was surprised to find her quite cheerful. She said she felt all right except when she tried even to lift her head from the pillow. All that day I tried to attend to her wants so that she would not have to move. She laughed heartily at Cliff's and my efforts to prop her up so that she could drink the soup I prepared. She chatted away gaily, speculating whether it would be a doctor who would come or a plane to take her away. I could see that even under these circumstances she was thrilled at the prospect of contact with the outside world.

It was nearly morning when Andy returned. He said he had run both ways on the trail. He had been able to get a ride from the Landing to Seward, but none of the doctors there were willing to come out so far. They persuaded him to take his wife to a hospital by plane. So Andy had contacted one of the bush pilots, flying out of Anchorage, who had promised to come for her next day. This was the kind of emergency trip they were frequently called upon to make; I could well understand the gratitude and affection people in the Alaska wilderness felt for these pilots and their small planes.

The weather turned warm that night, and it was on a dreamy, golden autumn day that a pontoon plane dropped into the lake and taxied to the Island beach. They made a place for Mrs. Anderson to lie on the floor of the cabin, and she was able to walk from the house with Andy and the pilot supporting her. Andy, forgetful of himself, made no preparation for his own departure, and left with his hair and clothes wildly disheveled.

I was depressed and full of foreboding, although I told myself that Andy would bring her back in a few days. My fear was not altogether for Mrs. Anderson—I was myself in a similar situation now. Mrs. Anderson had characteristics that I hoped I possessed, such as intelligence and practical ability, and besides these a loving family, but they were not enough. Her poor health, I believed, was not the cause of her troubles but rather the effect of her reaction to her environment. Now I would have to prove that I had the essential quality that Mrs. Anderson lacked—whether it was courage, unselfishness, patience, or whatever trait was needed to build one's strength for life in the wilderness. I prayed to be shown the way.

We did not return home that night; the Andersons' vegetables had to be gathered without delay and our help was needed. We all looked after the plane until it was no longer a speck in the sky, then started to digging potatoes. There was a bountiful crop; all next day we helped Cliff and Val store away great quantities of vegetables in the root cellar. Our own soil seemed very unproductive, but Andy had assured us that the soil on the Island had been no better when they came, and that it would not take long to build up. We did not have the animal manure as the Andersons did, but planned to use fish for fertilizer.

"Make a signal fire if you need us for anything, and we'll come over," Jack told the boys as we pushed off in the boat.

"You've done enough," Cliff answered. "We'll get along fine. You must do your own work."

A mountain of it was in fact waiting for us at home. First, Jack had to make a balcony, by laying poles across the rafters in the rear of the cabin, and a ladder to reach it, where we could store our small supply of food. The room was divided—at least in our minds, for there were no partitions—into two parts. The front part contained our beds, covered with monkscloth spreads and piled with green and rose-colored cushions; in the rear, with the balcony overhead, was the kitchen. We also had a long carved walnut table that had been shipped with our beds. This I placed near the stove for magazines and books and the gasoline reading lamp. We reserved two wooden boxes for seats and nailed up the others on the wall to serve as additional shelves. We used a folding card table for dining. Somewhere Jack found enough boards to use for kitchen shelves to hold the food and dishes we used every day, and I covered them with oilcloth.

The winter before, while we lived on the Island, I had used Mrs. Anderson's sewing machine to make and line curtains of bright chintz for the four windows. I made brackets from the crotches of small alders, and curtain rods from peeled spruce poles, all of which were sandpapered, stained, and waxed.

Andy had watched me stitch the curtains, and was most interested in my plans.

"I'll have to find some way to hang them on the poles," I told him. "I need rings so they can be pulled across the windows, but I forgot to order them."

"You could make rings from the leg bones of moose," he suggested. "I've got plenty of them. Let's go to the shop and I'll show you how." He fixed the bones securely in a vise and sawed off sections the size of regular curtain rings. When they were rubbed down with sandpaper they looked exactly like ivory.

Jack said the gravel floor would likely be cold in winter, so he scouted up enough boards to make wooden "rugs," one in front of the place where the range would stand and one by the heating stove, with a wool hooked rug on the latter to keep our feet warm when we sat reading or listening to the radio. Unk, however, objected to lying either on gravel or bare boards, and appropriated the rug as his own.

The kitchen range was uncrated, and its foundation prepared in the rear of the room. The bill of lading stated that it weighed six hundred and fifty pounds. It was impossible for Jack and me to budge it alone, and we doubted that we could move it even if we had Cliff to help. I didn't fancy cooking all winter outside the front door, but could see no solution to the problem.

Then, one cold, frosty morning we heard a chorus of motors coming from the lower end of the lake. Soon we could see three large dories, with several men in each, and we ran down to the beach to meet them. They looked like bearded pirates and I felt very glad Jack was at home. Suddenly one man stood up in the bow of his boat and waved his hat. Who could it be? When they were close enough we recognized Floyd Betts, an old friend from Juneau. He was in charge of a sizable crew of men making up a government survey party. They had left their camp on the lower Kenai River and were looking for moose. The boys looked positively silly, grinning through whiskers of various degrees of luxuriance grown proudly in the wilderness.

"I've been trying to get up to see you all summer," Floyd said enviously. "If my wife would only agree to live like this."

The range sat there suggestively in all its heaviness and bulk. Everyone had to walk around it to get into the house. "Let's ask them to help us move it," I whispered to Jack.

Floyd heard me. "What's that? You want this stove moved? Come on, boys!"

There was not room enough around the range for all the eager young hands that were anxious to help. It was soon deposited in its ivory-enameled splendor on the foundation in the kitchen.

Jack pushed the stovepipe up through a hole in the roof, and I made a fire. Soon the teakettle was bubbling, and I made coffee and served bread and jam to the whole crowd.

"Can't you just camp here and get your moose nearby?" Jack suggested. "You're sure to find some at the Lick just over the hill."

"Wish we could, Floyd answered regretfully. "But we want to go on to the head of the lake and try for some sheep on one of those peaks."

We stood on the beach and listened until the sound of the motors died away. Jack was grinning happily. "Gosh, what an easy way to get the stove moved!"

"It was a miracle, darling," I answered. "I'll never doubt miracles again. If we're ever in great need, help always comes —remember how the Indians brought Andy a motor last winter?"

Jack's hand tightened on my shoulder, and he smiled at me. I think he believed it too.

The range, with its reservoir for hot water, took all

the drudgery out of cooking. The oven was wonderful—it even had a thermometer! I liked it better than the electric range I had cooked on in Juneau, and the smell of wood smoke was clean and good.

A couple days later, as we lingered over breakfast, Jack surprised me with a question. "How would you like to take a trip to the Landing before the snow begins to fly? Any morning now we may wake up and find the ground covered. After all, this is your second year here." He looked at me very solemnly. "You may not know it but you're getting queer."

"Me getting queer!" I laughed. "It's you! It always starts with seeing queerness in others."

"It'll do us both good," Jack answered with a grin. "I'll have to go on a few errands anyway before winter. Can you be ready by this evening? We'll spend the night at the river cabin and walk the trail tomorrow."

"I'll be ready," I assured him. "But what about Unk?"

"We'll take him with us."

The sun had already set when we arrived at the little cabin, near the beach where the swift Kenai River burst out into the lake. It was comfortable and secure, with bunks and blankets, and we had brought our sleeping bags. That tiny cabin never seemed strange to me; it had an atmosphere of friendliness and welcome. Long ago Andy and Hank had built it for just such needs. Bags containing beans, flour, and sugar hung from the rafters, out of reach of mice. There was always enough for a chance visitor who might be hungry but we had brought our own food and enough to leave some for the next person who came by. There was also a pile of shavings and kindling by the stove. Jack soon had a fire going, and I laid out supper.

Next morning, after cutting enough wood to replace what we'd used, we set out. The trail was dry underfoot and yellow leaves drifted down on our heads. Jack led the way at a steady pace. He swung along smoothly to reach his destination as quickly as possible while I tended to dawdle. Jack would not allow this for there was always danger of meeting a bear on the trail. I had rehearsed in my mind how I would climb the nearest tree, but Unk frisking along in front of us reminded me that if a bear appeared he couldn't climb to safety. I tried not to think about that.

A number of moose moved through the trees like big prehistoric animals. Suddenly a large bull with heavy branching antlers appeared in the trail ahead. Jack stopped and motioned for me to do so. He shouted, but the moose paid no attention—just stood staring at us.

Unk could not have failed to see the moose but turned and ran back down the trail whence we had come, barking furiously. Jack and I watched him with amusement. We had also seen him indulge in practicing this bit of acting when an unfriendly dog appeared, running from one danger and pretending there was a greater danger somewhere else.

It is generally agreed that a moose will not attack a human being unless he comes between a cow and her calf. This one did not appear to be hostile, but he was stubbornly blocking the trail.

Jack took from his belt the "six-shooter" he always carried with him on the trail. It was a large revolver, considered powerful enough to stop a brown bear. "Don't shoot him!" I screamed.

Jack chuckled. He aimed far above the moose's head and pulled the trigger. "That's something he'll listen to." The moose wheeled and ran swiftly up the hill, racking like a cow with stiff hind legs.

An opening in the trees appeared around a bend in the trail, and there was the beginning of the highway. My feet had begun to drag a little; it had already been a ten-mile walk, with several more miles to come.

My steps became slower and slower. More and more often Jack had to stop and wait for me to catch up. After a couple of miles we came to an inviting log by the side of the road. "You rest here," Jack said. "The Landing's only about four miles further. I'll go and get Nick Lean to come for you or I might meet a car on the way."

"I don't believe I could walk another mile, Jack. I didn't know I was so tired."

"Sure you won't be afraid?"

"Oh, no!" I said with false bravery. "There's nothing to be afraid of. Unk will stay with me."

Night was coming, and it was a very lonely place. We had met no one on the road and had not passed a sign of human habitation. I fervently hoped that all the neighborhood bears were at home eating supper with their families. I took off my shoepacs and rested my tired back against the tree. Unk was tired too; he lay down with a huge sigh and fell asleep.

I must have dozed, too, for when I looked around it was dark, and the stars were out. How quiet it was! It seemed that Jack had been gone for hours. I heard the sound of a car and soon saw the flash of its headlights. As it pulled up beside me I recognized the genial gleam of Nick Lean's white smile. Jack had come too—presumably to start a search if I had vanished.

While Jack sat in the store and drank Cokes with Jack Lean, I yearned over the wooden crates in the back. Some of the contents could be seen through the cracks.

We had made the mistake, in the enthusiasm of building our house, of having our furniture shipped to the Landing. We later realized how difficult it would be to bring it to the cabin; indeed, with Andy away it was now impossible, and we had to arrange for its storage over the winter.

A year had passed since these possessions had been packed, but we had lived a lifetime since then. How far we had come. Our way would never be easy, I knew now, but we would have to go on. Here were my treasures that I was trying to drag with me. I wanted the new life but could not give up the old. Shelter, food, and warmth were offered by the wilderness on its own terms, and if Jack and I could accept the offer and live like Indians it would be much easier. But I knew we would continue to struggle to preserve something of a way of life we valued. We were pioneers.

We had to take back with us every pound of food we could carry. Jack scolded and insisted that I not try to carry so much. "You'll only have to discard it on the trail," he warned.

"I'll take the can of baking powder, five pounds of butter, three dozen eggs, and three pounds of bacon," I insisted. "That's all." I could feel the drag on my shoulders, but felt I could manage. My pockets were crammed with mail.

Jack's pack weighed almost sixty pounds. "This won't be bad this time of year," he said, thoughtfully hefting it. "I couldn't make it through snow."

"In this life a man's only as good as his back," Jack Lean said, smiling.

"You're right," Jack said, "and I've found that I have a poor back." But he swung his pack on his shoulders with a grin, and we started off in the gray morning light.

We saw no bears and few moose near the trail this time. We rested often, and I was far from exhausted when we came in sight of the welcoming little cabin. We intended to spend the night and leave for home early next day.

But next morning a terrific wind rattled the windows, and we could hear the roar of the surf while we were dressing. With Unk at my heels I followed Jack to the beach. At the water's edge, where the wind could strike us squarely, it was hard to keep one's feet. The "white horses" were again kicking up their heels in a frenzy of excited galloping. Jack shouted something to me, but the wind struck the words from his lips before I could hear. I shook my head to indicate that I had not heard, and he came close and yelled in my ear, "Glad we pulled the boat up high on the beach."

I nodded. Thank God, our boat was safe.

It was the time of equinoctial storms and we knew the

wind might last for days, so we made ourselves comfortable. Jack made pancakes and they were especially good, for we had plenty of butter. Unk enjoyed them as much as we did. I gathered driftwood and Jack sawed it up for the stove. The stove was half a fifty-gallon oil drum, with a door and damper fitted into it. Known as a Yukon stove, it was very effective, and ones like it were in general use all over the interior of Alaska.

Jack and Unk went for a long walk on the beach, and I found some old magazines to pass the time. "How does it look?" I asked as Jack opened the door.

"Not very good," he answered, "but you remember the wind usually dies down at daybreak. Another night won't hurt us."

We were up early, but daylight came without a lull. All that day I watched the tops of trees bend and toss outside the windows. The lake was not visible, but the pounding of the waves filled the cabin. By midafternoon, however, the wind had lessened. The trees stopped tossing, and slow waves slapped fretfully at the rocks along the shore.

We walked along the beach and scanned the sky. "It's getting late," Jack said uncertainly, "but I sure hate to spend another night away from home. If the wind doesn't get any worse, we'll take a chance." There was only a little wind now, although dark storm clouds still moved overhead. We had never known the wind to die down and then start up again.

The motor sputtered at the first pull on the starter cord, and we were off. At first the waves were of no consequence, but the further we drew from the shore, the higher they became. The boat, which had very little freeboard, began to pitch violently.

"Your eyes are big as saucers," Jack shouted, grinning. But I was not deceived; I knew he was worried too. I was petrified with fright. Unk scrambled into my lap, seeking shelter and comfort, but I could not hold him—my hands were occupied in clinging tightly to the sides of the boat.

It was somewhat reassuring to watch Jack deftly meet the waves as they rushed at us. He turned the bow slightly before the impact so that the boat did not meet the waves head on. The motor ran smoothly except when the propeller was lifted out of the water on top of a wave, and it raced madly. Dear God, I prayed, don't let the motor stop.

Jack shouted something that I did not hear plainly, but I thought I heard the words "Safety Bay." We were almost opposite Safety Bay, but it was on the other side of a mile of frenzied water. We would be swamped if we turned.

Andy had often told us to run in to Safety Bay to escape from a storm, but I thought we could never make it now— it was too far away. I closed my eyes tight and tried to pray. My thoughts reached out, but terror wiped out everything. I knew nothing but the pitching and dipping of the little boat and our utter helplessness.

Suddenly the motor stopped, and my heart stopped too. "Oh, God! We've struck something," I whispered. "In another minute we'll be in the water."

My eyelids had been pressed so tightly together I could not see clearly when I looked about. Jack sat smiling at me, the oars drawn up and resting in his hands. The water was calm! Unk jumped out of my lap and barked loudly.

"Whew! I hope we never have to go through that again," Jack said. I noticed that his hand shook as he lighted his pipe before starting to row to shore.

"So this is Safety Bay!" I looked about gratefully.

Jack was puffing on his pipe. "Yes, I stopped here once with Cliff. Look at the lake out there!" He pointed to the angry waves that sped by the narrow entrance.

We were drenched from the spray, so we hurried to gather a stock of wood before there was complete darkness and built a driftwood fire under the arms of a big old spruce, where there were burned fragments of former fires. Fine white sand covered the beach where we spread our sleeping bags.

But I could not sleep because of the strangeness. I was comfortable but still nervous from our narrow escape. Unk slept close beside me. He was wakeful too, often sitting up and staring tensely into the blackness around us. Jack slept peacefully, and I was careful not to waken him when I threw logs on the fire.

When it was light enough we could see dark clouds still streaming overhead. But surely we could go home now; the water in Safety Bay was motionless. Jack climbed to the top of the cliff where there was a view over the lake. He shook his head when he returned.

We would have to be there for some time, and I thought of food, but there was nothing to cook in but the bailing can from the boat. I boiled some eggs. "Will you open this can with your pocket-knife, Jack?" I asked.

"What's this?"

"It's a can of sausage. I brought it for our Christmas morning breakfast."

"We'll never need it more than we need it now." Jack pushed his knife through the tin and opened it. "We can eat moose meat for Christmas morning breakfast."

I brought some clean white birch bark for plates. We ate sausage and eggs, and took turns drinking good hot tea from the bailing can. The food tasted wonderful!

Through the day Jack made several trips to the top of the rock, and it was late afternoon before he was satisfied that it was safe to leave.

The boat was tossed about when we reached the middle of the lake, where the wind from the glacier had a fair sweep; but we were becoming seasoned and the bright sunshine was encouraging.

All was peaceful and in order when we arrived. Home had never looked so good.

Early next morning we saw flames and thick smoke rising from the Island. "It must be something important," Jack said. "Come on." I expected Unk to prefer staying at home after our recent experiences but he ran eagerly ahead of us to the boat.

The boys were waiting for us on the beach. "I see we made a big enough fire to bring you," Cliff said, grinning. "It's lonesome over here. We got a moose and have a hind-quarter for you." We were indeed grateful for the gift.

We had brought a letter to Val from his father. His mother had left the hospital and was much better. They were coming by train to Moose Pass and on Friday would reach the Landing.

"Why, that's the day we left," I remembered. "We would have seen them if we hadn't gone that day."

"If you left the Landing Friday, where have you been all this time?" Cliff asked in surprise.

"We were held up by the wind at the river cabin," Jack replied, and carelessly, like a seasoned frontiersman, he added, "and one night at Safety Bay. I couldn't risk traveling in that little boat—not enough freeboard."

Jack now stopped all other work and concentrated on fuel. The two stoves devoured an unbelievable amount of wood, and he took his rifle ever morning and rowed to the Point to saw up trees.

I begged him to let me handle one end of the crosscut saw, but after my first attempt he said, "I can do better alone, hon—you ride the saw."

Tears came to my eyes. I had tried so hard. "I can learn. Just show me how."

"No," he said gently, but firmly. "I must get the sawing done and you hinder me."

At any rate he did not object to my piling up the limbs to be burned after the snow had fallen. Jack was very careful to clean up all debris from his cutting. There was little undergrowth, and the forest looked like a park.

Andy had written that he would send a radio message before he returned, but weeks passed without a word. A few

days before Thanksgiving we saw a strange craft traveling
toward the Island. It looked like a queer sailboat moving
slowly before the slight breeze.

"Must be Andy," Jack said. "He's made a sail out of a
tarp."

"That's a clever way to keep from having to row," I said.
"I wonder if Jessie came with him."

"I don't believe there's more than one person in the
boat," Jack answered, squinting his eyes. "We'll go over in
the morning and see what's going on."

We found that Andy had come for Val. "I've built a
cabin at the Landing," he said. "It will be convenient to have
it, and I want to keep Jess there through the winter where she
can see a doctor occasionally. We'll be home in the spring."

"Do you think we can get Hank to haul our supplies?"
Jack asked.

"The river's already too low for his boat," Andy answered. "Now that the trail's in good shape I can get away
for a few days any time and bring them with the horses. I
intend to take the horses back with me and leave them at
the river cabin—there's hay there for them. No need for you
to worry."

"It will be serious for us if you find you can't make it."

Andy answered easily. "We've spent many a winter here
on a diet of moose meat and beans I carried down the trail
on my back."

"We can do that too," Jack replied, with tight lips.
"But we won't if it can be helped."

I knew how much Jack wished to be independent and
how it hurt him to have to ask for favors, but at the same
time I realized that he was not sure enough of his ability to
get along in the wilderness—to go it alone. He was learning
his lessons surely but slowly and painfully.

CHAPTER 7

THE PUT-PUT OF Cliff's motor Thanksgiving morning gave notice that we would have a guest. The weather was clear and so very cold an early freeze-up seemed likely.

Cliff wore ear muffs and his long blond cowlicks flopped as usual in his eyes. As he warmed himself by the stove, he sniffed with relish. Then he went outside and brought in a jar of goat cream from the windowbox where he had left it to cool. "No matter what you have for dessert," he said, chuckling in his characteristic way, "whipped cream goes good with it. But I'm glad it's pumpkin pie."

Jack came in and smiled when he saw our visitor. "Do you suppose you could lend me a hand?" he asked. "I'd like to get the windcharger up."

"Sure. Whenever you're ready."

"No need to hurry," Jack said. "Take time to get warm."

Cliff held his hands over the stove and flexed his fingers. "Y'know, I'm worried," he said slowly. "If this cold keeps up I'm afraid Andy'll have trouble bringing your groceries. He might get the freight down the trail with the horses but there might be too much ice to bring it across the lake in the boat, and yet not enough for a long time for the horses to pull a sled over."

"So far we're not suffering," I said.

"Maybe not yet, but still I'm worried. And I don't have much faith in Andy's being able to get away from home. When I was at the Landing Jess lay in bed all the time, crying. He wouldn't have the heart to leave her."

"It can't be helped," I assured him. "We're learning to be patient."

"I had planned to batch this winter at Egyptian Bay and trap," Cliff continued thoughtfully, as if burdened with responsibility for our welfare. "John has decided not to come back because he thinks he'll be drafted in the Army. I may be too for that matter—"

"Do you want to go, Cliff?" I interrupted fearfully.

"No, I don't," he said fervently. "I couldn't bear to shoot a man."

"I pray that you won't have to." The ominous rumble of war was coming closer all the time but I could still hardly believe it.

Something was still on Cliff's mind. "I must live at my camp six months of the year in order to homestead it," he went on, "but I'll have to stay on the Island most of this winter and look after the stock. They have a lot of food there, and I won't need mine, so I can loan my groceries to you. Tell me what you need, and I'll bring it next time I come."

"Oh, Cliff," I exclaimed, deeply touched by his generosity, "that would be wonderful! We need 'most everything. But then I would worry," I said hesitantly, "for fear we couldn't return them to you."

"Oh, I can always get more. I probably haven't what you would order, but I have dried fruits of several kinds, tea, coffee, sugar, flour and some other things.

"Have you any shortening?"

"Oh, yes. Two big cans."

A burden had been lifted from our shoulders. How sweet

and thoughtful Cliff was! He understood our problems better than we did ourselves.

Jack and Cliff worked several hours hoisting the heavy windcharger to the roof peak. When the work was finished they were cold and hungry.

"I'd get that lock washer for you from Andy's shop," Cliff said, "but I want to leave for Egyptian Bay early in the morning."

"I'll run over to the Island in the morning if you're sure he has some."

"Oh, yes, he has some. And I wouldn't advise letting the propeller turn without it; you might have an accident." They securely tied down the rope with which the charger was controlled so the propeller could not turn.

Cliff was our first overnight guest. After a big dinner we played pinochle until late, and he set out his sleeping bag on the floor.

I always wakened if the wind rose in the night. This time it started with a rush. The windcharger was released with a wild whir and the entire house shook. Jack was only one jump ahead of Cliff as they dashed outside. There was a heavy crash and, soon, another, followed by dead silence.

I shivered in my bed—the windcharger was gone. I had been looking forward to having at least one electric light to read by that winter, and already we had not dared to operate the radio for a long time, for fear of exhausting the battery.

The men came back and put on more clothes. They took a flashlight to examine the damage, but there was little to be seen in the darkness. Jack brought in a big splinter from the broken propeller. The trouble had been caused, of course, by the missing lock washer. No lights for us.

We were glad to see Art Frisbie again. "How did you get across the lake?" Jack asked.

"The water's so low now I could make my way along the beach to Egyptian Bay. I made a fire there, and Cliff saw the

smoke and came for me." Art was very interested in all that
we had accomplished. "You're going to have a nice place
here," he said, looking around with approval.

"I've been wanting to go for mail," Jack said, "but it
stays so cold and I'm afraid the freeze-up will start and I
won't get home."

Art pulled some letters from his pockets. "I brought
your first class mail—all I could carry. Had to leave your
packages."

"Oh, thank you, Art!" I said. "Jack won't have to go
now."

"I wouldn't go now unless you have to. We'll soon be
able to skate across." He went on eagerly, "It's great to be
back again. I'm anxious to get to work on my place."

When the leaves had dropped, moose could often be
seen on the hillside behind the house, and as the weather
became colder more and more of them appeared. Sometimes
three or four would be silhouetted against the evening sky
along the rim of hills. The hills made a beautiful background;
the view of them from the windows was as interesting as that
in the other direction over the water.

Jack wasn't able to go for mail before Christmas, so
there were no messages from the outside world. The lake was
again dictating to us. The water was forbidding and dark; so
still that it seemed to be holding its breath, waiting to receive
the ice. Heavy fog hung low over the water and once more
had come the tender frost to silver the trees and earth, too
beautiful for description.

Christmas, 1939, our second in the wilds, was a point to
look back from. Our progress had been slow, but at least in
the past year we had gained independence from the Andersons and had a comfortable home of our own—there was
plenty to rejoice in and thank God for. But, as I baked
cookies and trimmed them with fancy frosting the dark day
before Christmas, there was a lump in my throat that I
couldn't get rid of.

I mourned because we had no radio and no Christmas music. Our Christmases had always been gay and exciting, with people about us. This was another of the adjustments that I would be called upon to make in our new life. The future appeared only as one adjustment following the last one, on and on through the years.

When we started for the Island early on Christmas Eve snow had begun to fall in heavy, fluffy flakes—Christmas snow. The temperature had risen a little, but firm ice already connected the Island and mainland.

Cliff had made a gorgeous cake. "It turned out good, didn't it?" he crowed, "but I didn't know how to make frosting."

We had coffee with him and Art. The lump in my throat became bigger and harder, and I was barely able to smile and answer when I was spoken to.

"We put up a few decorations," Cliff said, indicating faded paper bells he had hung at the windows. The bells were more than I could endure, and I very nearly burst into tears.

The snow was getting deep and we could not stay. The boys came to the beach to watch us start out across the strip of ice. "We'll expect you early tomorrow," Jack said. "Don't be fashionable and wait till dinner time to come."

Jack walked ahead and did not see when I let the tears have their way. I was thinking of other Christmases. I was a little girl in South Carolina, hugging my new china doll, and my brothers were shooting firecrackers before dawn on Christmas morning. I didn't like the firecrackers very much, but it was exciting. How wonderful Christmas had been then!

My thoughts leaped across the years. Jack and I were standing in the door of our Juneau home, with a background of candlelight, the room filled with the fragrance of flowers, welcoming our guests. I choked back the sob in my throat.

As usual, when I found myself shedding tears, it was time to take stock. I winked my eyes, and by sheer will power

I flung off this mood. It will not always be like this, I reminded myself. It will take a little time, but the years ahead
will be filled with progress. And what better occasion could
be found for experiencing a real Christmas? Some of the joys
were missing, but there were no distractions, no worry about
what to give, no hectic rushing to get things done. All that
Christmas had meant to me in the past was swept away.
Instead of a fleeting thought that it was the birthday of our
Master, I now had unlimited opportunity to reflect on His
coming to bring fulfillment to the world. My heart filled with
love and gratitude for the tiny Babe whose cradle was a man-
ger, and suddenly the cold, snowy world was very beautiful,
and it was normal and right for us to be there.

As long as I live I shall remember that scene and the
peace that came to me. I have only to shut my eyes and concentrate a moment to bring back the lonely lake shore, my
feet sinking into the deepening snow, Jack's dim figure barely
visible through the falling flakes, and a truer realization of
Christmas flooding my heart. I ran to overtake Jack. Without
a word, he reached out his mittened hand for mine and we
walked home side by side.

Unk, who had preferred to remain at home in the warm
cabin, welcomed us with joyful yapping. I had fastened spruce
boughs to the beams, and hung red-berried kinnikinnick
wreaths at the windows. I wanted very much to strew evergreen twigs on the floor as they did in medieval times, but
Jack put his foot down. "We'll be picking up all the needles
on our hands and knees," he said crossly.

I had neglected to order ornaments and candles and had
planned not to have a tree that year. I was glad I had changed
my mind. I made ornaments of eggshells—after carefully
blowing out the contents through holes pricked through the
ends. I didn't know Jack was paying attention, but he came
in later with some feathers.

"Where did you get these?" I asked. "They look as if
they came off a Plymouth Rock chicken."

Jack chuckled. "They came off a dead hawk." He looked over my shoulder as I was painting the face of a red-cheeked girl on a shell.

"Just what I need for trimming hats!" I laughed, and glued the feathers on at a jaunty angle. I also made Chinese sages with slanting Oriental eyes and spruce-needle mustaches.

Jack cut a star from a tin can for the top of the tree and glued bits of glass along its edges. He helped me string cranberries too.

Our perfect little tree stood on the table against the wall with festoons of cranberries draped over it and the brave eggshell ornaments hanging from its branches.

Jack covered the kerosene lantern with red cellophane and placed it behind the tree. The whole tree was suffused with the rosy light, and the star was outlined with sparkling gems.

It was the most beautiful Christmas tree we had ever had! We brought our supper close to the stove so we could look at it as we ate. I wanted everybody to be happy and fed Unk bits of forbidden cake from my plate. What if it did make him fat? This was Christmas.

When our holiday was over Jack turned his attention to getting fresh meat. I hoped I only imagined that he was uneasy as he prepared to leave. It was the first time he had hunted alone. "I'll have to get a moose close to shore," he explained, "where the ice is thick enough to bring it home on the sled." He strode off through the snow with his rifle on his shoulder.

That day he had no luck, but next morning, as it grew light enough to see, three moose could be discerned almost in our backyard, browsing in the place we had staked off for the vegetable garden.

Jack loaded his rifle and watched from the window. He was very deliberate. He waited until the light was stronger and then, having chosen a tree to hide behind, crept out of the house. In a few moments I heard the one shot that was necessary, and the ordeal was over.

I helped him move the body about so it could be skinned. Jack ordered me off while he performed the unpleasant task of disembowelling. Even though sickened by the smells and blood, I wanted to stay and help. But Jack said, "Run along, I know you!"

The butchering required the entire day. Next morning the joints, which he had separated with an axe, were frozen stiff. We carried the big pieces to the house slung on a pole, each of us bearing one end, and hung them behind the house. What a lot of meat! It looked like enough for the rest of the winter.

Between Christmas and New Year's the lake froze over completely, and once more it was a highway. Jack made ready to go for mail. The trip would be much longer and harder since he had to cross the lake on foot, going and coming, for there was too much snow for skates.

This was the first time I had been alone. Jack would be gone about four days, and getting on by myself was just another of the adjustments I must make.

Darkness came early on those winter nights. I dreaded lighting the gasoline lamp. I had watched Jack do it many times, and it always made me nervous when the flame flared up before settling down to a steady purr. The first night I left the door open so that I could seize the lamp and throw it out of doors if necessary, and turned it on carefully and applied a lighted match. It was taking longer than usual to stop flaring! I was terrified I would have to throw it out, but the flame subsided at last.

I built up the fire in the stove and had a good book from the Andersons' library to read. Unk lay on the couch beside me, with his head in my lap. Art and Cliff were only a mile and a half away, and I could have seen the light in the Andersons' home if it had not been hidden by a rocky bluff.

There was nothing to fear—nothing ever happened at night
—but my book did not hold my attention. How black it was
outside the windows! Somebody or a wild animal might be
looking in at me. I jumped up to pull the curtains across the
windows. We never did that when Jack was at home.

Something moved in the blackness outside and my heart
leaped. But I refused to panic. It was probably only a limb
of the birch tree near the house, waving in the wind. I peered
out, my face pressed close to the glass. Then I could see in
the dim light cast from the window a yard-long mournful
face staring back at me. Socrates, minus his horns, was standing only a couple of feet from the window. He look as if he
were lonesome and wished I would invite him in. I pecked
on the window and heard him crash off through the brush.

Next morning I was looking out across the frozen lake,
as I did many, many times while restlessly waiting for Jack's
return. In the direction of the Island I saw a black speck—
probably a moose. I finally recognized it as a man, but not
Art or Cliff.

A strange young man with a rifle over his shoulder was
approaching over the ice and walking up from the beach.
He grinned amiably at me. He was an Indian. "I'm Alec
Wilson," he announced. "Is Mr. Sharples here?"

I quieted Unk's barking and answered, "No, he isn't. I'm
Mrs. Sharples. Come in, won't you?"

He came in and sat down. "I spent the night with Cliff,"
he explained. "He told me your husband had probably gone
to the Landing—I'm sorry to miss him. I just wanted to get
acquainted before I left for home."

"Where is your home?"

"I live at Kenai. My wife and baby are there. I often
come up to Skilak."

"Oh, are you one of those who came last year and loaned
Mr. Anderson a motor?"

"Yes," he answered with a grin.

"That was the most wonderful thing that ever happened!" I said. "We couldn't have stayed here last winter if you hadn't made it possible for us to get our supplies. We are very grateful."

Alec no longer seemed a stranger and we chatted easily. He told me he went to Bristol Bay every summer to fish for the canneries; in a good season he made a lot of money. In winter he trapped along the lower Kenai River, the outlet from Skilak to the sea. He had been "looking" his traps and decided to make the folks on the lake a visit.

"My folks have lived at Kenai a long time," he told me. "One of my grandfathers was a Scotch sea captain. He liked Kenai and didn't go back to Scotland. My grandmother was Russian and Indian, and the rest of my family's all Indian."

I was interested in his speech. He evidently had had more than an ordinary education. "Where did you go to school, Alec?"

"I finished the grades at the government school at Kenai, and then I was sent outside to a government industrial school in Oregon."

"But you came back to Kenai?"

"Yes. I don't like it anywhere else."

Since Alec was our first guest in some time I prepared an abundant meal, which he ate appreciatively. I told him our plans for improving our place, and he listened without comment. "We're anxious to get our garden started," I said. "We're going to use fish for fertilizer; we hope to get a net before spring."

"I think I can help you with that," he said quickly. "The canneries discard their nets after one season and some of them are good as new. I'll bring you one when I come again."

"Oh, that will be wonderful!" I cried gratefully. What an unexpected answer to our pressing need! "We'll be glad to pay you for it," I added. "We tried to get one in Seward but there are none in the stores there and Sears, Roebuck doesn't show them in the catalog."

"There's no fishing around Seward. You have to get them where there are canneries."

Alec thanked me for his lunch with quiet dignity, and shouldered his rifle.

"Do come to see us again," I said. "My husband will be back in a few days. He hasn't caught a coyote yet, and he'd be interested in talking to you about trapping."

"Thank you. I'll be here before spring and you can count on the net."

The sun shone brightly next morning. I was confident that Jack would come that day. In midafternoon I called Unk and we set out around the Point and headed toward the upper end of the lake. There was not a living creature to be seen on the flat expanse of ice. On and on I walked until I became discouraged—I must be more patient. As I looked intently for the last time before turning back I saw a little black dot. The dot seemed to be stationary, but I knew it was Jack, steadily walking toward home.

I tried to make Unk see him. "There's Jack!" I cried, pointing, but Unk only pretended he saw something. He barked and ran around in circles, but when I ran toward Jack, my joy adding wings to my feet, Unk raced ahead. Tired as he was, Jack started running too, and we all met in breathless excitement. I knew by the relief I felt that I had not been at ease since he left.

I asked my usual first question. "Was it a hard trip, Jack?"

"Not very. I'm glad it didn't snow any more."

"Did you bring a lot of mail?" I asked eagerly, almost running to keep up with his long stride.

"Quite a lot. Wait till we get home and I'll give it to you."

"Is Mrs. Anderson any better?"

"I didn't see her, but Andy said she's about the same."

These questions were the obvious ones, but I wished for the courage to ask him if he had done any drinking at the Landing. I knew the store was a meeting place for the men there, and it was reasonable to expect that there would be drinking. No doubt liquor, or beer and wine at least, was sold there. Otherwise we had not been in contact with liquor since coming to the lake. My fear and hatred of it had lessened, but I wondered. Jack showed no signs of it, but I could not induce myself to ask.

A few mornings later Art came striding purposefully over the ice. I knew before he spoke that he had news.

"A radio message came from Andy," he said. "He suggested that you and I haul your freight with the horses. What about it, Jack?"

"I'm willing to undertake it if you think we can."

"There wouldn't be anything hard or dangerous about it," said Art. "I thought you might pay for having the freight hauled just as if Andy were doing it, and we'll give him the money. The poor devil needs it. When will you be ready to start?"

"Tomorrow."

"Is Mrs. Anderson worse, Art?" I asked.

"I don't think there's been any real change, but she's certainly no better. You'd hardly know her. The doctor put her on a diet. She's a shadow of herself."

Jack and Art made their plans. "It will take half a dozen trips between the Landing and the cabin," Jack said to me. "We'll store all the freight in the cabin, and then we can get it across the lake even if we have to bring it in a boat." That meant I was not to expect them until they appeared.

When they were gone I spent most of my time watching at the window. I never got used to the waiting. More than a week later, with Art in the lead, one of the horses drew a heavily loaded sled around the end of the Point.

I ran down to the beach and helped remove the tarp. "Isn't that apples I smell?" I sniffed.

"I brought a box of them," Jack said.

My craving for fresh fruit rose up strong within me. No dried or canned product was a satisfactory substitute. The men lifted out the various cartons and boxes and piled them on the beach. One corner of the apple box was loose. I tore at it until I could reach a juicy red apple. I held it in my hands and savored its rich aroma before biting into it. "Um-m!" I mumbled. "I never tasted anything so heavenly."

Art and Jack looked like unshaven tramps. It was the first time I had seen Jack really dirty. They wanted to go back to the river cabin that night for an early morning start on the trail, so while they took their shirts off and shaved and washed over a washtub of hot water, I cooked dinner.

"Was it hard to tie the freight on the horses so it wouldn't fall off?" I asked.

Jack and Art exchanged indulgent smiles at my naive question. "We used Andy's packsaddles," Art explained.

"I didn't know he had any packsaddles," I said.

"Oh, yes," Jack added. "He used them when he guided hunters."

Without taking time to answer any more of my womanly questions, they were gone again.

Finally the last sled load was delivered and Jack and I stacked our year's supply of food neatly away on the balcony. The hundred-pound sacks of sugar had become damp and hardened like solidified cement. I was to learn that this was normal—sugar never arrived in any other condition. It had to be pounded up and I learned to compensate for the lumps in measuring for a recipe.

Surprisingly, a new propeller for the windcharger, which Jack had ordered on his last trip to town in late fall, had come. Jack made sure this time that no washer was missing. The propeller picked up the slightest wind, and its vibration shook the whole house. I did not object to the noise—the louder the better—since it meant that our battery soon would be charged.

Jack showed me how to snub the rope and stop the machine if the wind became dangerously strong. One had to wrap the rope around a large spike driven in a log and tie it securely, then tie it around another spike and, passing it back to the first spike, tie it securely for a third time. "Did anyone show you how to do this, Jack?' I asked.

"No, I figured it out to keep the darned thing from working loose again." Jack had taken another step in self-reliance.

I had to practice before I could tie the knots properly. There was sufficient wind to keep the charger going quite steadily. We tested the battery every day and soon decided we could risk fifteen minutes of news every day on the radio. Without a radio to keep us up to date, we had become completely confused about the day of the week. The Anchorage radio station announced each evening the day of the week and of the month for the benefit of prospectors, trappers, and others in remote places. We found it was really Wednesday, while Jack thought it was Tuesday and I Friday.

Jack had obtained a dozen snares. "I'll set them on the shore on the far side of the Point and in East Bay," he told me. "I must be careful not to interfere with those that Cliff has set out. He says February is the best month for snaring coyotes; it's their mating season."

Often coyotes could be seen crossing the ice, but the sly creatures took care to be out of range of a rifle. Every night their "Yip, yip, yip, e-e-e-ow" could be heard on the still air.

When Jack came home with his first coyote slung on his back, he was as happy as a little boy with a new pair of skates. He studied again the Game Commission pamphlet which gave instructions for skinning them and worked industriously.

I was busy on the typewriter and glanced up as Jack came in, closed the door, and leaned back against it. "It doesn't seem possible I could have done such a thing," he said, the picture of dejection.

"What happened? What did you do?"

"I was following the instructions closely. The pamphlet said to leave the bone of the first joint and the foot of the left front leg attached. If it's detached it's disqualified for bounty. When I'd finished, I found I'd left on the right foot."

"Well, that's not a catastrophe. You'll know better next time."

He was still desponent though, as he went out again, muttering that he could kick himself.

I went on typing. The door flew open. "I was wrong!" Jack shouted excitedly. "I was looking at it wrong! I did leave the correct one on. Come and see what a fine skin it is!"

Jack's delight revealed to me how important it was to him to capture his first coyote, with its promise of future income. He had proved that he could do it, and we had taken one more step toward independence. I was happy too. He would be so proud to show it to the boys.

CHAPTER 8

A SUDDEN SOFT SPELL, with howling wind, took the ice out down to the end of the Point, and all the upper half of the lake was free again. The heavy ice ended abruptly and we could step from the ice into the boat. Thin ice formed over the open water every day or two, but there was just enough wind to break it up.

At twilight one day in late March two figures appeared far out from shore, moving toward the Island. We wondered how Art and Cliff could have passed earlier without our seeing them.

The mystery was explained next morning before daylight when they came to see us. They both looked strained and ill at ease. Something must have happened and they appeared unable to tell us what it was, but talked nervously of unimportant things. Apparently each was waiting for the other to begin.

"We were surprised to see you coming home last night," I said. "We hadn't seen you crossing the lake earlier."

"That was Andy and Val you saw," Cliff answered. "Jess died last Friday."

"Oh, Cliff!" I gasped.

"I don't know much about it," Cliff went on soberly. "She was taken suddenly and died soon after they got her to the Seward hospital. Andy is bringing her down to the Island to bury her. He left her at the river cabin and came on last night to see if the ice was strong enough to bring the sled across. Art and I are going up after her; Andy thinks we can make it all right by being careful."

"Oh, poor Andy!" I said. "We must go over to the Island at once, Jack."

"I don't know," Cliff answered uncertainly. "He probably wants to be alone."

"Well, we'll wait until you get back tonight then."

But the boys did not return that night. I could not sleep for worry. The weather turned warm and springlike; rivulets were running over the ground. It was as if there was a stirring all around us. Spring had surely come.

Jack and I went about silently, waiting. Anxiety for the safety of the boys and shock over the unexpected turn of events hung heavily over us. I wanted very much to go to see Andy and Val, but Jack said, "No, Cliff told us to leave them alone." There was no possibility that the boys could cross the ice now; over half the lake was open water.

The tension had become almost unbearable when at last we saw Andy and Val walking across the ice. Andy looked as if he had not slept for weeks. "We came to borrow your boat and sled," he said tensely. "I must see what has happened."

"The ice is dangerous now, isn't it?" I asked fearfully.

"We'll keep close to shore," Andy answered. "We'll pull the boat on the sled when there's ice and use the boat when we come to open water. If the ice should break we can hang onto the boat."

"I'll go with you," Jack offered, "if you think I would be of help."

"I may need you very badly. Anything could happen."

And, indeed, a terrible thing could have happened—Art and Cliff could have been at the bottom of the lake with Jessie.

They did not return the next day or the next. Further inaction was intolerable and, on the fourth morning after they had left, I decided to walk to the Island and take care of the chickens. The weather was stormy and cold, so I had little difficulty in persuading Unk to stay at home. Unk was beginning to show some of the infirmities of age and his short coat no longer provided enough protection from the elements.

The sight of the big box of rough boards, lined with flowered chintz standing in the middle of the living room floor would not have shocked me so much if I had not been overwrought already. I hurriedly fed and watered the imprisoned chickens and, without re-entering the house, turned toward home. It was then that I caught a glimpse of two black dots on the ice near the Point. Soon they were close enough for me to recognize Andy and Val. "Where's Jack?" I called, weak with fear.

Andy's ravaged face broke into a reassuring smile. "He's all right. We left them all safe at the river cabin. We need my big boat and a motor," he went on. "The lake's full of floating ice, but we'll start right back and try to get through."

Even as we stood talking I could hear a low roar from the head of the lake—the wind was rising.

"Oh, Andy!" I wailed. "Why did it have to be at the time of the break-up?"

He did not answer me, but gazed desolately into the distance, his shoulders drooping wearily. Val looked frightened and as if his whole world had collapsed.

"We would be caught in the dark if we tried it tonight," Andy went on. "We'll try to get some rest tonight and come by for Jack's motor in the morning."

During the night the wind reached gale proportions and continued all next day. No boat could travel on the lake, so there was nothing to do but wait. Another night rolled by, and there were signs of clearing. Andy and Val came as the gray dawn was breaking. The weather was still unsettled, but I was cheered by the thought that Andy could make it when no one else could.

Val had developed a severe cold and his cheeks were flushed with fever. Andy's eyes were now haunted and he appeared to be near collapse. He hastily gulped the cup of coffee I offered him, then lifted the outboard motor to his shoulder, and he and Val hurried down the trail and started across the ice toward the end of the Point, where Andy's heavy boat had been beached all winter.

When they disappeared around the end of the Point I was once more alone. I must wait with only suspense for company. Each morning, as soon as I could make out in the gray light the end of the Point where they would first appear, I took my station at the window and left it only when it was too dark to see. I could not sleep.

The wind blew incessantly, and all became unreal. Was Jack drowned? Had Andy and Val now joined the others—all drowned? How long would it be before someone came for me, or would I stay there until I went mad?

It was a hideous thing to be unable to bury her and lay her to rest. I thought she must be resisting Andy's efforts to bring her back to the Island that she hated—she had told me once that she hated it. Could that be it? Did her strong will have power after death? Dear God, I must stop thinking such things.

Days passed but I did not count them. The wind still blew. One morning as I gazed out the window, trying through will power to force Jack to materialize on the ice, Unk jumped up energetically and went to the door and stood there. "Do you want to go out?" I asked, and opened the door.

Unk drew back from the open door and looked at me. His tail wagged deprecatingly, but his eyes said, "Come on, we've moped in here long enough. Let's get out there!"

We ran around the Point close to the shore. The hump-backed Point, covered with a dense evergreen forest, pro-

tected us from the wind shrieking over our heads. Unk happily
sniffed and rooted in the moss under the trees. When I
crossed to the side exposed to the elemental fury, I stood on a
bald cliff and the wind almost took me off my feet. I shrank
from looking at the lake, but it fascinated me. How helpless
I was and how powerful it was! The wind took my breath
away and I turned my back to it until I could breathe again.
Icefields had broken away from the bays and as far as I could
see the floes were restlessly lifting and stirring. The floating
ice curbed the waves, but the entire expanse seethed like a
giant cauldron of boiling water.

That night the storm blew away and subsided. I slept
a little from sheer exhaustion and woke to a heavenly morning. I could see from the window where the thick ice ended—
a lot of ice had gone out.

As I watched, the nose of a boat pushed around the end
of the Point. It stopped at the edge of the ice, and I could see
black dots around it. My relief and joy over the return was
swallowed up by the realization of what it was that was being
transferred from the boat to the ice. It was too far away for
me to see clearly and my eyes were dim with tears, so I closed
my eyes and did not try to look. That was Jessie Anderson on
the sled. No, it couldn't be! I remembered her hearty laugh—
so full of life; she had nothing to do with death.

I did not expect Jack to come so soon, and when I heard
him at the door I was so startled I screamed. "Are they all
safe?" I asked in a trembling voice.

"Yes," he answered simply. He didn't look like himself.
His eyes were sunken and his unshaven cheeks hollow. "Gosh,
I'm tired," he said, "and dirty too."

I quickly emptied three pails of water into the wash
boiler on the stove to heat. "Sit down, honey," I said, and
handed him a cup of coffee. "The water in the reservoir is
already hot, and your bath will be ready in a minute. Eat a
little now and I'll have a real meal for you after you've
bathed."

Between bites he told me a little more. "Art and Cliff are taking her to the Island. Andy has a grave ready, and the boys will bury her."

"The boys will bury her! Where's Andy?"

"We put him ashore—the poor devil's nearly crazy. He and Val will walk the beach until they reach the ice."

When Jack was bathed, dressed in clean clothes, and was eating hungrily, I heard more of the story. "Art and Cliff left the river cabin with her that first day. After about five miles they decided the ice wasn't safe, and they went ashore and left her on the beach—"

"They left her alone on the beach!" I interrupted.

"They had to leave her there until we came with the boat," Jack answered grimly. "It couldn't be helped. The boys went back to the river cabin, thinking it would turn cold that night and the ice would stiffen up, but instead it got warmer."

I was sobbing uncontrollably. "It's all wrong, Jack. It's ugly, and she loved beauty so."

"Try not to think about it," he said, wearily. "Everybody did the best they could."

"There wasn't much to eat at the cabin, was there?" I asked.

"At first we had oatmeal and rice and the makings of pancakes. Then the oatmeal was all gone and we had rice and pancakes with bacon grease for butter. We ran out of coffee and Cliff volunteered to go to the Landing and get some food. He brought bacon and eggs and coffee." Jack helped himself to another slice of roast.

"We thought we would get away the next day so we ate the bacon and eggs in one day. It was lucky we had coffee when Andy came back. He wouldn't eat—just drank coffee. The last two days we ate the potatoes that were there. They had sprouted and we thought they wouldn't be good, but they tasted fine." Jack was now able to grin.

"I'm sorry there isn't any dessert," I apologized.

"I don't want anything more than this bread and good butter and jam. Nothing ever tasted so good to me before."

Jack looked human again and leaned back on the couch smoking his pipe contentedly. "How is the wood supply holding out?" he asked.

"We have very little," I answered, "but don't think about it until we've both recovered from this."

Surprised at this reminder, he asked solicitously, "Did you have a bad time too?"

"I'm glad it's all over anyway," I answered. I would never tell him of the hysterics I had indulged in.

Jack found we had no fuel at all and, over my protests, left to saw wood on the Point. He worked at that all the rest of the day. He seemed to enjoy doing everyday necessary things.

Art came and talked to me. "Frost was going out of the ground," he said, red-rimmed eyes staring out of his tired face. "The grave was full of water. We kept bailing it out but it filled right up again." His voice broke and he added, "We couldn't find any lid for the coffin."

"Oh, Art!" I sobbed. "Wasn't there anything to protect her from the mud?"

"She was wrapped in canvas." Art put his arm around my shoulders and we wept together.

Andy and Val were leaving to work in a gold mine far in the interior of Alaska. Andy made ready as if driven, running from one task to another, emptying and repacking boxes and trunks, giving instructions to Cliff, haggard, worn, and ill-looking. There were chickens, ducks, geese, goats, and horses to be taken care of. "Would you like the house plants, Mrs. Sharples?" he asked.

I remembered Jessie saying, "If you ever get a greenhouse, don't expect me to give you slips. I got them all the hard way."

I burst into tears. "I couldn't, Andy—oh, no!"

Andy looked helplessly from me to Jack. Jack understood

and came to my rescue. "Of course we'll take them, Andy," he said. "Thanks. I can make a place for them by winter, and we'll give them good care."

We arranged to buy the chickens but left them on the Island until we could make a place for them. They could now be turned out to scratch in the bare places where the snow had gone.

Andy worked all night and by noon the next day was ready to go, taking with him the pair of old geese for someone at the Landing. All the young geese had perished with the cold during the winter.

Jack and I went out to the end of the Point where the open water began, and watched as our little motor slowly drew the heavy boat over the water. A loud honk from the old gander sounded above its sputter. Andy turned and waved at us.

All through that bright spring afternoon I stood with my elbows on the windowsill, gazing at the small portion of the Island visible from our place. Art had pointed out the spot where they buried her, and I could see the sun shining on the white trunks of the two birch trees that grew above the grave.

I ached with depression such as I had never known. I ached for all pioneer women, and some of my pity was for myself. Would I be able to go ahead and keep my balance? I was afraid. It was all the same to her now whether she lay under palm trees or northern birches. I hoped that she did not care any more at being left on that deserted island, surely the loneliest place in the whole wide world.

Jack understood my mood. He quietly did any necessary household tasks and did not suggest that I leave the window.

There was no time for morbid thoughts in the busy days that followed. The ice had vanished, and spring brought again the many tasks that must all be done at once.

Jack took Art to the river cabin when he had to leave. I was not depressed to have him go; the summer would be short, and soon we would all be together again. Art filled an important place with us. His enthusiasm matched ours, but he had much more than that in ability and resourcefulness.

Jack returned that day at sunset. Unk and I ran down to the beach to meet him, as we always did. "Bet you're surprised that Art has bought Hank's place at Cottonwood Creek," he said, as I helped him pull the boat up on the beach.

"I can hardly believe it. Why?"

"He found that the cement he brought down was too old and wouldn't harden when he used it on his basement. I think he got a little discouraged and Hank offered him his place at a good price. I don't blame him. The house is already built—he's getting out of a lot of hard work." Art must have really been disheartened to give up Fryingpan Island—he was so attached to it.

It was a shocking surprise to learn that Cliff intended to leave too, to get a job for the summer. There would be nobody left. Before he went Cliff did many helpful things for us. We were to use the Island garden that year, as ours would not produce yet, and he plowed it with a horse. He, Jack, and I talked at length about the future. We agreed to combine our resources with the boys' and buy equipment—particularly boats and motors. Little did we know, however, that the gathering clouds of war would make many of our plans impossible.

"When Art and I come this fall," Cliff said, "we'll get things settled." He suddenly appeared to be much older and no longer a boy. "I expect to make a trip to Seattle if possible. My mother wants me to come home—I've been away three years." His cheekbones reddened as he added shyly, "There's a girl in Seattle, too. That's why I need money now."

"Wonderful, Cliff!" I cheered. "Won't we have fun visiting you at Egyptian Bay! By that time we'll know all the secrets of the lake and can help you train her."

We all laughed, but a silence followed. Cliff said thoughtfully, "I'm afraid this life is hard on women."

Only four milk goats remained. The buck had died that winter, so there would be no milk, and we had no shelter for them. Cliff felt that the goats and horses could make their way through the summer on the Island. "We'll let Andy decide about them when he comes in the fall," he said. "I doubt if he lives here again, though."

At first I was a little frightened at the realization that we were absolutely alone, with no one to counsel us. If Jack was confident I would be too; but our future in this man's world, where women were secondary, really depended upon Jack. I watched him closely after they had all left, but he went quietly about his work as if nothing unusual had happened.

On an unexpected rainy day, Jack sat on a wooden box by the stove sharpening his saw with a file and humming "My Bonnie Lies over the Ocean" softly to himself. The wholesome smell of baking bread filled the cabin. The knowledge that we two were alone, with no other human beings within a day's travel, weighed on me heavily as I went about my household duties. "My bonnie lies over the sea," Jack's low bass droned on, accompanied by the squeak of the file.

"Jack, do you feel that we can go on here?" I suddenly asked.

Jack's file squeaked several times before he looked up and answered simply, "Why, sure! We know what to expect now. Of course we can."

My spirits lifted, but I felt impelled to probe further. "Andy was willing to do the hard work and suffer inconveniences because he loved this kind of life so much. Do you really love it, Jack?"

"If you're asking me if I want to stay," he answered, with an easy grin, "I've never had any other idea. Don't worry about me. I'm willing to work because I love it too."

He didn't ask me if I loved it enough—he knew that I did. My doubts vanished, and Jack picked up his tools and went out into the sunshine. The skies had suddenly cleared.

A cloud of pale green immature leaves made all the birches shimmer in the warm sun. Frost left the ground around the door, and there was a sea of mud into which our feet sank as we came and went. "Let's pave the space in front of the door with flat stones, Jack," I said. "This mud's terrible."

"All right," he answered impatiently. "I'll gather some flat stones when I can find time, but we need wood now."

"I know where there are a few. I'll get those to start with, and we can add them as we find them." I had learned that the best way to get Jack started on a new project was to begin it myself. He would then take it out of my inept hands.

That day I began collecting flat stones on the beach. On the more distant beaches I picked up suitable stones and placed them on big boulders so that they could be found easily when we came for them in the boat. Bears were coming out of hibernation and I was always watchful.

I was much freer after I learned to row the boat. At first I floundered about with the oars, but in a short time I became skilled enough to venture some distance from the shore alone. The new sense of freedom was wonderful! I visited areas that were new to me, but Jack made me promise I would never venture far from shore. He need not have worried—I had a horror of brown bears and hoped if I ever met a bear face to face it would be very black. Black bears are considered harmless to humans, but some expert told us that one brownie in twenty would charge on sight; and he also warned us that it might be the twentieth that we met first.

I paddled along the shore with Unk in the bow, sitting upright like a black figurehead. When we traveled with Jack, Unk would climb into my lap. I could not repulse him even though his wet feet were cold, and soon he would be sleeping contentedly, leaving all responsibility for my safety up to Jack. But now he was alert, peering into the depths of the bushes when we passed. If he growled, or seemed unduly interested in something on shore, I continued to paddle. It was not likely that even the most enraged bear would come into the water after us. I never pulled the boat up high on the beach but tied it to a rock and left it afloat so that I could jump in and cast off in a hurry if I heard a crackle in the shrubbery.

The unfamiliar beach I landed on one day was farther away from home than I had ventured before. I became deeply interested in a small bulbous plant growing in the crevices of a large rock. I knew it was *Lloydia serotina,* for I had seen it growing on a mountain top far above timberline, but I was certainly surprised to see it here so near sea level. I walked on, looking for more of these plants. Jack had once said, "Do be careful when you're out alone. You get so absorbed when you're looking at flowers you could walk right into a bear's den without knowing it."

"I wouldn't do any such thing," I answered. "I look around every minute." But Jack had been right as usual. I didn't walk into a bear's den, but when I glanced at the boat which I had securely tied to a rock, it was some distance from the beach and the slight breeze was rocking it gently out into the lake. The rope had slipped off the rock.

I thought I could wade out to the boat, but found the water much too deep. Even if I didn't mind getting wet, I might go in over my head, and the water was too paralyzingly cold to swim in. It was too dangerous. What would Jack say to me for losing our only boat? If I left it and ran home along the terrifying bear-infested beaches, the boat would be far out in the lake by the time he got there, and he had no boat to use in rescuing it.

In despair I stood there with my hands clenched in my pockets. I suddenly realized that one of my hands was fastened around a ball of twine. Jack always carried twine in his pocket. It often came in useful, and I had acquired the habit. I don't know how I got the inspiration, but I grabbed a jagged rock and quickly tied the end of the twine around it. Then, running as close as possible to the edge without getting into the water, I threw it with all my strength to the boat, already much farther away from shore. My string was not

long enough, and the rock splashed in the water two feet
short; but I was confident now and waded out to my knees.
I threw the rock into the boat, holding tightly onto my end,
and was able to pull the boat gently to the beach. I was weak
with relief. Unk gave me a severe look, which said plainly,
"*That* was very careless—don't let it happen again."

"I won't," I promised out loud.

The vegetable garden on the Island now demanded
most of our attention. The ground was very rich, and the
plants were soon growing lustily. But weeds grew just as
lustily. We pruned the raspberry plants and cultivated them,
and hoed the strawberries. We ate lunch in the house and
made a fire so that we could have a hot drink, but I escaped
out of doors as soon as possible. I could not rest in the house;
it was filled with the past. Mrs. Anderson's artistry was part
of its very substance, and her presence would remain as long
as the house remained. Her empty chair stared at me.

Our own home was wonderfully improved with the stone
terrace that Jack laid in front of the door, with house plants
in tubs decorating it. There were some lovely blooming cycla-
men plants that Mrs. Anderson had raised from seed—one
pot for each of the windows. "They're so beautiful," I said
to Jack. "I'm glad we did take them."

Many of the most interesting wildflowers grew along the
shore. I learned where they could be found and enjoyed making notes of their blooming and seeding dates. I had walked
along one beach many times without seeing the large planting of Lady-slippers I found in full bloom one day in June.
There were dozens of the lovely waxen blossoms, with pure
yellow sepals and brick-red spotted sacs, pushing up through
the coarse beach grass. It was strange that a beautiful orchid
should be growing there; they seemed out of place. In late
summer the place would be covered by high water.

The most important event of each day was the seven
o'clock news on the radio, followed by personal messages.
One day in May, while the sun was still high in the sky, we

listened to the news carefully, since it was our only source of information concerning what went on in the world. When the news came to an end, a voice said, "I shall now read the messages," and we received our first one: "To Mr. Jack Sharples, Skilak Lake. Cannot come before going fishing; leaving net hanging on tree near head of river on south side." It was signed Alexander W. Wilson.

Jack had not untied the large bundle when he brought it, and we spread it out on the beach. There was a complete net, with leads and floats, and many yards of extra net. We wanted two nets, one to anchor out from my little island and the other on the Point.

"Andy told me that if I could get some net," Jack said, "I could use the leads and floats from the old rotted one hanging on his fence. I'll run over now and get them, and we can start getting them ready to put out."

When Jack returned we examined the complete net to see how to make up another one. "I can't understand it," Jack said, baffled. "How in the world was the rope woven into the edge of the net like this in one continuous cord?"

"Let me see," I said. It looked easy. "Couldn't we start at one end of the net and weave it as we go?"

Jack brushed my suggestion aside. "No, we'd get it all tangled up. We'd have to have some kind of a tool or something."

"We'll just have to cut the cord, Jack, and tie it each time."

"All right," Jack agreed reluctantly. "It's all we can do."

Alec later laughed at this. His flying hands wove the cord in and out with a carved wooden shuttle. He could "rig" a net in a few minutes, but it required a whole day for Jack and me to tie our strings.

Jack set up one of the nets from the little island, and within an hour had caught a large Dolly Varden trout, weighing eight pounds. It was delicious after the long winter of moose meat and canned food.

We would not be going to the Island so often after the garden was under way and could not leave the chickens uncared for. "I must make some kind of an enclosure for them," Jack said. "I don't see why there would be any objection to our taking some of the wire from the old mink pens that Hank Lucas built at Cottonwood."

"Andy made his chickenyard of that," I answered. "You can tell Art when you see him."

The trip to Cottonwood required a whole day. About half an acre was enclosed by the eight-foot wire fence, and remnants of many breeding dens could still be seen. Hank and George had operated the mink farm for years before Hank's health failed. He could not live there because of his arthritis. I could imagine how Art would energetically start making improvements the minute he returned, but he probably would not raise mink.

The staples had to be withdrawn, and wire cutters used to separate the widths of mesh. My thumb was adorned with a big blister by the time Jack said he had enough. He rolled the wire in a compact roll and loaded it in the boat. We took enough for the chickenyard and also for part of the fence he intended to build around the vegetable garden.

How welcome fresh eggs were! We had not had any in months, and canned dried eggs were only good for cooking. The old hens were a mixture of every type and color. I was delighted with them; they reminded me of skinny pioneer women who had survived many hardships. I thought of perfect names for them—Myrtle, Carrie, Emma. But I realized I could not let them be individuals—I might learn to love them. I remembered the old saying, "Don't name it if you're going to eat it." Mrs. Anderson had told me they had difficulty in carrying their chickens through the winters until they got the strain of hardy mixed ones. Their horny feet indicated that some of the hens were several years old, but it was surprising how many eggs they laid.

Our vegetable garden was to be one hundred feet square.

It was sheltered from the wind by the hill and there were no big trees to obstruct the sun. It was also near the beach, with a smooth trail to wheel up fish for fertilizer. The ground was covered thickly with a tangle of evergreens. Jack patiently cut the sod in sections, lifted and pounded it, and shook the soil off. Then he spaded the ground and removed roots and stones, and it was ready for the fish. Jack and I had been married twenty years, but I was only learning now some of his traits of character. He completed, with almost fanatical thoroughness, any job he started.

I selected the best salmon at the beginning of the run for canning, while they were fresh and shining silver. Later, as they grew more travel-worn on their journey to the spawning grounds, they became inferior; the flesh was flabby and the red showed through to the outside. They were no less effective for fertilizer, though.

Mrs. Lean at the Landing had told me how to smoke fish before canning them, and this made a variation upon the plain canned salmon. We cut the fish into strips lengthwise and rubbed the strips with a mixture of brown sugar and salt, and laid them in a wash boiler overnight before curing them.

Jack was very busy building fences. "If I smoke the fish in Andy's smokehouse," I complained, "I'll have to stay over there all night. I couldn't stay alone, Jack."

"Why not? You'd have Unk for company. I don't want to lose any time from my work."

"I know your work's important, but I couldn't possibly stay there alone. I'm sorry I'm such a coward."

Jack grinned at me teasingly. "Could it be you're afraid of ghosts?"

"I know there's no such thing as a ghost, but I just couldn't do it."

So we spent the night on the Island together and slept in our sleeping bags on the bunks in the little cabin. I knew I was being unreasonable, but I could not make myself sleep in Mrs. Anderson's bed. Daylight lasted all night and the

cries of waterfowl floated lonesomely over the water. The
mewing of a gull sounded like a baby crying.

As soon as I finished canning the smoked fish another
job awaited me. Rows must be made in the garden to receive
the fish so that they could be distributed evenly. I used stakes
and string and had just finished making the rows when the
heavy salmon run actually began. When the run was at its
height big salmon could be seen jumping all over the lake.
Jack emptied the two nets twice a day into the boat and carried the fish to the garden in the wheelbarrow. Such a smelly
job it was! Blow flies swarmed over the fish, and it was sick-
ening work to cut them up and bury them. Jack worked out a
system. He laid the big fish end to end in the rows, and with
a sharp knife cut each of them into several pieces. It was my
work to cover them with soil.

"A bear dug up some of our fish last night," Jack announced at the breakfast table one morning.

"Oh dear! I hope it doesn't come back and disarrange
our rows."

The bear came again the second night. "Guess I'll have
to watch for it tonight and shoot it," Jack said reluctantly.
"Darn it!"

But that very morning when Jack planted the first wheelbarrow load and went back for more the bear came brazenly
for its breakfast. It was very busy and I could see it plainly—
a little fellow, hardly more than a cub. It heard Jack coming
and, with a frightened grunt, disappeared among the small
trees.

"I don't want to shoot it," Jack said impatiently, "but
this won't do."

The little black bear must have hidden close by and
watched us, for as soon as we left he came back for more
fish. It looked like the illustration of a child's storybook. A
bow of red ribbon around its neck would not have seemed out
of place. It came cautiously to the edge of the clearing, looked
around intently, turning its head from one side to the other,
then began to dig industriously. I tried hard to frighten it

away. When I shouted and Unk dashed after it, barking threateningly, it scampered into the woods, looking back over its shoulder.

Jack sighed, went to the house, and got his rifle. Poor little bear! Jack skinned it and nailed the pelt on the outside of the house, rubbing it with salt. Occasionally he worked at it, fleshing and scraping it. We offered it to Unk for a bed, but he would have none of it—he probably disliked the smell.

Afterward, as I looked back, it did not seem possible that Jack, with so little experience, could have accomplished all that he did that second summer. He became very thin. Near the end of the season he told me he had taken the fifth hitch in his belt; but he was sun-browned and wiry and had the appetite of a stevedore.

One day as we gardened on the Island, I grew tired of stooping and weeding and, to straighten my back, went for a walk around the forlorn, deserted premises.

There was an extensive strawberry patch by the barn, but in the previous seasons it had not produced any berries. Mrs. Anderson complained bitterly about this and told me it was because the weather was always too dry at the time moisture was needed for forming the fruit.

I lifted up a handful of the vines and could not believe what I saw—the luscious fruit hung in heavy clusters. "Jack!" I shouted. "Come and look!"

Jack was in no hurry to leave his work. When he arrived I was cramming strawberries in my mouth greedily. "Holy smoke!" he said, and began to grab handfuls and eat them too.

One of the few good rains must have come just at the right time, and all the strawberries that the Andersons should have enjoyed through the years ripened that summer. I never got over feeling guilty about them. We picked gallons, and on returning a week later there were more gallons for the picking. I filled all the jars I could find on the Island with strawberry jam, and canned much of the fruit for sauce.

Jack had cut logs for a chicken house over the winter

and towed them across the bay. He pulled the heavier ones up the trail from the beach with block and tackle. I watched admiringly. "When did you learn to operate a block and tackle?"

"I never learned. There's only one way to do it."

"I wouldn't know which end to attach," I said, laughing. Men just seem to be born with know-how about machinery.

The logs had dried nicely in the woods, and most of them were light enough to be carried on our shoulders, each bearing one end. It's no easy matter for one man alone to build a log cabin, but the chicken house grew staunchly, and Jack put on a roof of tar paper. We had bought two cold-frame sashes from Andy, and one of these, puttied and strengthened, was used for a window on the south side, to catch the winter sun.

I always liked that little house and enjoyed keeping it clean. The chickens were my charges. I gathered moss that grew thickly under the trees on the Point, and spread it out in the sun to dry for litter.

Gradually both Jack and I acquired a growing confidence in our ability to cope with wilderness conditions. We really had accomplished a great deal. But this was the easy season. We didn't yet know how it would be facing the rigors and isolation of winter—perhaps, as now, completely on our own.

CHAPTER 9

JACK FINISHED WIRING the chickenyard, and the hens joyfully took possession of their new home. "Before I start another job," he said, gathering up his tools, "I'll have to go to the Landing and arrange for Hank to bring down our furniture. You want to go too? Maybe it isn't so good for you to stay here so long without a change."

"I don't really care about going," I said blithely. "You won't need me, and I'd be uneasy about the chickens. Unk and I can stay alone."

"Well," Jack said, "I can't make you go. But I don't want you getting queer for lack of company. How long has it been since you've seen a woman?"

"I don't remember. I like men better anyway."

"Cut the comedy now," he said sternly.

Even I was a little surprised at my own audacity. Before, I found waiting at home while Jack was away a difficult, lonely, fearful experience. But now I found I could face the prospect with equanimity. Evidently I was getting used to our isolated surroundings and was learning to face the challenge of remaining alone there. I was, in fact, rather proud of my pluck.

Fortunately, Jack made good time, and was back even before I expected him.

"Hank agreed to bring our freight," Jack said cheerfully as we walked up to the house. "But he said it might be a couple of weeks before he can come."

"I'm glad of the delay," I remarked. "We're far from ready for the furniture. It'll be hard to find a place for it."

"I know," Jack answered gloomily. "Guess I'll have to get busy and build a bedroom. There won't be any room for us in the house until I do."

"Oh, Jack!" I protested. "You have so much to do already, and it will be such hard work to get the logs."

"Have you a plan?" he asked irritably. "There's no use arguing; we can't do anything but build another room."

"Yes, I do have a plan," I answered. "I thought about this all the time you were gone. If you'll get some poles and continue the balcony across to the wall to make a complete attic, we could put our beds up there. You could finish cutting out the door in the back of the attic," I went on eagerly, "so in summer we could enter from outside, and we'd have a small opening at this end, with a ladder, to use in bad weather."

Jack looked interested. "You have all this worked out, don't you?"

"It'll work," I insisted. "We would have room then for a good deal of the furniture. The dining table could go here, and the highboy over there."

"I only wish," Jack said, "I'd had sense enough to make the attic higher. It would have taken very little more work to make a complete second story." He paused. "But it's a fine idea anyhow."

Adding more to the balcony was not difficult, but the poles of its floor were rough and unsightly underneath, and I wished that we had peeled them. "Jack!" I said, "I've an idea!"

"Another one?" he answered. "What now?"

"We have two rolls of heavy kraft paper with our freight," I went on excitedly. "I ordered it from the catalog because I thought it would be useful. It's very strong, and I think if we tack it on the ceiling underneath the poles it would look much better."

"It would at that," he admitted. "It would keep dust from coming down too."

"We can have a door here by the fireplace, with an outside stairway leading to the door in the attic, and fix a cute little guest room up there."

Jack looked about solemnly. "I didn't know we had a fireplace."

"You idiot! I'm talking about the fireplace we'll build some day."

"Oh! *That* fireplace! I might have known."

We had just finished all our preparations for the furniture when the first boatload arrived. Three trips were necessary to bring it all.

The rickety card table was folded away, and we dined on polished walnut, with sterling silver and fine china. Not a piece had been broken on the journey. There were chests of drawers for our clothes, a comfortable couch, upholstered chairs. The old Seth Thomas clock ticked majestically from the top of the highboy.

All the rest of the furniture went into the attic, packed close under the eaves, with the beds in the middle. I should have been very happy to have my possessions again, but for some reason that I could not explain, I was not. Those pieces belonged in an old, established home in the East—they were out of place in a log cabin in the wilderness, their feet resting on chips to keep them level on the gravel floor. I wanted to apologize to them and explain that it would not always be like this.

While Jack labored with clearing, fishing, and building the chicken house, I laid out paths and brought gravel from the beach. When they were graded and gravelled, we had

comfortable walks to the boat landing, to the chicken house
and to the vegetable garden. Then I laid out a walk at the
edge of the lawn, through the wildflower garden, and down to
the beach. Unk had learned when he was a puppy not to run
through the flowers, so very little coaching was required to
keep him on established trails. However, he had some ideas
of his own and carefully proceeded to cross the lupine bed at
the same place until his feet made a well-worn trail.

The walk to the beach passed through a cleft in the
rocks, where I made steps of well-braced logs. Below was a
little rock-floored cove, entirely sheltered from view of the
house. Here I boiled water in an oil can and did the laundry,
the galvanized iron tubs sitting on wooden boxes. I hoped
eventually we could have our own water system with a gasoline pump and a reservoir tank in the attic, but meanwhile
this was better than having Jack carry water up the hill to the
house. He never complained, but sometimes I wished he
would gripe out loud instead of stoically accepting a job and
leaving me to judge by the set of his shoulders whether or not
he enjoyed the work.

The water of the lake, having flowed so recently from a
glacier, was far too cold for swimming, but in that little cove,
sheltered from the wind and with a nice bonfire going, it was
fun to bathe in one of the washtubs. One day I was thus en-
gaged, feeling secure and untrammeled, when all of a sudden
I heard a motor alarmingly close at hand. While I looked
around wildly for a nonexistent place to hide, the boat appeared—it was far out and proceeding down the lake. There
was little consolation in the thought that it was too far away
for its passengers to pick out details on the shore—I shuddered to think they might have been using binoculars.

The busy summer of 1940 rushed by. In September,
when we could expect the first frost at any time, we became
even busier preparing for winter.

We picked gallons of the low-bush cranberries that grew
around us so abundantly, and stored them in the rootcellar.

Their juice, sweetened and mixed with water, made a sparkling drink that we never tired of. It didn't ferment but kept well in jugs closed simply with a cork.

The crop of cranberries varied from year to year. The blossoms were sometimes injured by late frosts, or the arid hillsides on which they grew might be so dry that the berries failed to form. But when the crop was normal there were acres so thickly covered with fruit that at a distance the ground shone red. Raspberries, red currants, and two species of blueberries also grew wild, but the moose cropped off the branches in winter and greatly curtailed their fruit.

Cranberries also proved to be a splendid winter tonic for the imprisoned chickens. They greedily consumed those I stored in the rootcellar, and when they were released in the spring they enjoyed the berries that had remained on the plants over winter. Freezing spoiled the flavor for us, but the chickens didn't seem to mind. These were also the chief food for bears when they emerged from hibernation.

Our tropical shrubs had their tender leaves nipped by frost before they could be brought inside. We took them to the attic, and then fastened the door which Jack had made from coldframe sash. Actually, it would be too warm and dry for the plants up there, but they would exist until another spring. Like the chickens, they were accustomed to hardships.

The garden on the Island produced lavishly that year and we stored quantities of vegetables in Andy's rootcellar. The bins of potatoes, beets, carrots, and rutabagas, and the heads of cabbage with the roots attached hanging from the roof, gave me a wonderful feeling of security. Home-canned meat, fish, vegetables, and fruits, and all my jellies and jams, were stored in one end of the attic, along with our shipped-in groceries, which included a barrel of butter in brine. I found our onions did not keep well in the rootcellar, and planned to try them next year in the warm, dry attic.

Mrs. Anderson had made gallons of relish of celery, cabbage, onions, and the small tomatoes that refused to ripen. I had learned how welcome this relish was in winter, so I made rows of jars, using her recipe. A spoonful on a serving of cabbage, from which winter had drained the flavor, did much to reedem it.

The most beautiful season of the year, the golden Indian Summer, which we always enjoyed for a few weeks after the first crippling frost, now gave place to real cold. Winter was no longer a gentle hint. "Here I am!" it announced, "you've had long enough to get ready." As if they had agreed among themselves, the hens produced not another egg after they were confined, in spite of being pampered with a fire night and morning.

Jack could never keep far ahead of the appetites of the two stoves. He strove constantly, without success, to build up a reserve. When the garden had been harvested, he turned without a pause to sawing wood on the Point. My days were spent in unpacking whatever articles we had room for and repacking those that must be stored. There were many books, and Jack made bookcases from disassembled crates.

All one day the fog hung low over the water like a soft gray blanket, and we listened to the ghostly honking of invisible flocks of southbound geese.

"I hear three flocks out over the lake," I said, straining my eyes to pierce the gloom.

"There's another one!" Jack answered, as a faint bell-like clamor sounded from the north.

"And another!" I cried. "Hear it? It's over the Island." Five flocks at once; all through the day at least one of them could be heard in the sky.

Twilight came early. "Isn't that a motor, Jack?" I asked.

"Probably more geese," he answered and went on splitting wood.

"Yes, it *is* a motor," I said, and started for the beach to listen. Jack followed, and the sound of the motor grew louder. The fog was so thick it seemed to press down upon us.

The motor stopped, and we could hear the thumping of

oars in oar-locks. The water was black and motionless. It must be Cliff, I thought. "Cliff!" I called, my voice echoing.

"Yee-o-ow!" came Andy's voice in reply.

"You might know nobody but Andy would be crazy enough to travel in such fog," Jack said.

As the boat touched the beach, Jack grasped the bow and held it steady, and Andy and Val jumped out. I was more excited over their arrival than the occasion warranted and chattered like a magpie. Was this the effect of isolation? I determined to watch myself.

Andy was anxious to get to the Island, but they stayed to have dinner and tell us the news. It seemed to me that Val had grown a foot while away—he was going to be a tall man. He was now fifteen years old and had changed surprisingly. I noticed that he joined naturally in the conversation and listened to what others said without interrupting them. More contact with people had given him new poise and self-confidence.

The first letter I opened of the handful that Andy handed me was from my sister Sue, who was teaching in a government school for Indians in Seward. For several years she had taught in such schools in southeastern Alaska, and spent her vacations with us. She wrote that she found war-conscious Seward rather trying, and was looking forward eagerly to spending next summer with us on Skilak. I wanted her to come but I dreaded it too. If she considered Seward trying what would she think of our primitive home?

Also in the mail were letters from Art and Cliff. Art was working in Seward and would not come down to the lake that winter. I did not want to open Cliff's letter for I had a premonition of what it contained. I was right. Cliff's mother had begged him to stay in Seattle until he was drafted into the Army. John had already gone and, with the war situation as it was, Cliff was sure he would be called before long. As soon as he possibly could he would come back to Skilak Lake.

These were two blows in quick succession. And we knew

Andy couldn't stay either. He said he had to return to the
Landing next day and would take any mail I had ready. We
were going to be alone on the lake that winter.

"Could you use the horses, Jack?" Andy asked.

"I'm afraid I couldn't take care of them," Jack answered
thoughtfully. "I could use them for hauling logs, but I would
have no food for them."

"How about the goats? I'll give them to you."

"I would gladly pay you for them if I could keep them,"
Jack said, "but we have no shelter for them and they would
be trouble for me here on the mainland." He added with a
grin, "I don't fancy staying awake at night wondering if
they're safe from coyotes."

"That's true," Andy said. "You'd have no hay for them
and no shelter. I'd better take the horses back to the Landing
with me. The goats may get by on the Island. If they can stay
in the barn they'll be fairly safe from coyotes."

"Only three of the does are left, as far as I know," Jack
said. "I'll look for them whenever I go over there, and when
it gets real cold I'll cut down some birch for them to browse
on."

"That's all anyone can do. It would be very hard to keep
them here."

The heartache with which I watched Andy's boat towing
the horse scow away next day proved how much I had looked
forward to company that winter.

The cold steadily increased and the lake froze over
before Christmas. Every year it behaved differently. There
was infinite variety in its moods and whims.

As soon as the ice was good, Alec Wilson appeared. "It's
hard work getting my heavy fishing dory over the shoals in
the river," he said, smiling broadly, "so I waited for the ice."
Jack paid him for the net. "I didn't charge you this much,"
he said, but he kept on grinning and pocketed the bills. As he
drank the coffee I made for him, Alec asked, "Have you put
out any snares yet?"

"Only the dozen I got," Jack answered. "I set them out close by. I could do better on the other side of the lake and around the glacier, but I don't like to leave home so much. Cliff wrote me to use his snares if I need them, and I intend to set out some more."

"They ought to be out now," Alec said. "Since Cliff won't be here this winter, how would you like to have me trap with you? Two can always do better than one alone."

"That would be fine. I'd like to work with you and learn more about it."

I was a little disturbed; we had so little room I wondered if Alec could live with us. It would only be for the winter, though, so I said nothing.

Alec had an uncanny way of seeming to read my thoughts. "I saw Andy in Seward," he went on, "and he told me I could stay in the cabin you lived in on the Island. I don't think I'll have the woman and baby come."

Alec placed his sleeping bag on our couch and produced a clean towel and soap from his pack. He wished it understood that he was not asking for favors, as indeed he was not. He helped Jack saw wood, pulling the other end of the crosscut saw, and when he noticed the pails were empty, he carried water from the hole we had cut in the ice. He would walk into the house with quiet dignity and sit down with his hat on; he never removed it except at meals. After staying a week and helping Jack set out more snares, he promised to come back right after Christmas, shrugged into his pack, and left.

"Would you mind not having mail before Christmas?" Jack asked apologetically. "It won't happen again. When Alec's here he won't mind going."

Since Andy had brought mail a month before, I assured Jack I could stand it until after the New Year.

So, in 1940, we spent our first Christmas alone on the lake. The weather was glorious, with frost all over everything. I put a "welcome" wreath on the outside of the door. After all, I thought, somebody might come. Next morning the wreath was completely frosted, looking like a beautiful confection. This time we had candles and many ornaments for our Christmas tree.

When we found that the gifts we had ordered for each other would not arrive, we each made a list of small tasks that each could do for the other; we agreed not to ask anything really difficult—just a few small chores. My requests included bracing a leg of my bed that wobbled and squeaked, and I also asked for a knob to the lid of the cooky can—Jack could make one from an empty spool I'd saved. We never threw anything away. For years afterward, under different circumstances, I had to overcome the impulse to stop and pick up every board lying beside the road, indignant over such waste. Jack asked that I set over the buttons on his shirt collars, since they had become too small, and would I please make him a date cake?

On Christmas Eve, when it was almost dark, I decided to make another wreath and went down behind the chicken house for some spruce cones. Suddenly all around me in that frozen world there was a swishing, lisping horde of birds. They were the size of large sparrows. Some of them—no doubt the males—were almost wholly bright red, others more somber. They seemed to have no fear of me, and one lit on my head and cooed softly. When it flew away another came and scratched into the material of my cap. Evidently they either did not know I was a human being or that I had power to hurt them. They settled all about me on the small spruces and busily shelled off the scales from the cones. I was astonished at the speed with which they worked. When I noticed their peculiarly shaped beaks I knew they were crossbills, although I had never seen any before. I watched them in awe— it was a beautiful Christmas present for me.

The usual still cold weather came in January. It seemed to me that Jack became more silent each day. He was impatient for Alec to come back, but it annoyed me that he let it affect him so much. He seldom looked in my direction and spent the days doggedly sawing wood.

On one long winter evening Jack and I sat side by side on the couch, leaning back against the cushions, one electric bulb serving us both for reading. This time had always been happy and our companionship sweet, but in spirit we were now growing apart. The moonlight lay on the snow in unearthly beauty. I grew restless and put on my outdoor clothes, hoping that Jack would come with me for a walk, but when Unk and I left the house he did not even ask me where I was going.

The snow was crisp, squeaking under my feet. I walked out to the top of one of the highest cliffs at the edge of the lake, which gave the illusion of being on a mountaintop. The moon etched purple-black shadows of the stiff little spruce trees on the snow, and spread a milky radiance for miles across the flat plain of the ice. The air was clear and translucent; the silence was eloquent as thunder.

The moonlight suddenly seemed to waver. The light surrounding me was now pale green, and as I looked, it became a shifting, flickering, ghostly yellow, changing to delicate pink, then lavender, and back to green. It was too lovely to be borne. I closed my eyes, and when I opened them the color was gone, leaving nothing but pure light, soft and yet intense. I knew this was Northern Lights, but I had always before looked out on it; this time I had been in the midst of it.

Unk, sitting at my feet, whined. It was too cold to stand still, so we moved onto the ice and ran far out toward the end of the Point to get warm. As I walked back, it was not the light that entranced me but the stars. They were so close overhead I felt that I could reach out and grab a handful. They gleamed like candle flames, expanding and contracting. Some were pale; some glowed deep red. I picked out the Great Dipper, hanging at eye level, and Jupiter, shining bright and blue-white near the horizon.

I was still thrilled over my experience when I returned. Jack had gone to bed.

The intense cold continued. One morning, as we breakfasted by lamplight, Jack said, "The goats can't find much to eat now. I'll go to the Island and cut down some birch so they can get the buds."

Jack walked far ahead of me as we crossed the ice. Some distance from the Island beach he stopped, looked down at his feet, and waited until I caught up. "Well, there are probably no goats left," he said, pointing to some spots of blood in the snow and a bunch of tawny hair.

I was speechless with horror; coyotes had gotten at least one of the goats. "The others may be in the barn," Jack said, "but they wouldn't be likely to stop with one."

We could see the poor goat's tracks where the sly coyotes had driven her out into the deep snowdrifts. There coyote tracks were thick.

I shrank from going to the barn, but hoped the coyotes had been too cowardly to pursue the goats to the shelter. But we found coyote tracks all around the barn and not a sign of a goat. The Island had never looked so deserted and forlorn. "They might be on the other side," I suggested, but without hope. "They stay over there much of the time."

"Not a chance," Jack answered. "We would be wasting our time looking for them."

As we turned toward home Jack and I kept our own thoughts. Mine were depressed. The disappearance of the goats removed the last reminder of fruitful farmlife on the Island—it had surrendered to the wild animals.

It was strange that Alec did not come. As yet Jack had caught no coyotes, but there should be some in the more distant snares. When Alec comes, I thought, we will all be busy and happy again.

It was the end of January when a black speck appeared on the frozen lake. I soon recognized Alec's pigeon-toed walk. He brought us a fine rainbow trout that he had caught in the river.

"I've been looking for you every day," Jack said.

"I would have been here three weeks ago," Alec replied, "but I've been in jail."

"In jail!" I cried. "What on earth did you do?"

"I didn't do nothing. The deputy marshal at Kenai has it in for me. He threw me in jail with a couple of fellows because there was a fight at a dance."

I was indignant. "But that's not fair! What has he got against you?"

"He's always accusing me of being drunk," Alec answered indifferently.

Jack raised an eyebrow. "Have you been in jail before?"

Alec looked at him with a grin. "A couple of times."

I felt it was best to change the subject. "Tell us how you caught this trout, Alec. We've tried to fish through the ice out here in the bay, but never catch any."

"The fish are there, all right. I just put a little piece of bacon on my hook. But that was in the river. You don't catch them here in the lake because your lines are not long enough. The fish lie along the bottom in winter."

"We've used quite long lines," I insisted.

"Not long enough. The lake's awful deep—no one has ever found the bottom in some places. Andy told me he tried and there didn't seem to be any bottom."

Alec and Jack were off at once to check their snares. That night they brought back one coyote and hung it in the tent. Early next morning they left for the other side of the lake. I felt toward Alec as I had toward Andy. He was so capable. If anything should happen he would know what to do.

I was a little alarmed when I saw Jack returning alone in late afternoon, pulling the sled. I ran down to the beach to meet him; he had two coyotes. Unk looked at the carcasses suspiciously, walking stiff-legged and slow up to smell them.

"Where's Alec?" I asked.

"He said he needed groceries and wanted to go to the Landing," Jack answered. His face inside his parka hood was burned red by the cold. "I don't think he had any money, so

I told him if he would make the trip for me and get the mail and some tobacco, I would give him five dollars. I sure dreaded a trip through the snow."

"I'm glad, Jack. Alec is going to be very useful to us."

"I think so too. I didn't have any money with me, of course, but I gave him a note to Jack Lean.

Next afternoon Alec returned, seemingly unwearied. Before dark he skinned one of the coyotes, with Jack looking on. Then he showed Jack how to stretch the skin on a board. "You'll want to stay at home now and get your work done," Alec said. "I'll take the run alone on the lower south side tomorrow." Alec was taking care of us just as Andy had done.

Meanwhile I had been working with my wildflower seeds, making a mailing list, and collecting data about the seeds I would offer. I also sent an advertisement to be inserted in a horticultural magazine. But for the short time that remained of the season we all gave our entire attention to trapping. One day when I walked to the Island I noticed Mrs. Anderson's chariot with its pointed prow. I knew it would be much better than the sled for the trappers, but when Andy had offered it to me, I had thanked him but left it there. I had a superstitious feeling that Jessie still controlled her possessions. But now I pushed it home for Jack and Alec; they needed it. I tried to persuade Unk to ride, but he would not, and ran ahead barking. Jack had some misgivings about using the chariot, for the same reasons I had. Alec overcame them. "Why not?" he said practically, "we won't hurt it."

When Jack and Alec took up their snares at the end of the season, they had fourteen coyotes in all. I never dreamed they would do so well the first year. Alec tied the skins in a bundle to carry on his back to Kenai, where he would have them certified by the game warden and sent to Juneau for the bounty. The Game Commission would then forward the skins to a fur dealer in Seattle for sale.

"Next year we'll really make some money," Alec said confidently. "There's a rumor that the beaver season will be opened around here next spring. If it is, we'll make several thousand. We'll have to get a license for my woman and Ada, and all of us work at it. There's a limit of twenty for each person." I smiled to myself. Evidently we were all one big Indian family. "This is the best place in the country for coyotes," Alec went on. "We'll get a good price for these skins too; they've gone up in price since there's danger of war."

If my seed business was a success, along with the encouraging prospects for trapping, we should make enough money in the future for our simple needs. But then, I had never really doubted that we would. We still had enough in the bank to carry us through several years—with our low cash expenditures—but I looked forward to the day when we would be truly self-sufficient.

CHAPTER 10

THE WARMTH OF the sun was increasing daily, but the nights were bitter cold, and the ground remained rock-hard. I began opening the door in the chicken house for an hour each bright day at noon, and the chickens scurried out into the sunshine, scratching happily in the few bare spots, each one singing shrilly in a different key. As a recompense for this favor we received one egg on the second day, on the third day three, and soon the hens were in full production. We ate eggs every meal, three times a day, until our taste for them was sated. I was proud we had brought our hens through the winter so successfully.

The spring of 1941 had come and our third winter on the lake had ended. The approach of summer demanded preparation. I hummed to myself as I pricked off tiny seedlings of cabbage into a bigger box in the window. Was that Unk howling? Where on earth was he? I opened the door and listened. He never went far from home, but the howls were coming from the rocky cliffs on the other side of the curved beach. I hurried in that direction, pulling on my coat as I ran. I could hear Unk howl lustily and then stop for a moment as if listening before howling again. "I'm coming, Unk!" I called. "I'm coming!"

A slight path, worn by moose, coyotes, and other wild animals on their accustomed rounds, wound along the top of the cliff, and Jack had set a snare low in the trail. Long-legged moose stepped over it, but it was just the right height to catch an unwary coyote.

Unk's head was caught fast in the snare, and he had pulled the wire very tight around his neck. I had never examined a snare and didn't know how to loosen it. I pulled it tighter and Unk panted, his tongue hanging out. I would have run for Jack, but Jack was on the Point sawing wood, and I feared Unk would choke to death before he could get there. I must handle this alone! I hated myself for being an ignorant fool. Unk did not struggle but by now was breathing in labored gasps. I saw the mistake I had made by pulling on the wire. When I had pulled, the loop became smaller, and it looked as if it could not be reversed.

Now I studied the mechanism carefully. There was a little hump in the lock, and I pushed on it experimentally. Thank God! By holding down the little hump I could open the loop! Unk coughed and shook his head, looking at me reproachfully. I hugged him in a spasm of gratitude for his intelligence in ceasing to struggle. The coyotes were doomed when caught for they struggled as long as life lasted.

Two days later, as I worked around the stove, I noticed that Unk was sitting close to the wall under a shelf and watching me intently, his eyes following every movement I made. Then he attracted my attention with a sharp yelp, and I saw that a string from a bag on the shelf had fallen off, and a loop hung down a short distance from the floor; Unk's head was thrust through the loop. He could easily have withdrawn his head, but it was plain that he thought he was in a snare, and that if he moved it would close about his neck. I loosened the string and his whole body shivered with relief.

The ice that spring had gone out down the length of the lake, but in Dawson Bay it held on tenaciously. The April days were calm, and with no wind to hurry it the ice lay on the water and rotted. The days were bright and shining but the nights were still cold.

We had had no mail for more than a month, and there were several items of business for Jack to take care of at the Landing. "I won't wait any longer for the ice to move," he said. "I'll take the boat on the sled to the end of the Point where the ice ends. Can you come and give me a hand?" I ran down the trail after him, with Unk close behind.

The sled carrying the boat slid smoothly over the ice, although the surface was very soft. Jack pulled with the rope and I pushed from behind. When we drew the boat up on the shore of the Point he tied it at stern and bow in case of a wind.

As we recrossed the ice, Unk ran ahead and reached shore first. Jack, with a coil of rope on his shoulder, walked on, and I, as usual, dawdled. The bright sunshine was lovely and warm. I could hear the scream of gulls from their nesting grounds on the rocky islands far away; they always came as soon as the ice was gone. I noticed something that was new to me—a kind of singing from the ice. It stopped when I stopped, and when I took a step there came a little vibrating hum like the twang of a banjo string.

I hastened to catch up with Jack when suddenly, without the slightest warning, one foot broke through the ice. I dropped to a sitting position, one leg dangling in deep water, the other sticking out before me. I held my breath; more ice might break if I moved and I would go in entirely.

Jack had almost reached the shore but heard me gasp and whirled around. He started toward me, and the ice broke under his feet, but the water was shallow there and did not reach the tops of his rubber boots. "Don't move!" he shouted to me.

I sat there, breathing shallowly, trying to make myself light, not daring to move. I remembered how Andy's horse had drowned; if I went into the water I would be drawn under the ice. I tried to pray, but I was too terrified to do more than whisper, "God, God."

Jack ran along the beach, and out of the corner of my eye I saw him disappear behind me. I dared not turn my head to see what he was doing. I could not see Unk on the beach, either, but I could hear him whimpering. Of course, he would sense that I was in danger.

What was Jack doing out of sight behind me? He called again, "Don't move," and he sounded reassuring and capable. "I am going to throw the rope to you," his voice said quietly. "Don't move until you can reach it easily. I've made a loop in the end. See if you can get it over your head and shoulders."

There was a thud beside me but the rope was out of my reach. Jack pulled it back and tried again. I moved just enough to grasp it, but that tiny shift of weight was sufficient to make the ice break beneath me, and down I went into the water. Instinctively I threw my arms up, still grasping the rope. How cold the water was! It was like acid burning the skin from my body.

Down I sank below the surface! I swallowed water, fought for air, and swallowed more water. There was a terrible pressure on my chest—I was drowning. I had never learned to swim, but I struggled. Then I felt the air on my face; I had risen to the surface again. I heard Jack's voice, far away. "Hold onto the rope! Hold on tight; I'm going to pull you to good ice." Somehow I had managed instinctively to clutch the rope end and now the rope was taut. I did not go under and I could breathe again. Gasping and choking, I reached the edge of the ice and put my arms out on it, but it broke in front of me. At each movement I made Jack took up the slack in the rope, and I did not go under again when the ice broke.

"Keep on breaking the ice," Jack called, and I obeyed.

Still holding the rope, I pressed on the ice and it continued to break. Then I could not break it any more, and rested with my arms on the ice. I was so very tired.

"Hold onto the ice," Jack yelled. "Don't move till I tell you. Stay as you are and let go of the rope."

No, no! I could not give up the rope, but it slipped from

my hands, and I was left hanging there bereft of my only link with Jack. I clung to the shelf of ice, praying it would hold. When the water stopped pouring over my face from my knitted cap I could see Jack, quickly pulling the rope back and again throwing it to me. This time it fell within my reach! How wonderful it was to be attached to Jack again! "See if you can get the loop over your head and shoulders," Jack directed in a calm voice. "Put your arms through the loop. You're going to be all right—don't be afraid."

I no longer felt the icy water, but when I tried to lift my arms they felt as if weighted with lead. Somehow, with my fumbling hands, I managed to do as Jack told me, and the rope tightened around my chest. Straining to lift myself with my arms as he pulled on the rope, I felt my body scrape over the edge of the ice, and then I was lying flat on top of it. I couldn't lift a finger. Again the rope tightened under my arms and I felt myself being pulled over the ice like a sled. Jack's face appeared, bending over me; then everything went blank.

I found out afterwards that Jack had run along the shore until he reached the shade of the group of big spruces. The sun never touched the ice there, and he knew it would be firmer. He had come as close to me as he could, and pulled me to him on the ice.

The next thing I knew Jack was carrying me to shore. He slipped on the ice and fell. "Just help me up," I croaked. "I can walk." I thought my strength was coming back, but when I tried to walk I fell on my face. I could feel the cold again; every fiber of my being ached. The rope was still around me. I felt it tighten once more, and again Jack was forced to pull me along by it. Finally we reached the shore. Unk jumped on me in wild joy. He had understood the danger and had not tried to come to me on the ice.

We were only a little way from the trail. With Jack half carrying me I staggered towards the house. "We're almost there, hon," Jack said. "Just a few more steps now."

Soon we were inside the warm cabin. I stood dazed, shivering convulsively, while a pool of water formed at my feet. Jack helped me get rid of my sodden clothes. I fumbled with the laces of my shoepacs but finally gave up and Jack took them off my feet. He must not have known where I kept my pajamas, for he brought me a pair of his own flannel ones. While I struggled into them, he dashed up the ladder and brought our two sleeping bags. One of these he arranged on the couch and I fell exhausted upon it. He zipped it up to my neck and tucked the other one around me. I was dimly aware that he had placed a very hot water bottle at my feet and was rubbing my hair with a towel. The stove was red hot. My teeth were chattering like castanets, but I began to feel the heat and the delicious comfort. Soon I could not hold my eyelids open.

When I awoke the stove was still red hot. I was dripping with perspiration and threw back the sleeping bag, but Jack sprang from the circle of lamplight to tuck me in again. "No, no! Stay covered up. Do you have a pain in your chest?"

"I don't think so," I mumbled vaguely. "What happened? Did I fall through the ice, Jack?"

"I'll say you did. How do you feel? Are you warm enough?"

"I feel all right, and I never was so warm in my life. What time is it? I'm hungry."

Jack pointed to the clock. It was just three o'clock. It was black outside the windows so I knew it was 3:00 A.M. I had slept more than twelve hours. Unk jumped on the couch, and I had to turn my face into the pillow to keep him from licking me in the mouth.

Jack hovered over me. He wouldn't let me sit up, and after I promised to stay covered up he went to get food for us. He had not eaten either, and he made sandwiches and hot chocolate and brought a tray. "I fed Unk," he said. "I tried to make him go outside, but he wouldn't leave you. He's watched you every minute."

"It was a miracle that you could save my life, Jack."

"I could do it only because I was carrying the rope. If I hadn't had that rope!"

"But you did have it, and you knew what to do. It was wonderful!" We sat looking at each other fondly. I knew Jack was thinking, as I was, that there was constant danger in our life, and that we had only ourselves to depend upon in an emergency.

Jack was very solicitous of me for several days. When he did not think I saw him he often peered into my face anxiously, but I suffered no dreadful effects from my cold bath and was soon able to do my share of the work.

The fall before we had selected a long pole, perhaps fifty feet in length, ten inches in diameter and tapering to a point. We peeled it and towed it home, and there it had been seasoning for a flagpole.

Jack dug a deep hole. "I think we should wait until somebody comes," he said. "We can't raise it alone."

"Oh, please let's try!" I exclaimed. "I've wanted a flagpole ever since we came. The flag would mean something—it would identify us to the planes that fly over." At that moment a gray Army plane roared low overhead.

"I didn't know you cared that much. Well, I'll try." Jack painted the pole green, tarred and charred the butt end, and strung a rope through a pulley at the top. Then he worked the butt end into position near the hole. "Here's where I need you," he called to me. Jack held the weight of the pole on his shoulder and I slipped a log under it. Then he straightened up more and raised the pole a few more inches. I placed a log on top of the last one, and we continued until he could not reach high enough to lift the pole any farther.

I thought impatiently that we would have to wait after all, but without explaining Jack wired two long poles together at one end, spread out the legs and placed this as a secure prop under the flagpole. "I can do this faster if you will help me," he said. "I will move one leg and will tell you when to move the other. Hold it steady now."

Jack moved one leg of the prop forward a few inches and the flagpole was raised slightly. He motioned me to move the other leg and I did so carefully, fearing that I would not do it properly and it would be my fault if the flagpole fell. We followed this procedure several times until it was almost upright. However, the butt end hung up on the side of the hole and stubbornly refused to move down to the bottom.

Jack had fastened a pulley with a long rope at the top for raising and lowering the flag. Now he attached each end of the rope to a nearby tree, so that it was doubly secure. He loosed one end of the rope and pulled carefully. Suddenly— Swoosh!—down it slipped into the hole. After that it was an easy matter to adjust. Jack shoveled in dirt gradually and could straighten the flagpole easily by pushing on it, without danger of its falling.

We made a few adjustments, and finally, viewing it with squinted eyes from all directions, we could find no fault with it. Jack fastened the flag to pulley rope and pulled it up hand over hand. When it reached the top, and the breeze caught it, it flapped sluggishly for a moment, then floated proudly at full length. Jack and I gazed at it in silence. Unk raised his bristles and barked at it, then turned to me questioningly.

We both laughed. Jack stooped down and, lifting Unk's head, pointed his grizzled muzzle toward the flag. "That's Old Glory."

When Jack spaded our garden the soil showed much improvement, and we decided this would be the last year we would have to use the Island. Another frost was unlikely, and I tried out the new earth by planting one row of each important vegetable in it to see how they would grow there. The spring sun warmed my back pleasantly as I dropped parsnip seeds in the row. I could hear Jack's hammer blows.

He was taking out the glass door in the attic and replacing it with a screen door.

There was nothing quite so heavenly as the smells of spring. Unk was enjoying them too. He crept under the fence and ran, sniffing, up into the woods. I didn't call after him for I knew he would not go far.

Suddenly, like a clap of thunder, I heard a dreadful scream. It was like the cry of a human being in agony. A coyote must have attacked Unk, I thought, as I flew in the direction of the cries.

Jack was just ahead of me. He hadn't stopped for his rifle; he, too, must have thought it was a coyote that he could scare away. There had been a couple of quick screams, then silence, then a fresh burst. Jack called, "Unk! Unk! Where are you?" I was close behind—both of us were running.

I stumbled and fell, so it was Jack who first saw the big brown bear. The bear had heard us coming and calling. It stood on its hind legs, gave a "woof," and looked at us, but did not charge. Instead, it turned and disappeared among the trees. We would have been quite defenseless.

First Jack, then I, called and called, but there was utter silence. "I only hope he isn't suffering," Jack said shakily. My throat was locked in ice. "We must find him quickly," Jack added, "but I'd better get my rifle. No use risking our own lives—that bear was in an ugly mood."

We started back for the rifle. Jack had been working that winter, when the weather permitted, on excavating a rootcellar back of the garden, and where the path Jack's feet had worn crossed a little knoll, sat Unk waiting for us. He looked as if nothing had happened.

I turned and lifted my face to the sky, my eyes closed. "Thank you, God," I whispered, "for sending him back to us." Blindly I followed when Jack picked Unk up in his arms and carried him to the house. I spread a cloth on the couch and Jack laid Unk down on it. The dog did not appear to be suffering, but his eyes stared unnaturally. He looked from one of us to the other as if asking us to take care of him as we always had done.

Jack examined him; I could not look. "Ribs broken," Jack muttered. "The bear did it with a blow of its paw. I'm afraid he can't make it, hon."

"Yes, he will, darling. Remember that God sent him back to us."

Unk seemed dazed, but lay quietly with his nose on his paws. His eyes did not close. I saw, each time he breathed, a bubble of blood formed and broke over a little hole in his side. I did not show this to Jack—I refused to think about it.

Jack rested in his sleeping bag on a chair and I sat on the couch beside Unk and watched through the night. He did not move once in those hours; I knew that it was instinctive for dogs to lie quietly until wounds healed.

When we began moving about in the morning and disturbed him, it evidently agonized him to move. He whined piteously if I moved so I sat by him. I noticed that he was more contented if my hand was close to his head, and I left it there through the long hours. Jack and I talked very little and in low voices when we did. Occasionally Unk would struggle to sit up, panting and whimpering.

As the second night came on he grew more restless. He couldn't lie still any more, but tried to sit, tried to lie down, looking first at me and then at Jack with suffering eyes. I talked to him soothingly. I told him the pain would go away and he would get well if he lay still. He looked at me earnestly. He seemed to understand me, or at least the tone of my voice; once he licked my hand.

Jack walked, walked, up and down the room, out the door, down to the beach and back, over and over. He came in from the outside and knelt beside me and laid his head in my lap. He was crying. "Let me do it, hon," he begged. "He asked me just now with his eyes. Let me do it."

I did not need to ask what it was he wanted to do. "If he were our child, Jack, would we shoot him because he's suffering? He would see you pointing the gun at him, dar-

ling." I stroked Jack's forehead tenderly. "He'll live; God sent
him back to us." I still believed with all my heart that Unk
would recover.

The hours passed. Unk's whimpering turned to cries of
agony. I could never explain how it came to me to give in. It
was as if suddenly I saw clearly that this was the customary
thing to do when a dog was injured and suffering. I could
not hold out stubbornly any more. It wouldn't matter to Unk;
he wouldn't feel it. Jack came through the door. I smiled at
him and said, "I'm ready." I rose energetically. "Let's take
him outside on the blanket. I'll take this end."

Jack took up the other two corners and we carried Unk
out into the sharp morning air. He was quiet. I don't know
if he was unconscious, or if he understood that at last something was being done to help him.

It was about three o'clock. The sun had not yet come up
over the Point, but the sky was rosy red; swallows were
twittering from their nesting boxes; the tops of the mountains
were on fire. I lifted my eyes "unto the hills from whence
cometh my strength" and did not watch Jack make ready.
"Will you stand by me?" he asked in a whisper. I knew what
he meant.

"You know I will, darling." I held Jack's left hand. The
hand that held the revolver was very steady.

"Where do you think we should bury him?" Jack asked
when we had rested awhile.

A grave had always been a horrible thing to me. I
couldn't bear to bury Unk in the ground, mark the grave with
his name, and afterward look at the place and remember. But
I didn't know what else to do. "I'll leave it to you, dear,"
I answered.

So by Jack's decision we rowed far out and consigned
Unk's little maimed body to the cold waters of Skilak Lake.
I was content to have it so; there would be no place to look
at and remember.

CHAPTER 11

WORK WITH ONE's hands is a potent remedy for heartache. I could cease remembering Unk's death only when I was too tired to think. As the green shoots of lupine appeared the trail his feet had worn was clearly defined; I don't know why that reminder should hurt more than all else.

I did not speak of this to Jack, but one day I saw that Unk's trail had disappeared. When I looked closely I could see that the ground had been dug up and lupine plants set out where the trail had been.

I was grateful to Jack. How had he sensed that I could not bear to look at it?

Time passed very swiftly as we planted the garden and performed the work that always assailed us at the beginning of a new season. Soon it was June and time for Sue to come.

A visit from my oldest sister, who had guided my childish footsteps, meant much to me. Sue was my first teacher when she was little more than a child herself. She was still teaching children who were not her own, and although she had yielded to my pleadings and had come to Alaska to teach Indian children, she had brought South Carolina with her. At any rate, Sue's opinion was very important to me, and now she was to visit me in this strange new world that I instinctively felt would not meet with her approval.

The prospect of her arrival brought home to me our complete isolation. I should go all the way to Seward myself and bring Sue down to the lake. She wrote enthusiastically of the walk through the woods and of traveling in a small boat, but I knew her eagerness was born of ignorance. I knew she could never walk the trail. Hank might bring us down the river, but the streams that fed the river were still frozen at their source on the mountains, and I expected that the river would be too low until July. What to do with Sue in the meantime? She planned to come as soon as school closed. I became nervous and jittery trying to figure it all out.

But all my anxiety was needless. When I reached Seward, and we talked it over, she suggested brightly, "Let's charter a plane. I'll gladly pay my share."

Immediately my thoughts began darting here and there. If I didn't have to walk I might find a power saw for Jack . . . we needed a new strain of chickens. The possibilities took my breath away.

"Oh, yes!" I replied, choking back my excitement. "If we share the expense it shouldn't be too much. How wonderful of you to think of it!"

School would not close for several days; meanwhile we set a day for our return. I sent Jack a message to be radioed from Anchorage—a great convenience which the radio station provided without charge. No one in the wilderness failed to listen in at the time for broadcasting messages. It was the old-fashioned farm telephone adapted to frontier life.

Seward had changed greatly since my last visit. The Army had taken over and olive-drab uniforms were much in evidence. The atmosphere was tense and fearful, and some citizens were digging air raid shelters in their backyards. The Army guarded its secrets well but there were rumors that a military installation, with several thousand soldiers, was soon to be established there.

Still, it was hard for me to believe that war was likely to come any day, or that the Japanese might drop bombs from the air, or that the whole world would be changed overnight into chaos. I spent a happy and busy time collecting my booty to take home.

The school where Sue taught was a government boarding school for Indian children, with a farm connected to it. The superintendent agreed to sell me two young Rhode Island Red roosters; I thought I had better take two since something could so easily happen to one. Also I obtained from him a setting of eggs. Old Red, as we called the youngest and best-looking of the Anderson hens, was clucking when I left home, and I only hoped the mother urge would not wear off before I got back.

On a visit to the dentist I was led, because of his kindness and interest in our life on the lake, to tell him about Unk. That night I was surprised to have him phone me. "I have a dog for you," he announced. A dog? I could only gasp. "Some friends of ours have a beautiful nine-month-old dog that they can't keep in town," he went on enthusiastically. "She has a kind of heedless nature, but your place would be perfect for her."

"What kind of a dog is she?" I asked absently. At the moment I never wanted any dog but Unk.

"She's a mongrel. Her mother's a brown spaniel, but she looks just like an Irish setter. If you'll come to my office tomorrow around noon, I'll drive you there when I go to lunch, and you can decide if you want her."

I lost my heart to the lovely creature the moment I saw her. They had her chained in a shed, and her golden eyes, with pupils so large they appeared to be black, tried to tell me how she hated to be chained, and I longed to allow her the freedom of our hills.

The pilot said I could take anything I wanted, since the

plane was chartered. I looked for a power saw, but with the emergency there was not one in town. One storekeeper suggested that we order one and gave me an address in St. Louis.

I bought tools, material, paper for my seed catalogs, bananas, oranges, and some fresh vegetables so that we might have salads until the garden produced lettuce and radishes. I never dreamed when I left home that I would accomplish so much. And the crowning stroke, as we boarded the little pontoon plane that bobbed on the water in the Seward bay, was the copper-colored dog that tugged at the leash I held.

We would arrive in twenty minutes instead of walking all those weary miles and waiting for wind and weather. Would Jack and I ever have enough money for a plane of our own? It was the dream of every man in Alaska to own one. What a way to conquer the wilderness!

We followed Resurrection River, winging through the canyons between the high, snow-crested mountains. Upper Russian Lake, lying among the peaks, looked like a big dewdrop that had settled there.

"Looks like a lonely place," Sue commented, and there was a note of misgiving in her voice.

The plane droned on for only a few minutes and then we were over Skilak Lake.

"This is our lake, Sue!" I cried excitedly. "We'll soon be there! See how beautiful it is? We can see it all from the air."

"It *is* beautiful," she answered, with gratifying interest. "I didn't know just what to expect."

Our lake looked much smaller from the sky, lying there placid and inscrutable—a mirror with blue sky and clouds reflected in it, embodying all the wild charm of a land on which man had made no real impression.

I could actually see the shape of the lake for the first time—like a map drawn to a small scale. Its outline was that of a huge fantastic animal. At the top of its head the Kenai River poured in most of the contents of the lake; then the head elongated into a nose that ended with the dirty, seamed heap of the dead glacier, its substance slowly disintegrating and seeping away in a milky, silty stream that flowed from beneath the age-old ice to add its contribution to the lake.

The lake contracted below its head and formed a long neck, with a mountain as its Adam's apple. The cluster of bare gull rocks, reflecting the sunlight, was like a jeweled ornament at its throat.

Below its neck grew a big swollen body, but from my eagle's eye viewpoint I could hardly believe it was five miles across at the widest place. Caribou Island and its satellites were green blobs on the blue water.

Beyond the islands the lake contracted abruptly, with a decided tail at the end. Here the Kenai River, after resting awhile in the deep lake bed, once more resumed the work of emptying its waters into the ocean at Cook's Inlet, thirty miles away.

"There's Jack, Sue!" I squealed, as we banked sharply for a landing. "He's running the flag up to welcome us."

Thank God Jack was all right! Each time I was compelled to be separated from him in nagging uncertainty and silence, I was to experience, as at that moment, an almost painful sense of relief and gratitude that he was safe.

The plane struck the water with a jar and we taxied gently to the beach.

The dog was the first one out. She leaped in the water and swam ashore. Jack looked at her incredulously, but I could not take time to explain. Grinning happily, he stood in the water in rubber boots and reached up, first for me, then Sue, and gave us a lift that bounced us onto dry land.

I forgot that Sue was there as I anxiously watched my precious freight being unloaded. Jack held out his hands to receive from the pilot our belongings—Sue's suitcases, my canvas rucksack, many cartons and boxes.

"She told me to handle this with care," the smiling pilot warned, as he handed Jack a box. "I think it's eggs."

Next came a crate containing the two roosters, their

heads sticking up through the ventilation holes, viewing the scene with alarmed eyes. Jack muttered "Gosh!" under his breath as he set the crate down on the beach, whereupon both roosters gave out a loud squawk.

All this was simply routine for the bush pilot. Without alighting, he checked to see that nothing was forgotten; then the motor whirred and he was ready to go again.

"Gosh, don't go yet," Jack shouted. "Can't you come up for coffee? I made a cake."

The pilot smiled regretfully. "Sure wish I could, but I'm due in Kasilof right now." He backed the plane away from the beach, turned around in a wide arc and a fountain of spray, and with a grin and a wave of his hand, took off into the distance.

"Look at the roosters I brought, Jack!" I pointed out proudly. "And I've a setting of eggs. Is Old Red still clucking?"

"More than ever. She gets furious when I make her get off the nest to eat." He added in a low voice, "Where did you get the dog?" his averted head telling me mutely that his sorrow for Unk was still very much alive. It was going to take a long time for the mention of the word dog to fail to bring Unk's image to mind.

"Dr. Wagner, the dentist, gave her to us," I answered. "I was so surprised." I felt nervously that it was necessary for me to defend her. "We're going to love her, dear. Isn't she pretty?"

With only her plumed tail visible above the wild roses, she went ranging far and wide like her birddog ancestors, paying no attention when I called her. "She's just a puppy and hasn't been trained," I explained.

"I brought you a present, Jack," I went on, to change the subject, "a sprinkling can, so you won't have to use the old rusty gasoline can to sprinkle the floor."

"Gosh, thanks." He gazed at me intently. "I can't stand having you away."

"Why do you sprinkle the floor?" Sue asked, her question jerking me back to her presence. I had forgotten to tell her about the gravel floor. She stood uncertainly on the beach, a shiny purse in her gloved hand, clad in a stylish suit, with a little flowered hat atop her gray curls, and I was suddenly overwhelmed by the futility of an attempt to explain any part of our life to her. I decided to show her silently as best I could.

Jack had cleaned the cabin, even wiping dust off the wall logs. He had made a very good cake and had picked a large bouquet of wild roses. Tears came to my eyes when I saw all he had done so Sue would have a good first impression of our home. "We don't want people to think we live like Siwashes," he explained.

When we placed the fifteen brown eggs in the nest, Old Red carefully arranged them with her feet and settled down happily, crooning softly to herself. She had no time to think of the new roosters, but the other hens cackled excitedly when they were released.

The plants in our new garden seemed to have jumped out of the ground, judging by what remained of them. Sick with disappointment, I saw that most of the seedlings were only leafless stems. On all sides, small birds, sparrows, juncos, and an occasional one that I could not identify, had hatched their broods and were busy feeding their fledgings and teaching them to fly. The open level ground of the garden provided a fine training field, and the tender leaves of lettuce and mustard just the diet they needed. When the cabbage and cauliflower plants were put out the birds set to work at once and picked them down to the ground. In desperation I had covered the plants with newspaper, held down by handsful of earth, but this did not deter them. Flocks of birds in all stages of development swarmed along the rows; when their sharp little eyes spied an opening, one would dart under the paper, followed by others who picked off their salad with con-

secrated zeal. They paid not the least attention to us and we
could not make them fly away.

"Jack, what on earth can we do about it?" I bawled. "It
will be like this every year."

"I'll just have to shoot them. There's nothing else to
do."

Just then a white-crowned sparrow, sitting on a nearby
fence post as he waited for us to leave, broke forth in joyous
song.

"That's what he thinks of your plan, Jack. We'll just
have to put up with them."

The trouble was that we loved the birds despite their
depredations. The small spruce trees around the house provided ideal nests for both the sparrows and robins. The
sparrows were the chief nuisance but the robins were not interested in our garden plants, since they subsisted only on
bugs and worms and had to work hard for a living. I also discovered in a small spruce the nest of a pair of gentle Bohemian waxwings with five large speckled eggs. The dark-headed
juncos hatched their young on the ground, in little mossy
indentations under clumps of cranberry, revealed only by
their "Chit-chit!" warning when the dog came near.

In Juneau I had come to know the golden-crowned
sparrow when it arrived early each spring for a few days on
its way farther north. Its "one-two-three" call, the notes the
same as "Three Blind Mice," now sounded on every side.
When I first heard it my first summer on the Island, Mrs.
Anderson and Val had translated its song, "Oh my dear,"
but Andy said he had heard prospectors call it the "No gold
here" bird; the more superstitious would leave off prospecting
if they heard it nearby.

The vegetable situation was not as serious as it first appeared. When the birds taught their fledgings to fly they
were gone as suddenly as they had come. Most of the plants
survived and under the stimulus of long, sun-filled days soon

grew more leaves. And the peas and potatoes, we found, were immune.

The Andersons had not suffered this difficulty because they had many weeds. Mrs. Anderson laughingly told me, as I helped Cliff with the endless weeding of their vegetable garden, how chickweed had come to the Island. She had had a canary and one day had noticed a plant of chickweed that apparently had been imported in hay Andy bought for the horses. She carefully pruned off a branch here and there to give to the canary and kept the plant to produce seed. The next year there was an abundance of chickweed—enough for the chickens as well—and after that there was an annual battle to keep it out of the fertile rows.

Andy said we could not help having weeds eventually. I did not want weeds, but they were better than shooting the song birds.

To make the spring complete, in just three weeks Old Red became the mother—at least by proxy—of eleven fluffy yellow chicks.

We spent much time on the Island weeding and thinning the garden there. At first we took Sue on all our trips in the boat, and I invited her to go with me when I visited the beaches to collect wildflower seeds. She seemed to admire the beauty of the rugged scenery, but she was frightened of the water and quaked at the mention of bears. It was necessary for Jack and me to spend every daylight hour at work during the short summer, and Sue gradually began staying at home, reading or knitting.

"The wind might come up sometime when we are on the Island so we can't get home," I warned her. "I don't believe we'll ever have to leave you overnight, but you must be prepared."

I didn't really think this would ever happen, but the very next day an innocent breeze, barely rippling the water when we crossed to the Island, increased throughout the day until by late afternoon the lake was lashed into dangerous whitecaps.

"We simply can't leave Sue alone all night, Jack," I said worriedly.

"We haven't any choice," he replied. "She'll be perfectly safe."

"I know she'll be safe, but I can still remember how scared I was when I spent my first night alone."

"Well, it'll be dark only a little while," he said firmly. "We'll build a fire on the beach where she can see it from the window. That'll tell her we can't make it."

We built a huge fire, piling on armloads of leaves and other green material to make a thick smoke. It was all we could do to reassure Sue and tell her we were thinking of her.

During the small hours of the morning I awoke in Cliff's little cabin. When I realized that the wind had died, I called Jack and, rubbing sleep from our eyes, we stumbled down to the boat and pushed off.

There wasn't a sound from the cabin as I ran up the trail. Curtains were pulled closely over the windows, but I rejoiced to see a wisp of white smoke against the dark morning sky.

"Sue," I called, "are you all right?"

There was a faint sound of her voice from within—at least she was there and conscious. "Open up, Sue," Jack joked. "We're Indians after your scalp." The door was fastened on the inside and it took Sue a long time to get it open. In addition to the heavy bar, she had piled against it all the furniture she could move.

When I saw that she was fully dressed and had not been to bed at all, I knew what a night of terror she had spent.

"Something sniffed at the door," she said tremulously. "I heard it plainly."

"Could have been a bear, of course," Jack said seriously. "But we've never seen one near the house."

"I had no light and I tried to be very quiet so it would think no one lived here and would go away."

Jack looked for tracks but did not find any. I knew very well how one's imagination could play tricks, but felt it was more tactful to say nothing.

We had been in no hurry to give the new dog a name. I wanted to study her personality and think of something that really suited her. One day we all stood watching her leap with long, graceful bounds, her ears flapping, her burnished coat flaming in the sun, and a name burst into my consciousness fullgrown. "Flash!" I said happily. "Let's call her Flash."

Unk had been my dog, and I wanted Flash to adopt Jack—it was his turn. But she began where Unk left off and was like my shadow. She made fun of me and never took me seriously, but there was an intangible bond between us. I could feel it in the way she sat, not *at* my feet but *on* them, leaning back against my knees as if this was her rightful place. She did this to no one else.

While she had none of Unk's sober responsibility, Flash was a lovable dog. Her expressive eyes shone with intelligence. "She has a sense of humor," I said to Jack.

"I wouldn't appreciate her coming tearing behind me the way she does to you," he answered, "and dashing between my legs."

I laughed. "Isn't it funny she doesn't do that to you?"

"I think it's because she knows I wouldn't stand for it," he said drily.

Flash's body was long and slender with a tiny waist. She wriggled and undulated ingratiatingly.

"She reminds me of a young girl who's well aware that she's pretty," Jack said indulgently, stroking her silky ears.

Flash loved the water. I had to watch when we were in the boat to keep her from falling overboard and pretending it was an accident. She would scramble back over the side, dripping and shaking water, and grin with her tongue lolling. She never drank from the beach, but would swim out some distance and lap.

What fun it was when she discovered her echo! She learned by chance that if she barked at a certain place on the beach her voice would echo from the wooded hillsides of Dawson Point, and it gave her endess pleasure. She often went back to the same place to bark and then stand, with her head cocked on one side like the puppy that she still was, listening to the ghostly reply.

Jack dug the rootcellar in a well-drained gravel bank and lined it with logs, working at it day after day from morning till night. Across the front he made a dry wall of rocks from the beach. The top was covered with many thicknesses of sod, and on that he spread gravel. Inside the door he made a little entry with an inner door. It was stoutly constructed.

"I don't believe any frost can force its way inside," Jack said, with great satisfaction.

"If it does, we can just put on some more gravel," I answered.

Potatoes grew well in our home garden that year—all we needed for winter. We made another thick application of fish between the rows. Our strawberries were a failure but there were more raspberries than we could use, and we gladly shared them with the birds. The robins also liked the berries and joined the small birds in gobbling them up.

Sue was always occupied at something. She helped me address my seed catalogues, and sewed and knitted. She seemed content, so I came to believe that she was enjoying herself as much as Jack and I were until the day when Hank and his partner George Nelson brought our supplies in their boat.

We had had no mail in six weeks. For my own self-preservation I had learned not to fret over what could not be helped. There was a handful of letters for Sue, and I was astonished to see tears rolling down her cheeks when I handed them to her.

"What's the matter?" I asked anxiously. "Are you afraid of bad news?"

"How on earth can you stand it?" she asked. I didn't know what to reply. I had grown at least partly used to our isolation, and no longer minded these minor hardships. Sue's tears, which might have been mine three years before, dramatized how much I'd changed. She could not have stood such things for more than a few weeks at a time.

We walked to the beach with Sue when she boarded her plane to return to her school. The same pilot who had brought her grinned from the cockpit. Sue's last words were, "You have a beautiful, beautiful place." I knew, however, that if she had not been so polite, she would have added, "And you can keep it!"

The hills again shimmered with gold, and the clump of flame and tangerine aspens at the mouth of the creek looked like a garden of chrysanthemums. Then the leaves fell and moose could be seen on the rim of hills behind the house. We brought our harvest of vegetables home in the boat and stored it in our lovely new rootcellar. I wanted Sue to know I had no doubts about our new life, but I had to make an effort to prevent her skepticism from rubbing off on me. I felt a little sad as the plane climbed into the air and disappeared behind the mountains, and walking back to the house I stayed very close to Jack.

Up to that time I had been collecting seeds and now I was prepared to offer them for sale. The covers of my catalogs had been addressed, with Sue's help, from a long mailing list, composed mostly from answers to my advertisement in horticultural magazines. I printed catalogs on a little Sears, Roebuck mimeograph machine, and had everything in readiness before asking Jack to take them to the Landing for mailing.

It was only then that I remembered about the stamps. We had never kept a supply on hand but relied on Jack Lean to have some on hand when our letters were mailed. I now realized in panic that there were three hundred and thirty-five catalogs, and the Leans would not have nearly that many stamps. The catalogs would have to be mailed at Moose Pass where there was a regular post office, and where there was a new postmaster whom I did not know. I hated to ask a stranger to put on such a quantity of stamps.

If only I could go and attend to it myself! But Jack would not let me go alone with so many bears and moose about, and somebody had to stay home and prevent our food from freezing. In my frustration I felt like a bird flying against a windowpane.

"Why didn't you think of stamps earlier?" Jack asked, his question so logical it infuriated me.

After days of fretting and worrying I decided the only solution was for Jack to meet the mail carrier at the Landing and give him the money for the stamps, trusting to his good nature and helpfulness. So I wrote the mail carrier a note. "It means so much to me," I wrote, "and I am sick at heart because I forgot to provide stamps in time. I hate to ask you to take care of this for me, but I don't know what else to do."

Despite the burden of his work, Jack managed to get away to meet the mail carrier at the Landing, and returned, after breaking his previous record, with the report that the mail carrier had promised to help me.

I was sorting potatoes in front of the rootcellar, and Jack was wheeling gravel for the roof. "That plane's flying low," I remarked, rising from stiff knees.

"It's going to land," Jack answered, already on his way to the beach. I was conscious of my grimy overalls as I followed him. The plane was taxiing to the shore when we arrived. A cold wind was blowing over the water and the plane bounced on the waves. As it stopped Alec sprang out.

The pilot tossed out some large bundles and boxes for Alec to catch, and with a wave to us, combining a greeting with a good-bye, he was gone.

"Well, Alec," Jack said, as we walked up the trail, "you must have made a killing at the fishing grounds this season."

"I did very well," Alec answered gravely. "I decided it was best to bring some food and my stuff here in a plane. I can walk home with a light pack."

After taking his duffel to the little cabin on Caribou, Alec stayed with us several days. He lent a hand at all tasks —carried water for laundry work, and pulled the other end of the crosscut saw with Jack.

Alec and Jack went for a moose and in only a couple of hours they returned with the meat in the boat, dressed and ready to hang up. I canned some of this meat, for it was unusually tender; Alec knew unerringly how to select a moose. He said he had timed himself once, and had shot one, butchered it alone, and dressed the meat in just half an hour.

As the leaves fell from the birches we could often see Socrates close by, moving through the trees. Alec took a more than passing interest in him. "He would make good meat," he commented. "When a bull gets so old he isn't interested in the cows any more, he's good and tender."

"Take care of yourself, Socrates!" I cried silently. "Don't stand and stare at a man with a rifle in his hand; he wouldn't listen to your philosophy. Run, Socrates!" Fortunately, we needed no more meat for awhile, and Alec made no move to molest the old moose.

Flash had never seen such quantities of meat as we now had. At the sight and smell of it she went capering about excitedly, getting in everybody's way. By standing on her hind legs she could reach the tip ends of several big chunks. Jack scolded her and whacked her rear with his glove. "Don't touch it again," he threatened, "or I'll wear you out."

Flash looked at me with her long yellow eyes, and I

knew she was saying, "Just wait until he goes in the house."
As soon as Jack disappeared she stood up and began nibbling
again, with no apology to me.

I was often made aware how different Alec's tastes and
standards were from our own. In many respects, he kept to
the ways of his Indian people. For example, he seemed to
enjoy my cooking very much, but one evening as we sat by
the stove after supper, he said, "White man's food means
nothing to me; I don't have to have flour and sugar. When I
kill and dress a moose the warm liver tastes good to me.
My drinking cup full of warm blood is better than any drink
that must be bought and boiled."

"Ugh, Alec! I can't bear to hear you talk of it!" I shuddered, remembering the gamy smell of warm flesh and blood
when Jack opened a moose's abdomen.

"I'm going to teach my boy the same," Alec went on
contemptuously. "I won't let him grow up to be soft."

Another time Alec said, "My woman has not been well;
she'll have a baby in April."

"Shouldn't you go home and see about her, Alec?" I
suggested. "Perhaps she needs you."

"The government nurse can take care of her," he answered indifferently. "It's what she's paid for."

I had never known a man so nonchalant and taciturn
about his comings and goings. A few days later at breakfast,
he announced that he would leave for Kenai that day, but
would be back in time to set out snares. He thereupon rose
from the table, slipped into his pack, and was gone.

More than a month had passed since my seed catalogues
had been mailed. I was sure to have some orders and inquiries, so I persuaded Jack to go for mail.

"This is a bad time of year to have your orders come,"
he said. "Couldn't you arrange to mail your catalogues in the
spring?"

"No, Jack," I explained wearily. "The seeds must be planted in the fall in order to germinate properly."

This was just another difficulty that I had not foreseen. There would always be delays and I would always have to depend upon others. We came out here to be independent, yet in small but important ways we still were forced to rely on other people, I thought fiercely. If I could only handle it myself!

It was a short trip, and Jack hurried back to his work. There was nothing about the catalogs in the letters he brought me, except one from a friend in Juneau, dated less than a week before, stating that she had not received the catalog yet. Something was wrong.

I thought drearily of what Mrs. Anderson had said: "No plans are ever fulfilled here. No dreams ever come true." Nonsense! I would learn from experience. I had expected difficulties the first year.

As the weather grew colder Flash acquired the habit of lying against the hot stove. She did not appear to feel the heat, and I often pulled her away when I smelled scorched hair. This habit especially annoyed Jack. One evening he scolded her about it and sent her back to her bearskin in the corner; he then climbed the ladder to bed.

Flash watched him disappear, looking at me with raised eyebrows that said very plainly, "Now that the old grouch has gone I can be comfortable." She flopped against the stove and began to smoke. We women understood each other.

"What's that I smell?" Jack called. "Is something burning?"

"I don't smell anything," I replied, laughing silently as I grabbed Flash by the leg and pulled her away from the heat.

Real cold came suddenly. The lake froze from shore to shore in late November. Soon after, Alec appeared, trudging tirelessly across the ice.

Jack became very busy getting ready his snares and traps.

Alec gave valuable instructions and made most of the de-
cisions. Jack gladly took his lead—Alec had a real instinct for
anything to do with hunting and trapping. But I knew that
Jack himself had learned a lot since we had come, and in a
way I wanted him to have the opportunity to get by on his
own. I didn't realize, however, how soon that opportunity
would come.

CHAPTER 12

ONE COLD DECEMBER evening the three of us sat waiting for six o'clock when the Anchorage radio station came on the air.

Jack turned on the set, and it buzzed for a few seconds before a voice said tensely, "This is Station KFQD at Anchorage. Honolulu was bombed by the Japanese this morning."

Alec, Jack and I stared at each other. We all got up and crowded close to the radio so as to hear every word. Complete reports had not been received, but it sounded very bad. It was not until long afterward that we learned, little by little, just how bad it had been.

"The United States has officially declared war on Japan," the voice said. "It is expected that war will be declared on Germany in a few hours."

In the days that followed, the Anchorage radio station broadcast the news all day long instead of waiting until six in the evening. Anxiety raged in Anchorage. It was the most important Army center in Alaska and might be bombed at any time. Women and children were being evacuated as rapidly as possible.

It was also reported that the Japanese might try to land anywhere along the coast of Alaska. When Alec heard this he decided to leave for Kenai to look after his family. "I'll be back in a week," he promised.

It all seemed unreal; this couldn't be happening in Alaska. There were urgent calls for workers in Anchorage and Seward. The Army was increasing the fortifications that had been started when I was there.

I found all this excitement increasingly contagious. "Jack," I said one day, "don't you think it is selfish of us to stay here when we're needed so badly? I'm not sure there would work for me, but they certainly need men."

"I can't see it," he replied. "We would have to abandon all that we've worked for here."

Bombers and scout planes were now flying over almost constantly. The radio told us that if the Japanese bombed Anchorage they would likely come from their aircraft carriers in the Gulf of Alaska. "We would be right in their route, wouldn't we?" I said, studying the map on the wall. "If we hear them coming I'll remember to turn out the light."

Jack chuckled. "They wouldn't waste a bomb on us."

We were very conscious of the planes going over, day and night, and we listened to the short-wave radio much of each day. There was a London station that we could hear plainly. Once it brought the stirring words of Winston Churchill. But the strain gradually lessened and I thought no more of leaving.

However, we faced another strain no less severe. Alec had promised to go to the Landing as soon as he came back, so Jack did not go. I brooded over the seed orders that I was sure had arrived. I felt frustrated, helpless, and miserable. I said nothing to Jack; he seemed to sense my resentment, but he never spoke. There was a frozen barrier between us, although I felt it would dissolve if we could have a good talk.

Being so much by ourselves, with no one else to talk to,

and at such close quarters in our small cabin, was beginning to take its toll of our nerves. Jack and I had often laughed about "cabin fever," but it was no joke. It was so hard to keep one's perspective under conditions like these!

One morning Jack prepared to leave to inspect his snares. I often wanted to go with him on these trips, but he was usually gone all day, which made it hard for me. This time, however, he planned only a short journey on our side of the lake. "Wait until I've finished washing the dishes, Jack," I said, "and Flash and I will go too. I'd love to have a good hike."

Jack did not say anything, but that was not unusual these days. I happily prepared to go and made some sandwiches.

I was shocked a few minutes later to see Jack walking rapidly over the ice, pushing the sleigh in front of him. Why on earth hadn't he waited for me? Could he have misunderstood me? No, I was sure he had not. He just didn't want me to go. I threw myself on the couch and buried my face in a pillow, sobbing forlornly.

I knew I must stop this vicious spiral of misery or it would kill me. I jumped up, put on my coat, and with Flash bounding ahead, ran down onto the ice, continuing blindly far out around the end of the Point. I was tempted to keep on and not be at home when Jack returned, but that would be foolish. Where could I go?

It was a gray, overcast day. The ice was covered with a thin carpet of frosty snow. The lake was dead, and the sky was an impenetrable dirty gray. There was no color or warmth in the whole world.

I would have to fight this somehow. I must keep my head. I straightened my shoulders and turned back toward home. I had come a long way and it was very, very cold. On the way back I had time to think. I knew that Jack was buried under a weight of responsibility in this new life, and that he had worries of his own. How foolish of me to expect him to think of me all the time. I was too possessive—he had a right to his privacy. My spirits lifted and I jogged along to keep warm.

It was dark when Jack came. I decided not to wait before speaking. It would sound more natural if I mentioned it at once. "Why didn't you wait for me, Jack?" I asked, trying to speak calmly.

Jack did not look at me. After a while he said quietly, "I wanted to be alone." There was nothing to say, and uncomfortable silence fell between us once more.

Christmas came. On Christmas Eve, after I had decorated the house and trimmed the tree, I cleaned the shelves and dusted and made the house tidy in keeping with the decorations. I carried some articles out to the tent, among them a flashlight of Jack's that had no batteries.

I could not put my finger on the cause of the heartache that persisted all through the morning. My pain lessened, however, when I remembered that Jack would soon come in for lunch, and I could show him my handiwork. There were kinnikinnick berries like tiny red apples among their small polished leaves, and branches of juniper, with their spiny metallic foliage heavy with blue berries. Candles on the tree were ready to be lit.

Jack came from the tent, walking very fast. He had the empty flashlight in his hand, and his face was livid with fury. "What did you throw away my flashlight for?" he demanded.

"I only put it in the tent out of the way," I said in astonishment. "It was safe there."

"You know perfectly well that you did it to annoy me!"

"What's the matter with you?" I screeched. "You're acting like a fool!" That was bad enough, but I couldn't stop. The words poured out. "You're conceited and self-centered! I'm sick of your drooping around!" When the words ceased I stood stunned and trembling.

Jack placed his precious flashlight on the shelf. His voice was controlled when he spoke, but cold and cutting. "And I'm sick of your constantly doing things just to annoy me. It's you who are conceited and selfish. You expect me to stand it and say nothing, but I don't intend to."

He rushed out, slamming the door. Oh, why had I spoken to him like that? I wept bitterly. We must be going insane!

If only there had been an understanding person there to talk to me and remind me that Jack and I were simply too closely associated in this little world surrounded by cold and ice. But I could not reason alone, so I was blind, and dissolved in misery.

Jack disappeared. I thought achingly that he might never come back, but after several hours he came in without speaking. I prepared supper, and we ate in silence. The Christmas music on the radio, which I had looked forward to for days, now seemed a mockery.

Christmas morning came after a wakeful, wretched night. Jack left the house without speaking, and I could not bear to think what day it was. I considered taking down the decorations and the tree but put it off. I could not even do that. The hours dragged by, until the dismal, gray day ended at last.

Darkness had fallen when Jack came in, closed the door, and stood with his back against it. I did not know why I did it, but I jumped up and ran to him.

He opened his arms, and we clung together. We drew back and looked into each other's eyes. I saw my own bewilderment and fear reflected in Jack's. How could this happen to us?

"You don't hate me, do you, hon?" Jack asked, and he sounded like a little child who had lost its way and was not sure even after seeing the lights of home.

"If you'll just stop hating me." I was laughing and crying all at once. "Oh, darling!" We clung together again.

I did not want to discuss what had happened, and Jack seemed willing to accept peace for its own sake. With an excess of energy I prepared our Christmas dinner, with Jack insisting on helping me with everything. How good the fried chicken tasted, and the plum pudding I had made ahead of time. In the candle-light our cabin glowed with happiness.

Days and weeks of the new year passed and Alec did not come. It was late in January when a message finally came over the radio. Alec was no longer in Kenai. He had gone to Anchorage to get work and was writing. We would be alone for the rest of the winter.

The ice was smooth as Jack skated away, pushing Mrs. Anderson's sleigh with his pack on it. He intended to "look" some of the distant snares and would then go on to the Landing for mail. It was mid-February and he had gotten four coyotes near home.

In the quiet of that evening I could not concentrate on my reading. It was when Jack was away that I missed Unk most. Flash, snoring from her bearskin, could never take the place of the little black head that had always rested in my lap as I sat on the couch. To get rid of the ache in my throat I called Flash to me and hugged her. I gave her a cooky, and she swallowed it at one gulp and drooled while I ate mine. I went to the window and looked out on the deep snow. It would be a hard trip for Jack. The highway would be blocked with snow, and he would have to walk all the way to the Landing. I knew I must go to bed and try not to think any more. To take my mind from my worries I mixed dough for bread to be baked next day and set it to rise.

I anxiously watched for Jack all through the usual four days of his absence, and had begun to dread another night of uncertainty when he came stumbling up the trail at twilight, his face gray with fatigue.

"I took some awful chances," he said, as he drank coffee and rested.

I was filled with concern. "There was deep snow, wasn't there?"

"Yes. A couple of feet in the trail, but that was not so

bad as the ice. I started across at the river cabin, but the ice wasn't good and I had to follow the shore for miles before I could risk crossing. I had to come away down opposite the Island, and then I had to pick my way among the water holes."

I sat beside him, longing to comfort him. "Thank God, you're safe. The lake is cruel, Jack. It always seems to be trying to resist us, or even to murder us."

"Don't talk like that," he said wearily. "It sounds morbid."

"I won't say such things any more," I promised, laughing to show I hadn't really meant it.

Jack had brought three carcasses of coyotes on the sleigh. Now there were seven. He had never done so well.

First I read the Christmas messages and letters from faraway friends and relatives. Sue sent us a pair of strong field glasses, for Christmas, to settle arguments about the identity of faraway black dots on the ice. Her letter told us of war conditions in Seward, with people groping through the blacked-out streets. I was very relieved to hear that she was to be transferred to southeastern Alaska at the end of the school term.

There was also a letter from Art. He was leaving for the States to enlist in the Marines. Another blow, but we had expected it.

Alec's promised letter told us that he was very sorry not to return, but that he had found his wife sick. He had no money to send her to the hospital when the baby came in April, so he felt that he should take a job. The tone of his letter was apologetic but obviously there was nothing else for him to do. We had already reconciled ourselves to getting along without help.

I waited until last to look at the many seed orders. My catalog had aroused much interest—not so much in gardeners as in botanists who wished to know what plants grew in Alaska. There was a letter with almost every order, and scores of inquiries of all kinds. The editor of a horticultural magazine asked me to write an article on Alaskan wildflowers, and I resolved to get to work on this at once.

"Listen, Jack," I said, laughing. "This one wants me to tell her how she can get a job teaching school in Alaska, and here are two asking about homesteading."

I had mailed the catalogs in September, but the orders were dated in February. Long afterward I learned that the postmaster at Moose Pass did not have sufficient stamps, and had to send away for them. His wife told me that she had personally put on the more than four hundred stamps. Of course, it had not seemed necessary to hurry, and the catalogs had been mailed only in time to be caught in the tie-up of boats immediately after war was declared. An order had gone out for all boats in Alaskan waters to proceed to the nearest port, and the boats were not released for three weeks. Then all mail was subjected to rigid censorship, as Alaska was in the war zone. But I was no longer unhappy— a new year had begun. Soon, I thought, there would be an opportunity to correct all mistakes.

At first the spring of 1942, the fourth we had spent on the lake, was only a sense of expectancy in the air, as if the world was slowly awakening from sleep but still too drowsy to move. The days lengthened, the warmth of the sun strengthened, and more brown earth was uncovered, but the lake still slept under a blanket of ice.

One morning, as I stared out of the window, I could hardly believe my eyes. "What in the world are those strange rolls all over the lake?" I asked. "Did you see them, Jack?"

"Yes, I saw them," he answered calmly. "I never saw anything like them before." He went on eating his breakfast.

My own breakfast could wait until I had taken a closer look, so I hurriedly put on my outdoor clothes and ran out to the shore. A light snow had fallen the previous afternoon, and during the night a brisk wind had blown from the north.

Apparently the wind had picked up handfuls of snow and sent them rolling over the surface of the ice. As they rolled they had gathered more snow until they were too heavy for the wind to move. Over the entire lake, as far as the eye could see, there were hundreds of such snow rolls. Many were as large as two feet long and a foot in diameter. Others had not become more than small snowballs. Each one had left behind it a clearly defined track across the snow. The strangest thing about them was that the rolls were all hollow, like a tube. The biggest looked like soft, white muffs.

We gave the chickens their liberty as soon as bare brown patches showed amid the snow on the ground. They reveled in scratching and picking at the earth. At first the hens returned to the chicken house to lay their eggs, but some of them discovered that it was more convenient to lay in the natural mossy hollows under the little spruce trees around the house.

One evening as I passed the chicken house, I stopped to see if there were any eggs. There were only two, and I laid them on a hummock of moss, intending to get them later. As I returned, there was Flash lying in the trail, her head cocked to one side, tossing an egg from one paw to the other. The other egg was only a shell—she had already eaten the contents. I blamed myself severely for putting temptation in her way.

"An egg-sucking dog can never be cured," I complained to Jack. "Now I'll have to shut the chickens up."

But Jack soon came in with the announcement that he had found a whole pile of eggshells where Flash had been at work.

"She can't get any more," I said hopefully. "They're shut up now."

"Some day you'll get careless and she'll slip in the chicken house," he answered, and added firmly, "We've got to teach her."

I had been trying to teach Flash, but she learned only what she wanted to. I promised to fix an egg with cayenne pepper and leave it where she would find it. Jack thought a good whipping would be better, but I couldn't bear it. "She won't know what you're whipping her for," I wailed.

Jack was very sure that she would know. He placed an egg on the lawn and cut a keen willow switch. In a few minutes Flash came capering along and spied the egg. "What luck!" She lay down, carefully broke the shell and began to lap the contents. I looked no further but shut out the whole scene with a pillow over my head.

Next morning Jack and I were standing in the yard when Flash came from among the trees, her whole body wriggling ingratiatingly. She went straight to Jack and laid at his feet a perfect egg, unmarred by toothprints. Neither of us could speak. Flash stood looking at Jack with her heart in her eyes; for once she paid not the slightest attention to me. We praised and petted her. But after that she never went near the chicken house, and we never knew of her eating another egg.

By mid-April the ice was gone except in our bay. Trapping season was over, and when Jack took up his snares on the other side of the lake, he planned to go on for mail. He was also, at long last, going to place an order for a gasoline-driven power saw, having had his fill of sawing wood by hand.

It was necessary to drag the boat across the ice in the bay, but this time we kept close to the beach—no more falling through the ice. Jack made me stay on the shore. "I'll have the boat to hang onto if the ice breaks," he said.

In early afternoon the fair morning weather changed to stormy black clouds and wind. The old lake seemed to enjoy making commotion after being bound up for so long. Whitecaps scudded by the end of the point and rain beat on the windows. Then four windy but untroubled days passed and it was time for Jack's return.

But he did not come. The wind rose again. Three more

days went by. Even Flash, who usually accepted any situation cheerfully, did not care for the raw wind, and when I let her out she was soon at the door begging to come in again. I spent a good deal of time letting her in and out and did not attempt to do anything else—but wait.

Each morning I tried to avoid looking at the racing waves, but I was drawn to the window by a force that was stronger than I. Then I rested my elbows on the sill and gazed out over the tossing sweep of water. Hour after hour I stood watching the never-ending movement. I would often drop my head in my arms and try to still my anxious thoughts, but to no avail.

"White Horses! White Horses!" With streaming manes and wild violence, they swept down the lake as if fleeing from some relentless fury. I watched their mad stampede until the dark mercifully blotted out the sight, but in the surging roar I could hear the unending beat of their hooves. Each night I went out to check that the rope which held the windcharger was not working loose, before settling down to try to divert my worries by reading.

The words now ran together in an unintelligible line across the page and I surrendered to my thoughts. I went over every foot of Jack's trip, beginning with the day he left. I helped him pull the boat up on the beach, so that it would be safe until his return. I walked at his heels along the trail through the expectant birches and aspens, and sniffed the wet fragrance of the woods so recently covered by snow. I heard the greetings of friends at the Landing. I was with him when he completed his business and started back with his heavy pack of purchases. It was as if by rehearsing his journey in my mind I might will him back.

Bad weather could be expected at that time of year, I knew. Jack had said something about returning to the Landing if he found, when he reached the lake, that he could not cross; now I wondered if he had not done that. If so, he would send a message to Anchorage to be broadcast to me. The message might have been delayed.

There had been, I thought, fourteen days of this when

the skies cleared. The wind gradually died until there wasn't enough to turn the propeller of the windcharger. The white horses sped by the end of the Point, but they were slowing down. Jack would be hungry, so I cooked a good dinner. The lull had come just after noon—he would be home before dark.

But darkness brought the wind again instead of Jack. The wind had changed. No longer were there gusts with little intervals of quiet between, but an unremitting, screeching intensity that I found almost unbearable. In the dim light I watched from the window the trees streaming away from the wind, bent far out of perpendicular, never released for an instant. Trees in a storm had always held an unreasonable terror for me. I could remember the crashing of limb against limb of the big oaks at home in South Carolina in a night storm, when it had seemed like chaos and hell. In my childish imagination, I expected to see the trees in the morning standing on their heads with their roots in the air.

The keening vibrated on my eardrums. I could feel the very house straining away from the wind. It seemed to be leaning like the trees.

I could not see through the darkness now. There was only the keening of the wind and in the background the roar of the surf. I put my hands over my ears and closed my eyes; I willed my thoughts to be calm.

Perhaps Jack had not been at the river cabin when the wind dropped in the afternoon. Of course, that was it! He had returned to the Landing and there would be a message. Time for the news in ten minutes, and I would have Jack's message. It would be like his voice in the room and would bring me peace. I turned on the radio and waited.

I was trembling when the voice in Anchorage began to read the messages. There was a number of them. Each time I thought, mine will be next. I could not accept it when the announcer said, "That concludes the messages for this evening." There *must* be another one!

I was completely off guard when the cunning suggestions came. *It's very plain. He started out in the little boat—you know yourself it has very little freeboard. The wind caught him in the middle of the lake—the motor stopped—he didn't have a chance.*

"No! No!" I screamed, so wildly I was frightened at my own voice. Flash stared at me with terror in her eyes. I must control myself.

It doesn't matter whether you control yourself or not. No one will hear you. You're all alone. I ran from one end of the room to the other, my hands clutched over my ears but the dry, diabolical suggestions of my imaginings pursued me relentlessly. *You're all alone! You're all alone!*

I shrieked to shut out the thought—again and again, hideous, insane shrieks. Flash cowered and trembled. But there was no stopping the awful thoughts that seared through me. *No one will come for months. You can't do anything. You'll go mad.*

Somewhere in my consciousness a spark of courage stirred. "No! No!" I sobbed. "It isn't so! It's a lie!" I seemed to be in a deep pit. A light appeared at the top of the pit, and I must not lose it. Wild denials poured from my lips. I gave no heed to the words I used, but I must keep denying. If I accepted, the light would disappear, and there would be nothing but darkness. Then I heard myself cry, "Water has no power to destroy if there is faith! Didn't Jesus walk upon it?" O marvellous light! I was out of the pit. The ray of light expanded until it surrounded me. Its radiance filled the room. Then a gentle, tender voice said, "Don't be afraid. Jack is safe."

The voice was unlike any I had ever heard. To this day I do not know if there was really a voice that spoke to me, but I knew that Jack was safe. Wonderfully, surely safe! O blessed peace! I fell on the couch like a rag doll and slept without even taking off my shoes.

The sun was shining in flashes through the black clouds

when I awoke, wonderfully refreshed. The gusty wind was normal once more. I ran out of doors. The house stood straight and sturdy. No trees were broken or uprooted. Millions of white horses raced by the Point, but they looked very different now. No longer stampeding, they chased each other in fun, prancing and tossing their manes gaily. Jack will come today, I thought, but if he doesn't it will mean only that he is being extra careful.

Not a vestige of ice remained. The little wrinkled leaves of the birches were unfurling in pale chartreuse—so unlike the green of other leaves. Spring had really come.

All that day I gathered wood from the hills behind the house. I could not use a crosscut saw as Jack did, but with the handsaw I soon produced a big stack. By night I was very tired but satisfied, and went to sleep as soon as my head touched the pillow.

Two nights later I was wakened by Jack's voice in the room. The wind had stopped hours before. When I could shake off the fog of sleep I greeted him quite calmly.

"Are you all right, hon?" he asked anxiously.

"Of course," I answered. "You can see that I am."

"It was awful," he groaned, "awful!"

"Oh, my poor dear!"

"Once I ran along the beach and cursed the wind."

"I was afraid you would get desperate enough to start out in the wind. Did you make a second trip to the Landing?"

"No, I stayed right there in the river cabin and waited. I wanted to be ready for any chance to cross."

I felt a calm, deep joy that he had come.

"I ate everything there was at the cabin," Jack said, munching toast and grinning at me in the lamplight. "I've a surprise for you," he added. "I brought back nine coyotes."

"Good heavens! Do you think there are more of them this year?"

"No, I think I am just getting the knack of catching them. Alec says some trappers catch very few, and others who follow the same procedure can always catch them. Gosh, I hope I'm going to be one of those.

"Don't count on it too much," he added cautiously. "I may have just had good luck this year. Alec and I together could do much better."

But I was overjoyed at the realization that Jack did not need Alec and could make his way alone.

We were startled by the roar of a powerful motor coming from the lower end of the lake a few days later. We had heard no other motor than our own since the year before. Who could it be?

By the time we reached the beach we could see that it was Alec, who waved at us.

"I thought you were working in Anchorage," Jack said, as he held the bow of the boat steady for Alec to jump out.

"I decided to give up my job when the fishing started," he answered, with a grin. "I had a few days before time to leave for Bristol Bay, so I came to see how you folks were getting along. I thought you might need help."

"It's good of you to go to all that trouble for us, Alec," I said gratefully.

"I like to help old people," he answered calmly.

Jack winked at me behind Alec's back.

I made sandwiches and coffee. "How do you like my motor?" Alec asked as he ate.

"Is it yours?" Jack asked.

"Yes. I had the money and thought I'd better get it. It's a twenty-two horsepower and climbs the river easy. I can bring your freight any time now."

"That will be wonderful, Alec," I joined in. "How's your wife and the new baby."

"Nancy's all right but the baby didn't live," he answered.

His head drooped on his chest. "My woman was unfaithful to me," he said sadly. "The baby was a blond with blue eyes. I made her tell me that I was not the father of it."

Jack and I sat looking at him. "She's very young and I decided I would overlook it," he went on, "but I told her I wouldn't have white sheep among the black ones. I whipped her—not enough to hurt her—and she swore she would be a good woman. His face was flushed with anger and his voice was harsh. "A white man took advantage of her."

"You were right to forgive her, Alec," I said.

"It was no good. I sent her back to Kenai, but I got suspicious of her again, and finally she told me everything. The boy isn't mine either."

Alec got up from the table. Thrusting his arms out, with palms forward, he shrugged his shoulders. "I'm through," he said. "The deputy marshal can take care of them. That's what he gets paid for."

"I'm sorry, Alec," Jack said.

"I don't want nothing now but to live on Skilak Lake and trap with you."

"We surely will be glad to have you."

"I think I'll build me a cabin," Alec went on.

"Where will you build?" I inquired with interest.

"On your side of the lake," he answered, smiling. He understood me. "Near the river. I like being near the river. I'll come as soon as the fishing season's over and get my cabin built before winter, and be ready to help you set out snares."

Poor Alec! He had been deeply hurt. But it would be wonderful for him to live on our side of the lake so that we could reach him no matter what conditions were.

CHAPTER 13

THE GARDEN HAD been planted and Jack was ready to start work on the greenhouse. The summer before Hank had brought down six coldframe sashes for the roof, several sacks of cement, and a roll of plastic; the cement had been stored behind the door all winter to keep dry. Andy had already sold us some glass coldframes, and we planned the building so that all these components fitted together.

At last my burning desire for a greenhouse appeared about to be fulfilled. Above all, it would extend the woefully short growing season. Plants would awaken weeks earlier in the spring, and beauty would be provided long after frost had blackened everything outside. I could experiment with difficult seeds and furnish advice to the specialists who bought them from me. There probably would be disappointments galore but also, I hoped, a few triumphs, and I looked forward to being able to dig in the good earth and smell its richness all through the barren winter.

Jack measured the outline for the foundation carefully. "The new power saw is probably at the Landing," he said, as he folded up his foot rule. "Before I start digging I'll go and see about having it brought down the river. I want to get it just as soon as possible."

Flash and I were alone for three days. I did not at all mind staying alone—at least not in the summertime when the weather was good, and there was so much to keep me busy. Raspberries were ripening, and I made our winter supply of jam while Jack was away.

"It was quite a trip," he said, when he came and was resting, "but home never looked so good to me before."

He waited until we had finished the favorite dessert of dried-apple dumplings that I had made in honor of his homecoming, before breaking the bad news. Power saws were not available for the duration. So that was that. Once again, I felt slightly guilty to be reminded how little we were doing to help in the war effort.

Jack swallowed his disappointment bravely. "I want to have all the rocks on hand before I start building," he said, changing the subject. "Let's go to work early tomorrow."

Jack was very particular about the kind and shape of the stones he used for the greenhouse foundation. He rejected many that I brought from the beach, and we finally went together in the boat to a distant beach, where the rocks were worn hard and smooth by the water. These would lie securely in the wall. Several boatloads of sand and gravel were also necessary.

We were leaving for home with a heavily loaded boat when a wind squall came up suddenly. Jack hurried to shove off the boat. "Let's wait, Jack," I said fearfully. "It'll soon be over."

"It's only a little way," Jack answered calmly. "I'll row close to shore. It *would* be dangerous to use the motor.

It seemed foolish to me to take a chance in the breakers— the heavy load made the boat difficult to handle. Spray dashed over its sides, and it wallowed low in the water.

"Let's go ashore, Jack!" I screamed.

"If we start to sink," he said, rowing calmly, "just hold onto one of the biggest rocks."

Good heavens! I thought Jack was going crazy!

When the bow touched the gravel of our own landing I had completely forgotten the danger in my perplexity over his remark.

"Had to get your mind off of it somehow," he chuckled, and dodged the rock I threw at him.

As I watched him measure cement and sand into the metal bed of the wheelbarrow, I heard a faint hum coming from far away. "Listen, Jack! Do you hear something?"

"It must be Alec. I hope I can have his help with some of this."

Another Indian, with a heavy, sullen face, accompanied Alec. It was late afternoon and time for dinner, and I busied myself at the range while Jack showed the Indians how he was building the greenhouse. They had brought their sleeping bags, so I supposed they planned to sleep on the floor. They had come to build Alec's cabin.

But after supper, when the men sat smoking, Alec said, "I've decided not to trap this winter. I can get my job back in Anchorage. We're both going there to work."

In the silence that followed this announcement I heard Jack draw in his breath slowly.

"I believe I should take advantage of the good wages now," Alec went on apologetically.

"I would like to have you here, Alec," Jack answered, trying not to show his disappointment. "But I don't blame you. The good wages are tempting."

I heard no more of the conversation. My mind was reeling. All alone for another winter! If we needed help there would be none—probably not even a visitor before spring! Now I realized how much I had counted on Alec. I was always fearful when Jack trapped alone.

"Will you take us to the river cabin in the morning, Jack?" Alec asked. "I'll leave my boat with you until I come for it—you might like to use my big motor."

When Jack had returned and was back at work on the greenhouse, he said, "I must learn not to depend on people."

"No," I answered, trying to help Jack not to care. "Alec is an Indian, like those in Fenimore Cooper's books. They were always slipping behind a tree and disappearing into the forest. Alec has just left us standing looking at the place where he was."

Jack chuckled. "That's right. I guess I should be able to get along without him."

I wondered if Jack was really as confident as he sounded. If he believed he did not need anyone to lean on, nothing was impossible to him. Of course we could get along; the Andersons had spent many winters alone on the lake.

"Are you going to try to find enough dry seasoned poles for the framing, or will green ones do?" I asked, as I watched Jack use a spirit level along the top of the foundation wall.

He found a place that sloped slightly and built it up with a trowelful of cement before he answered. "I can't build it of poles. It would be impossible to get it true enough. The sashes must fit exactly."

I was speechless. Why was he doing all this work if he couldn't go on? There was nothing but poles to build it of.

Jack must have been well aware of my suffering, but he was in no hurry to explain. "There're some heavy planks on the beach on the other side of the lake," he said finally. "They floated down the river when a bridge washed out; we'll go tomorrow and see if we can locate them." He grinned slyly. I could willingly have brained him.

With Alec's motor our little boat shot out of the bay like an arrow. Even with the weight of both Flash and me in the bow it reared into the air. I had never expected to cross the lake so quickly.

By the end of the day we had a big stack of planks piled on the shore. Flash, having worn herself out chasing terns, climbed into the boat and went to sleep on my coat. Jack did not need me in preparing the raft, so I went exploring along this unfamiliar beach, which was strewn with driftwood.

Great overturned bleached trees, with their roots standing far above my head, formed a forest around me. At first I was careful to keep in sight of Jack and the boat, but I found an unfamiliar little plant growing in the gravel and walked on looking for more.

All of a sudden I was startled by a shout from Jack. "There's a bear!" he yelled. "Run!"

I saw no bear, but I began to run. Then it occurred to me that I might be running toward it. "Where is it? Oh, Jack? Where must I run?" I ran wildly a few yards in one direction, sobbing and out of breath, then changed my mind and turned to run in the other.

"It's right in front of you!" Jack yelled.

"Where's in front of me?" I screamed, in walleyed panic. I knew Jack was on his way to help me, but he was taking a lifetime and I couldn't stop looking for the bear long enough to see him.

Then the bear and I, each trying desperately to avoid the other, met head on. The horrible upright giant stood between me and the low sun, which touched its tawny coat with a halo of gold. It was the culmination of nightmares that I had been having ever since we came to live on the lake. The very worst experience imaginable was to find myself with a big brown bear towering over me, ready to charge.

This bear had evidently been having trouble with his directions, just as I had, but we both quickly got oriented. The bear dropped to all fours and scrambled out of sight in the other direction, while I ran stumbling to Jack who had arrived with his rifle in position.

"Why couldn't you tell me which way to run?" I demanded, sobbing and collapsing against him.

Flash, whining anxiously, jumped on me and tried to lick my face.

"Gosh, hon! I didn't know what to tell you!" Jack tried to smile as he added, "You looked just like a frightened hen," but I noticed his hand that gripped the gun was trembling.

"Come on," I begged, looking back fearfully. "Let's get out of here and go home."

Alec's motor drew the raft swiftly home. Despite my fright the trip was worth it. Those good, sound planks were a godsend.

The three-inch-thick timbers, seasoned until they were like iron, proved very hard to saw, but Jack had laboriously ripped them into three by fours, they made a splendid framework for the greenhouse. After much careful measuring and use of the level the glass sashes fitted exactly. There was no opening for the cold to come through, and for further protection I tacked plastic all over the inside, forming an airspace.

Jack enlarged one window opening from the house to make a door, and built steps down to the greenhouse floor, three feet below ground level. With no outside opening much less cold could creep in. One section at the end was removable so that I could bring in soil from the outside, but could be tightly closed when not in use.

I had never seen a greenhouse like it, but I was counting on the airspace to protect my plants. Information I had from the university at Fairbanks warned that it was not practicable to operate a greenhouse through the winter in that part of Alaska, since lack of light prevented bloom and fuel consumption would be exorbitant. But I wanted a year-round home for green, growing things more than I had ever wanted anything before.

Jack used wide timbers to frame the greenhouse benches, and he floored them with small poles laid close together. A layer of small stones and gravel was laid on the benches for drainage, and good soil spread on top. A Yukon stove was placed under one bench, with its stovepipe thrust through the soil and on through the roof, where Jack had replaced one pane of glass with tin.

I had taken up pansies, parsley, and some other plants in the garden and had kept them in boxes in the tent out of the frost. Now I brought them in and planted them in the benches. The parsley made a beautiful green border around their entire length. I had also planted late nasturtiums in boxes, and these were just beginning to bloom. The tubbed shrubs, luxuriant in growth after their summer outside, were placed against the end walls. The cyclamens were blooming profusely, and I hung potted ferns from the ridgepole. It soon smelled like a greenhouse—of earth and dampness and growing things. Already the plants outside were blackened with frost.

Flash discovered the luxury of lying full length on the soil of one of the benches in the warm sunshine. She enjoyed it so much I wondered if I would have the heart to chase her out when I needed the room for plants.

Many good reports came from those who had purchased my seeds the year before. My orders the first year had amounted to more than a hundred dollars, and this was only the beginning. From my experience with seeds the preceding year I had learned much. I must get the catalogs off earlier. I had the stamps this time and all the other supplies necessary. True, I had only three stencils for the mimeograph, but the catalog was to be only three pages long. Last year it had been only two pages, but my list had grown.

The first two stencils had been run—they turned out well. But when I turned the handle on the third stencil there was a horrid ripping sound, and I found the stencil sheet torn from top to bottom! It was not annoyonce I felt but profound shock. I was trembling. Greatly shaken, I covered my face with my hands and waited for my agitation to pass.

My thoughts raced here and there for a possible solution. I might send to Sears, Roebuck for stencils, but Jack was desperately busy getting ready for winter, and I could not ask him to go now and mail the order. And I could not send my truncated catalog—all the ordering and shipping information was on the third page.

I walked slowly down to the beach and out onto my

little island. It was a peaceful Indian Summer day. Mountains and blue sky were painted on the quiet surface of the dark water. The lake had never looked more beautiful.

I must be sensible, I repeated to myself over and over, fighting despair. There was really no alternative. This was the end—at least for this year. Wouldn't it be sensible to wait until the war was over? But the war might last many years. I was aware of a need in my nature for an absorbing interest in which to lose myself. My whole being cried out that this was a good undertaking, and like a disappointed child I could only ask, Why can't I have it?

I must think. I was not being sensible. It was the war; nothing was normal. No, I admitted to myself, it wasn't the war; it was the lake. Even if there had never been a war, it was the lake that told us when we could go and what we could do. It lay there now, calm and indifferent, but in a few minutes it could change. White-capped waves, so high that no small boat would dare venture out, could suddenly appear, roaring an imperious, "Wait!" I must either yield to the dominance of the lake or prove to myself that it was not my master by accepting its whims calmly. I must learn to be patient, to adapt but not to be beaten.

My black disappointment had become only a light gray cloud when I walked slowly back to the house to tell Jack that I had given up my seed business "for the duration." I could even smile when I used the familiar expression.

Jack was putting the finishing touches on the greenhouse, carefully studying a fitting. He looked up at me with evident understanding. "I think you're very sensible," he said gently. We didn't mention the matter again. I put away the half-printed catalogs and the mimeograph machine.

After the first snow it was necessary to confine the chickens. I did all I could to atone for imprisoning them.

"They're so quarrelsome," I complained to Jack. "Just look at the way they peck each other. They're all bleeding."

"That's serious. Have you anything to put on their heads?"

"I'll mix some cayenne pepper and lard and try that."

But the pepper failed to stop them. They began picking feathers off each other and eating them with a gloating expression in their shallow yellow eyes. It seemed to give both picker and pickee great pleasure.

I brought a box and sat in the chicken house hours at a time, but while I scared one into desisting, others all around pecked insanely.

The chickens particularly liked to reach up and pick from those on the roost above the feathers that were so necessary to protect their poor legs from the cold. They soon stopped picking heads entirely and concentrated on leg feathers. The rooster's long awkward shanks became denuded except for a little white fuzz.

I read somewhere that darkness would stop feather-picking and hung a heavy blanket over the window to give them a complete blackout. But whenever I gave them enough light to eat their food by, they picked feathers instead of eating. They're like drug addicts, I thought.

As my efforts failed, I became hideously depressed about the chickens. I could not understand why it affected me so deeply and tried to hide my feelings from Jack. I had been giving the chickens mostly scraps of moose meat, cooked with root vegetables. I decided their diet was somehow lacking, and gave them a large portion of the grain that was supposed to last them until spring. It did no good. Even though the regime of darkness was partially effective, the damage was done, and no fresh feathers grew.

The thermometer outside the door registered lower and lower. There was still no need for heat in the greenhouse as long as the sun shone, but darkness came early. I made a fire in the stove under the bench in early evening and again at bedtime. As the cold increased, I began setting the alarm clock and coming down to rebuild the fire at 2:00 A.M. With drafts closed, the heavy pieces of birch held the fire for several hours, but it was taking a lot of Jack's wood.

The cold meant business that year from the beginning; each night the thermometer dropped lower. Frost formed on the inside of the greenhouse. It was a losing fight; I realized that I would oversleep some night and come down to blackened ruin.

Jack had to go away on an unusually long trip. Not only did he make his usual pilgrimage for mail and supplies, he also intended to "look" his snares on the other side of the lake for the first time that season.

I worked hard arranging the tubs of shrubs in the corners of the cabin until Jack could help me take them to the attic. Several of the potted plants I had to leave in the greenhouse, abandoned to certain death; I had never loved them and there was so little room. The cyclamens, still blooming heavily, went back to the windows. At any rate, the annuals had given me joy for an extra two months, and plans were forming in my mind. I could make mats of burlap, padded with sphagnum moss, to cover the glass at night. Primroses weren't hardy outside, but they might live with no other protection in the benches, and would bloom in the spring long before anything outside. There were still many possibilities. I was regretful but not depressed. It was wonderful to have even a restricted greenhouse.

At the first sound of the returning motor, I ran down to the beach to hear the news and see what Jack had brought. Huddled in heavy wraps against the cold, he closed the throttle and let the boat drift into the shore.

"Guess how many coyotes!" he called.

I thought there were at least three, since he looked so satisfied. "Four!" I guessed, and wished that I had said three. He would not have four so soon.

Jack shook his head, grinning.

"Five, then!" I knew there could not be more than five.

Jack sat there grinning, his hands resting on the oars.

"I can't stand it," I screamed. "Is it six?"

"More than six. Fourteen!"

"I don't believe it."

Jack landed and silently pulled away the tarp that covered the big pile of carcasses. "I got around to all the snares I had out on the other side, and there were coyotes in nearly half of them," he said. Gazing on his catch, he looked as if he didn't believe it either.

"I don't understand it," I said. "Natural conditions haven't anything to do with it. You had good success last spring, too."

"I don't know unless I have that knack that Alec was talking about," he said—adding with quick modesty, "It may just be luck. Of course, the trappers along the river have mostly quit to take defense jobs."

"Why, the bounty alone on these will amount to two hundred and eighty dollars," I said, still incredulous.

"Yes, and I learned at the Landing that good skins are worth at least ten dollars now."

The money held second place in my thoughts all afternoon as I tried to assimilate our good fortune. Jack was proving that he could sucessfully outwit the coyotes. The lift this gave his self-confidence was worth more than money could buy.

The winter of 1942-43 will go down in the history of Kenai Peninsula. The paralyzing cold came much earlier than usual. The lake froze quickly with the usual cannon fire of protests. It was too cold even for frost to form and I missed its gossamer loveliness. Jack kept a water hole in the ice covered but still had to cut several inches of ice each morning. The ice had never frozen so deep, and after a while getting water was like dipping it from a well. I was afraid to go near the hole; I knew if I slipped on the treacherous ice and fell into that abyss I would never get out again. There were no soft spells to cheer us that winter. Each day laid an additional thickness of ice over the lake.

Jack was losing in his contest with the woodpile, and he

had to put in more and more time on the Point sawing wood.

With an aching heart I watched him walk across the Bay every day with his rifle on his shoulder. More than ever I regretted our lack of a power saw. Jack had depended too much on the boys' coming back. The wilderness was telling us that we must pay a penalty for weakness and bad judgment.

The cold was too severe for just standing around outside. One must be active every minute. I helped Jack haul the sled-loads of wood across the bay from the Point. He pulled with a rope and I pushed from behind, using the axe for a lever.

There was not enough housework to keep me busy, and I was restless as I had never been before in my life. Plant study had occupied most of my thoughts for years, but now I carefully pushed it out of my mind. It would come again, of course, but I didn't want to think of it for awhile.

Our evenings had always been spent in reading and listening to the radio. The radio suddenly developed a lot of static and distortion. Jack spent hours tinkering with it, finally dismissing the problem with an irritable "I don't know anything about radios!" It did not seem possible that the sudden end of the war news could be such a calamity. The war became more horrible to me since I could not hear the details.

The days were so much alike it was hard to keep the dates straight, especially without the radio check. Jack and I were several days apart in our reckoning, and the mention of the subject always brought on an argument. I watched myself, and I saw that Jack did the same, to avoid quarreling.

Even in the middle of the day the thermometer seldom registered above twenty below. Jack mounted it just outside the window so that we did not have to go outside to look at it.

Jack always made a fire for the chickens in the mornings so that they would be warm and ready for their breakfast when I brought it. One morning he came in and closed the door very carefully. "Hon!" he began, tensely.

My taut nerves seemed to shatter into thousands of tinkling bits. Something terrible had happened! Only terrible things happened to us! I could only stare at Jack.

"The chickens are all dead, hon—froze last night. It's twenty-nine below."

"Oh, no, no, no! I can't bear it, Jack. I just can't bear it." Jack did all he could to comfort me, but my sobs tore at my heart.

"Don't go and look at them, hon. I'll take care of them. Don't cry like that." He placed his hands over my eyes as if trying to blot out my misery.

"We shouldn't try to keep animals, Jack," I said, after gaining a little composure. "It isn't fair if we can't protect them from suffering."

"They would have been all right," he answered, "if the silly things hadn't picked off their own feathers."

"I know, but I couldn't make them stop." I began to weep again.

"Don't cry any more, hon. I've always heard that freezing is an easy death. They just went to sleep."

I blessed Jack for that comforting reminder, and gradually got over my tears for the poor creatures.

CHAPTER 14

LOSING THE CHICKENS shocked me into a new awareness of the problems we faced. We would have to admit that we could not keep farm animals. The Andersons had never been really successful with them and they had had the protection of the Island. All this time I had hoped that we might have goats, along with the chickens, to provide us with milk, butter and eggs. But I now saw that this would never be feasible and I resolutely made a decision and put a period after it, but it left me with a heartache of disappointment.

In former years real cold did not start until around Christmas, but all records were now broken. The unremitting cold stretched on for weeks, and filled me with an unbearable restlessness. There was so little for me to do now that my seed business was gone, and I had no interesting work. I couldn't do anything for Jack; I seemed only to get in his way. I had never been like this before in my whole life. What was the matter with me?

Day after day the tension between Jack and me tightened. I knew it was senseless. The suggestion that I had lost Jack came to me over and over. Could I ever win back from him what I had lost by my wild hysterical words? I was scourged by remorse but powerless to reason it out. I couldn't reason with myself so how could I reach Jack? I must do something. I had never been one to accept a situation without fighting, but what was there to fight? It was opposing a shadow.

All these things were going through my head as I awoke one dark morning. Jack's bed was empty, and I could hear him downstairs making breakfast. The stove lids rattled as he added wood. Flash yawned loudly, and he asked with mock solicitude, "Well, did you sleep well?"

I was not quite awake and a thought that suddenly came to me at first seemed part of a dream. I sat bolt upright in bed. I had the answer.

If we were risking our happiness and our love by staying together then maybe it was better for us to be apart. The thought of being away from Jack made me sick at heart—the summer when I first came had been miserable for me—but the more I considered it the more I realized how logical it was. One of us must leave, and the more I pondered the matter the more sure I was that the person should be me.

I should leave, at least for the time being, and go to Seward, where I could get work with the Army. Jack could take care of the home and do his trapping, while without him, there was little I could accomplish here. After a few months, I knew our perspectives would be changed, and we would be ready to face, together, the challenges that now seemed only to drive us further and further apart.

I decided it was best not to wait. I would take the plunge at once and not think of how terrible it would be to leave. I got up and dressed quickly.

Before I reached the bottom of the ladder I began, "Jack, I've been thinking it might be a good idea for me to go to Seward and work for a while." I must control my voice better. "My friend Mamie Elwell wrote me that there's a terrific need for office workers in Anchorage, and it's the same in Seward."

Two Against the North

Jack turned a pancake and did not look at me. The griddle was too hot and the cake began to smoke, but he did not turn it again, although he was giving it very careful attention.

I came close to him and leaned my head against his arm. I could feel his heart beat. Why couldn't he say something? "What do you think of it, Jack?" I asked.

"How long have you been planning this?" he asked, too quietly. He tossed aside the burned cake and spooned some more batter onto the griddle.

"The idea came to me just now. I'd only stay a few months." I didn't seem able to put my thoughts properly into words. If I only knew what Jack was thinking! I went on, "We'll have to face the fact that we must have money to buy the equipment we'll need when the war is over." I waited a moment for Jack to say something, but there was only silence. I added nervously, "I don't have enough to do since I gave up my seed business, anyway."

Jack's arm under my cheek was as unyielding as the limb of a tree. Again the pancake began to smoke, although his eyes were fixed upon it.

"You fix the coffee, dear, and I'll make the pancakes," I offered, and Jack allowed me to take the spatula from his hand. He replenished the fire but still did not speak. His silence was intolerable—my control was slipping.

I tried to force him to talk so we could get to the bottom of it. "You couldn't go and leave me here," I said. "I couldn't get along without you one minute, but you could spare me." I was talking too fast. Jack turned his back and stared out the window. "I'm just not accomplishing enough," I went on. "You saw wood and I burn it." Heaven help me, I was saying the wrong thing.

At last Jack spoke. "When do you plan to leave?" He turned toward me, his face wiped clean of all emotion.

I waited for a moment for strength and poise, then

answered quietly, "I haven't really planned anything; I thought we could talk it over."

"Would you like for both of us to go?" he asked savagely, his lips tight and stiff against his teeth.

"No. I don't think you want to go. You could stay here and I would try to make enough money for a few expensive things we need, and we could then depend upon trapping to keep us going. Wages are high, and we can't do as much here until the war's over." My voice faltered.

"You're right. I don't want to go and I don't intend to; I like it here. But if you want to go, I won't stand in your way." Deliberately he reached for his coffee cup, deliberately ate his breakfast. It was as if we were separated by a sheet of ice.

Jack spoke again, tightly, "If you're planning to go and not come back, you're a coward not to say so!" He jumped to his feet and rushed out of the house. I knew better than to try and follow him. I thought I had failed.

Hours later Jack opened the door and came in. He sat down in a chair and looked directly at me. The rigidity had gone out of him. "I'm sorry, hon," he said. "I'm ready to listen now. I think it might be just as well for you to get away for awhile. I . . ." He swallowed and did not go on.

"It's all right, dear. I know we're both on edge, and that's why I really think it's a good idea. You were foolish to believe I didn't intend to come back. My home and you are here. How could I think of not coming back?"

The tension disintegrated like fog before the rising sun. Jack smiled at me. "Do you want to go right away?" he asked.

"Oh, not for a while yet—not until after Christmas anyway. I couldn't bear to be away from home at Christmas."

Many days of arguments and suggestions were required before we decided how I would get to the Landing. I very much wanted to go alone. The weather, while cold, was good for foot travel; it was too cold for snow, and bears were in hibernation.

Jack was adamant, however. "This cold makes it danger-ous," he said. "You might fall and hurt yourself, and you'd freeze to death in five minutes. I'll have to go with you."

"Oh, Jack! If the fires are out twenty-four hours every-thing we have would be frozen. You can't do that."

"Well, I know the whole trip in one stretch would be too hard. But, you know, there's an old trapper's cabin on the trail, halfway to the Landing. It's pretty ramshackle, but you could have a fire and spend the night. I'd go that far and then come home."

I was deeply impressed by his ingenuity, but appalled at the demands he was prepared to make on himself. "Oh, Jack! That would mean at least thirty miles for you to travel in one stretch."

"It wouldn't be much farther than walking all the way to the Landing from here—that's twenty-six miles and I've had to do that in a day. I can stop at the river cabin on my way back for a couple of hours' rest, and then skate home."

The plan began to look feasible, and my spirits lifted.

"I know what we can do, hon," Jack added happily. "I can skate and push you in Mrs. Anderson's sleigh. That will be a big help."

I would have to wear my ski suit to Seward for I could only carry a little food and my sleeping bag. It would be necessary for me to buy new clothes. That would be fun—I had bought nothing new except rough outdoor clothes in the five years since we had come to Skilak Lake. Hairdressing styles had changed; I stopped snipping off the ends of my hair so that the hairdresser would have something to work with. I also mended Jack's wardrobe and tried to think of all the instructions I must give him.

Jack made excellent cakes, but had never learned to make bread, so I wrote out instructions for it very carefully. I finished my list with, "Caution: Do not allow the sponge to become chilled," and pinned it on the wall near the stove.

He was reluctant to try it under my eyes. "These instructions are simple," he said. "I don't need to practice." But I insisted, got the paraphernalia ready, and turned the whole thing over to him. Then I went for a long walk.

The sponge was in the warm oven when I returned. I restrained myself from peeking. Jack came in at intervals and opened the oven door, studying his work judiciously.

"How's it doing?" I asked.

"It's rising all right. I'll make it into loaves now and it will rise some more."

Much later he reported, "It hasn't risen as much as I wanted it to. I'll build the fire up—it'll come up in a hurry as the oven heats."

Alas, through some strange chemistry the dough appeared to have turned to dark gray rubber, and the resulting loaves were impossible to eat.

"Shucks!" Jack said, grinning ruefully. "I'll just have to live on sourdough hotcakes like Alec does."

"Jessie Anderson told me I would have to 'get my hand in' before I could make good bread," I said encouragingly. "There's something strange about it. I always did it the same way each time, and finally it just seemed to give in and agree to be good. We'll try again tomorrow."

"I'll waste so much flour," he complained, "the next thing I'll be carrying a sack down the trail on my back."

I, nonetheless, knew how important good fresh bread was, and I drove Jack on until, after many trials, he became master of the tricky dough. He was proud as only a newly successful cook can be.

Christmas was coming. If only we had a radio! I knew it was silly of me to want it so deeply, but it just wouldn't be Christmas without the familiar music. After I had mentioned this to Jack the second time and saw his face grow pinched with unhappiness at not being able to do anything about my wish, I was careful not to mention it again.

We had often been disappointed in the past when our

gifts for each other had failed to arrive and had found it more satisfactory just to make a simple gift or plan a small surprise. Jack's footstool of the Christmas before, made of a polished section of a birch log with pole legs, had delighted me and for two years I had made good warm pajamas for him. He was by now well supplied with pajamas, so I had to give serious thought to what I would make.

Jack was particular about his headgear. "My bald head gets cold easily," he said. When the weather moderated, however, he would need something lighter than the heavy fur hat that he had bought from Jack Lean.

While he was away checking his snares on the other side of the lake and had stayed overnight at the river cabin, I ripped up his favorite plaid wool cap. The cotton lining was as good as new but the soft wool material had fallen to pieces. I had a strong, heavy red wool scarf and cut it up carefully, using the old cap material for a pattern. Covering the visor was tricky, but I stitched it carefully, and was surprised myself at the success of my work.

Jack came home two days before Christmas with nine more coyotes. That made twenty-seven for the year. He was proud and deeply pleased.

On Christmas Eve the weather was calm and even colder than before—twenty-four degrees below zero at noon! I sorely missed the loveliness of the hoarfrost which had brightened all our Christmases before.

Jack came in as I trimmed the tree. "Do you feel like taking a long walk?" he asked. "I have to go to Art's place this afternoon."

"I'd love to. What are you going for?" Jack apparently did not hear my question.

We crossed the Point and walked briskly over the ice. There was a thin coating of snow on the ice that made walking good. Flash loped ahead, the fringe on her legs burdened with loose balls of snow. We swung along with our shoulders touching.

"I've been trying to think of a special gift for you," Jack said. "It occurred to me I might bring over Art's radio and batteries. I know he'd be pleased to let us use it." He looked out of the corner of his eye to see my reaction. "The batteries should still be good, and I can replace them when he comes back. Would you like that for a Christmas present?"

"It would be simply wonderful!" I exclaimed. "The nicest present you could possibly give me." I laughed happily, hanging on his arm.

I thought of Art and Cliff and all the fine young men who had come to the lake. They were probably spending Christmas in lonely foxholes somewhere and I prayed that they be guarded from harm and brought safely back.

Jack pressed my hand against his side as we walked. There was a warm current flowing between us, and it was Christmas Eve. On the other hand, maybe it *wasn't* Christmas Eve—I had been marking the calendar very carefully but I had been wrong before. I desperately hoped that this time I hadn't gotten confused, for I wanted to celebrate Christmas along with the rest of the world.

There was only a whisper of sound when Jack turned on the radio in the frigid atmosphere of Art's deserted cabin. "We can't tell until it's warmed up," he said, "but I believe it will be all right." He strapped the radio and batteries on his packboard. It was a very heavy load, and he had to set it down on the ice many times and rest as we covered the two miles home.

Jack placed the radio by the stove to thaw while he brought in wood and I prepared supper. I had remembered to provide a can of oysters for stew. If possible, it was what we always had on Christmas Eve.

As Jack connected the wires I held my breath. I could not have borne it if there had been only silence and disappointment. The answer came in a burst of choir voices, "Look now, for glad and golden hours come swiftly on the wing;

O rest beside the weary road and hear the angels sing." We stood listening entranced. The lovely Christmas hymn was followed by the heartlifting announcement: "This is December 24th, 1942—Christmas Eve."

Jack tried on his new-old cap, pulling it down over his ears and admiring himself in the mirror. "Gosh, I sure needed this. My old one is a wreck. How did you keep me from seeing it in the mail?"

I proudly explained that I had not bought it, and showed him how I had stitched it on the sewing machine.

Jack had a fancy box of chocolates for me and six big red apples that he had brought on his last trip to the Landing. "I had a time keeping you from seeing them," he said. "There was nothing else at the store."

"I'm so glad they're a surprise, darling," I answered, with my face turned. Jack might not understand that I wept because I loved him so much.

With the New Year came moderation in the cold, but only sufficient to bring snow—lots of it. "Already ten inches deep," Jack reported at dawn. I had never taken a long trip on snowshoes, and we seldom needed them at all. It would be foolhardy to try to go now. Nothing to do but wait!

All day, all night, another day, another night, the fluttering flakes drifted down out of the gray sky. I can't stop it, I thought; nothing I can do will have the least bit of effect— the snow will keep falling if it's going to, even if I become so impatient that I lose my mind. I tried not to give way to hysteria. I wished that I had not waited until after Christmas, but I knew I could not have borne to go before. I wanted to weep, but feared what that would do to Jack. The house was too quiet; I turned the radio on, then off. The depth of the snow limited my movements so that I could only walk the trails that Jack shoveled to the waterhole and to the rootcellar. He shoveled them half a dozen times a day.

The snow was an awful nuisance, but I assured myself

each morning on awakening that the weather would soon turn warm and the rain would take it away.

Instead, the cold was only collecting reinforcements. As soon as the snow stopped falling, back came the cold. The thermometer dropped to thirty below and seemed to be fixed there. I thought the thermometer must be frozen and brought it inside to thaw, but as soon as I put it out again it went plunging back to the thirty-below mark.

Heat from the inside of the house melted the snow on the roof, and long icicles hung from the eaves, lengthening until they reached the ground. Such tremendous ones formed along the eaves over the greenhouse the glass was in danger. Jack placed boards and poles under them and carefully broke them off.

The crust of the deep snow was not strong enough to support the heavy sledloads of wood. The sled sank into the snow and runners stalled. Jack started digging a sled trail across the bay—a back-breaking task in snow over four feet deep. I brought another shovel and tried to help, but it was such an effort to lift the shovelfuls to the top of the snowy wall my arms cramped severely, and I had to stop. Jack told me gently he did not need my help. It was slow work, but he finally finished it, and we hauled over a large quantity of wood he had cut. It should have lasted until spring, but we both knew that it would soon disappear.

Moose came down from the hills. The small birch and willow shrubs on which they normally fed were buried under snow. Now they obtained their food from trees overhead, raking down the limbs with their long forelegs and breaking them off and feeding on the tender twigs and buds. Moose were all around Jack as he sawed wood on the Point, and came like hungry cattle to feed on the limbs of the birches he cut. Half a dozen or more stayed around the house and slept in the yard. The light was dim even at midday so that the bulls, whose horns had dropped, could not be distinguished from the cows. One moose stood out bigger than the others, and I knew that it was Socrates. He would move away when another moose came near. None of the animals paid any attention to Flash, and after a while she no longer bothered even to bark at them.

Time dragged on, each day like the one preceding. The wind blew and it became a little warmer. A gale roared in the night, and next morning Jack's sled trail could scarcely be distinguished from the surrounding flatness. There were no trees around the house that were big enough for wood, except the scattered birches. I felt that without them the place would have no charm; and I watched to see if Jack considered cutting them, but he did not mention it.

I tried desperately to think of some way to help when Jack doggedly began to dig the trail again. The shoveling required a long time, and when it was finished, we brought over all the wood he had cut. Then, without stopping, Jack began sawing down another tree.

All through the next two weeks Jack and I were very polite to each other. We had promised solemnly not to let "it" defeat us again if we could help it. My own case was a record manifestation of will power. I was so mad at Jack because he would not talk that I longed to pound him on the head with a stick of wood, but I smiled and spoke softly. There was nothing the matter with me; I was perfectly sane. It was Jack who was unreasonable, pig-headed, selfish and many more detestable things.

No more snow fell, and the sunny skies should have been encouraging, but it was very cold and there was no change in the monotony of our daily routine. Finally one day a minor irritation got the better of me. Jack took some food on his plate, tasted it and pushed it away. I tried very hard to prepare attractive meals and thought myself a pretty good cook. I intended to ask what the matter was with the food in a relaxed, even humorous manner, but my voice rose to a screech at the end of my question. That so unnerved me that I could not stop. Soon I was calling Jack names—a torrent of words poured from my lips, a destroying avalanche of accusation.

Jack escaped outside, slamming the door behind him. There was a dead silence in the room. Black despair engulfed me. He opened the door but did not come in—just stood there and let the cold fill the room. Then he spoke, "I've been making the effort of my life to keep from quarreling with you, but you're just impossible. Don't blame it on the weather or isolation or whatever it is that you try to excuse yourself with. There's only one thing to blame and that's your miserable, nagging disposition." He closed the door carefully without slamming it, and I heard his boots squeaking on the snow as he walked away somewhere—probably, I thought, out of my life.

I sat on at the table thinking. I was guilty, but there was no use moaning over something that had already happened. I would start at the present moment and go on from there. No matter what Jack said, both of us were victims of this situation, and the situation could not be changed. It was just this that I had hoped to avoid by my departure, but the weather had prevented me. Now my will power had failed me. I must relax in my mind and not just refrain from speaking the bitter words that I felt. I must stop feeling like saying such things. How could that be done?

Humanly there was no way. I sank into despair. Suddenly it came to me there *was* something that I could do. I could remember that Jack was unhappy too and stop pitying myself. With this awareness all my anger toward him vanished away —I never had stopped loving him. Peace flooded my consciousness.

Jack was gone for hours. It was quite dark when I heard his step outside the door. The peaceful feeling stayed with me, and I did not dread meeting him. I did not expect him to want to talk, and, indeed, felt no desire to talk to him. We sat peaceably side by side on the couch reading until bedtime.

There had been much talk over the radio about the coming total eclipse of the sun. It was of unusual interest to scientists, it was said, and if war conditions had not made this impossible they would have come from all over the world to Anchorage, where the eclipse would be complete.

That February day Jack and I talked and acted normally toward each other while we watched the moon slowly obliterate the sun. No one could remain unmoved at the weird sight. The darkness at noon was very unlike the darkness of evening and was more than a little frightening.

Suddenly Flash barked loudly and rushed down to the shore. Two dots were rounding the end of the Point—two men on skis. We dropped everything and ran to meet them. What a wonderful surprise! It was Andy and Val, our first visitors since October. They came shoving their skis along, their wide smiles answering ours.

"God Almighty," Andy said, "I was glad to see your smoke."

Val was laughing. "I shut my eyes when I came around the Point—I was afraid to look." At seventeen he was taller than his father, a fine looking young man, with easy manners.

"You could never be as glad as we are to see you," I answered fervently. "This has been an awful winter."

"Was it a hard trip, fellows?" Jack asked.

"Not at all," Andy replied. "We spent the night at the river cabin. You see, Jack told us you were coming right after the New Year, Missus. We hardly expected you after the snow was so deep, but we couldn't be sure you hadn't started and didn't get there. Everybody at the Landing has been worrying about it."

"Jack!" I cried excitedly. "I can go back with them."

"No, no," Andy said, shaking his head decidedly. "The snow's awful deep in the woods. You must wait."

"He's right, hon, but it won't be long now—it's getting warmer." Jack had called me by his favorite pet-name. He had come back to me.

In the evening we listened to the news and the men talked about the war. I was busy with my own thoughts. I could send a letter by them to be mailed to my friend Mamie Elwell in Anchorage. A commercial plane might be willing to come and take me to Seward.

I interrupted the conversation to ask for advice. They all thought my idea a good one. At least I could try, they advised, but it wouldn't be easy to charter a plane now because of the war.

I put all this into the letter, and told Mamie frankly what I could afford. She would understand.

Andy and Val spent the night with us, but skied to the Island early next morning for a quick inspection before returning to the Landing. The letter they carried was at last a definite step toward my departure. More than ever I realized how important it was.

Art's batteries were not very strong after all, and we could not charge them with our wind generator. We conserved them as much as possible, only listening each day to one period of news.

A week passed, and another. Then came a friendly, encouraging message from my friend. One of the airplane companies in Anchorage agreed to send a plane to take me to Seward as soon as the weather permitted.

Now that I was committed, I almost regretted it. Why couldn't I have let well enough alone? Perhaps I couldn't get a job. If I did, perhaps I couldn't do the work. In those years on the lake I had almost forgotten what office work was like.

With separation so near, Jack and I were drawn close together. Sometimes in the night I would waken and remember. How could I have thought of leaving Jack alone? But in the morning I would feel better. Spring was at the door. Jack could get along easily in summer, and I resolved to persuade Alec to come next winter. I would not stay more than one year; I would be back by March 1, 1944—not a day later.

I soothed my qualms of conscience with good intentions. I would send a radio message every week. My first act on reaching Seward would be to obtain batteries for Art's radio and get them to Jack somehow.

Jack promised to keep a diary, not missing a single day, and send it to me whenever there was an opportunity. I wanted to know what he did each day I was away. I watched for signs that he might be glad to have me go, but that was foolish; we were together again.

In spite of all my mental preparations, the arrival of the plane shocked me. Jack had just come in from sawing wood, when suddenly there was a roar overhead and we watched a small plane, with skis instead of wheels, swing out over the lake for a landing. As it touched the surface it sent up a fountain of slush on each side and came to rest near the shore.

"Well, this is it!" Jack said.

I was terrified and looked out the window, wringing my hands. "Jack, I don't want to go!" I pleaded. He quietly patted my shoulder and went to fasten my bags, which had been packed for weeks. "Now, hon," he said, "we've made our decision and we ought to stick to it."

Jack greeted the pilot at the door. "Will you have time for coffee?" he asked.

"Oh, yes," the young man answered, with a broad smile. "There's no hurry at all."

Jack became busy with the coffee, and my thoughts went hopping about—I must not forget important things.

"Take anything you like," the pilot said. "Remember this is a chartered plane; it's at your service."

"I believe I'll take my typewriter, Jack," I said. "It might be very useful, and you don't use it." We had already decided that I should take my sleeping bag. Otherwise I would be traveling very light—after all these years I would have to buy almost all new clothes.

The plane was like an enormous mosquito waiting to take me away, its red sides and silver wings shining in the sun. Slush was knee-deep on the ice, so I wore rubber boots and carried my shoes in my hand. Love for my home and terror at leaving it almost choked me as I climbed into the plane.

Jack and the pilot brought my bags. I changed from rubber boots to shoes and handed the boots to Jack. Flash tried to scramble in with me and I held her close for a moment; then Jack pulled her away.

"I'll listen for your messages!" Jack shouted as the door closed.

The pilot fastened a safety belt about my waist. I didn't want to be fastened down so, for it kept me from turning around and looking back. "You must," he said. "There's danger without the seat belt." Danger! I had forgotten there might be danger in flying.

The motors roared and as the plane swung around I saw Jack, with his hand on Flash's collar, standing there in the bright sunlight gazing after us.

I did not realize we were in the air until the pilot nudged me and pointed down. Far below, the lake was dark, with pools of water standing on the ice. Soon the lake was gone and we were flying low between mountain peaks. They seemed close enough for me to reach out and touch them. Jagged, sharp, diamond-pure, dazzling in the sunlight.

CHAPTER 15

I LANDED IN Seward only twenty minutes after leaving the lake. It was as if I had been suddenly and magically transported from one world to another.

In Seward it was cloudy, with a cutting north wind—not a sign of spring anywhere. Sidewalks were obliterated by walls of snow, piled as high as I was, which lined the streets. Snowplows had cleared only the center of the streets, where pedestrians dodged the heavy Army trucks that lumbered along with rattling tire chains.

It was very exciting. Old friends welcomed me warmly; my leaving home to enter into defense work appeared very commonplace to them. They said I had been wise—everybody was working.

Before looking for a job I had to accustom myself to being among people again. I visited the beauty parlor and was persuaded to have a permanent. It made me look strange and was no improvement. I shopped for clothes, but was disappointed to find the stocks in the stores severely limited on account of the war. I also wore a whole size larger and my shoulders were broader. That's from rowing a boat, I thought. I did not know myself; it was bewildering.

I immediately got a very congenial secretarial job with the U.S. Army Engineers. Immediately wasn't the word for it; I was eyed like a piece of prize beef when I applied, and I doubt that they would have let me out the door if I had tried to turn the job down. It was a far cry from my experience back in 1938. The office manager had seen my wildflower book and asked me to autograph a copy for him; he seemed like an old friend. Quickly the arrangements were made. I signed many papers, had my fingerprints taken, and after a perfunctory physical examination at the Army hospital went right to work.

At first I stayed at the hotel. I heard that rooms were impossible to find, but my friendly office manager found one for me in a private home with a view of the water and mountains. I took my meals across the street, with half a dozen women and three hundred men, at the Army camp mess.

The familiar little town of Seward had changed fantastically. Olive-drab Army buildings were spread out on the hill to the north and Seward itself, gorged with defense workers, now straggled up the hill toward the post. The result was not beautiful. Flimsy, clumsy structures, appearing very inadequate in this rigorous climate, perched along the new streets. But man could never do anything to spoil the beauty of Resurrection Bay, with alabaster saw-tooth mountains forming a ruffle around the edge.

My first word from Jack—half a dozen envelopes bulging with his diary—was mailed from Kenai. I went immediately to the last entry to make sure he was safe and well, then started at the beginning.

"After you left," he wrote, "Flash and I went back to the house. She cried for a while, and I am not sure if I did or not, but the house was empty. Cut down a tree—did the chores—got supper—read—radio till bedtime." So Jack told me more effectively than he could have in spoken words that he had suffered at our parting just as I had.

As I read the day-to-day account I came to an entry that

made my heart jump with joy. "Alec came today for his boat; he gave up his job to go fishing. I don't trust him entirely, but he says he isn't going to work at a job any more and will be back here in August when the fishing is over. He is living with his wife again and wants to finish his cabin on the lake and bring his family there to live.

Later he wrote, "I have a wonderful idea. When Alec comes after the fishing is over, I will get him to stay here and take care of the place and I will come to Seward to see you and have a vacation." That was something to live for.

Jack had cut out pictures from magazines to illustrate a kind of poster. They missed me when doing this: a man in a pinafore stirring something in a saucepan, with steam coiling to the ceiling. But they missed me most when doing this: a man reading a book, dressed in a fancy smoking jacket that I could never have induced Jack to wear in reality—but I knew what he meant. It would be when the evening chores were done and the supper dishes had been washed, and there was no other sound but the singing of the teakettle on the stove. Floating over the head of a picture very much like Flash were the words, "Where has she gone?" I pinned the poster on the wall and cried every time I looked at it.

When he took up his snares at the end of the season, Jack wrote, he had thirty-one coyotes in all. His pride shone through the offhand words.

My work was pleasant; there were friends, weekends at summer homes on the nearby lake, the latest movies at the Army theatre admission-free; but I lived only to receive those bulging envelopes. Nothing could hold my interest as did these accounts of the simple happenings at home.

I never knew when to expect them, so the arrival of the envelopes was always a heart-stopping surprise. During the summer two months passed between messages. I snatched the envelopes from the messenger and tore them open. First I found the last date and read the words he had most recently written—I must know if he was safe. Then I stacked the pages like a manuscript, chronologically, and started at the beginning.

Jack had the garden planted and everything was under control. I had written that the kind of batteries we needed for Art's radio were not available. Jack reported the batteries in the radio were almost dead now. So far he believed he had received all of my messages, but I had better not send any more. It would be wasted effort.

I came to an entry telling me that Andy had been down for a brief visit. That explained how I had received the mail. Andy had brought him a great quantity of mail, including many letters from me. With him were some people who had just come to the Landing to live, a seventeen-year-old girl and her parents. "I may be mistaken, of course," Jack wrote, "but I have a feeling that there is a romance between the girl and Andy." I didn't believe it.

It would soon be time for Alec to come, I read. I probably would not hear again before Alec came; Jack would come on his promised visit as soon as possible.

Late one night when the rest of the household was asleep, I heard a knock on the front door. It was not my responsibility to answer, but I grabbed a robe and slipped down the dark stairs. When I opened the door, there stood Jack. He whispered, "Is it all right for me to come in? Should I go to a hotel until morning?"

"No, no!" I whispered in reply. "Come to my room."

We crept up the stairs so as not to awaken anyone and talked until dawn. Jack was with me again, and he was safe! I was freed from the constant, clutching fear that he was lost or hurt or sick.

I was granted a full week's vacation to spend with Jack. We visited friends and were invited to many dinners and parties. One host served cocktails before dinner. I felt no apprehension as to whether or not Jack would accept. The old bugaboo of alcohol had almost faded from my memory in five years and more. I don't believe I would have minded if

Jack had taken a drink but he refused it simply and without attracting attention.

When we were on our way home from the party I mustered the courage to say, "I was surprised that you refused a drink, Jack. Don't you care for liquor any more?"

"It didn't appeal to me," he said. "I thought there was no use developing a taste for it again after being without it so long." His tone was natural. He was not pretending.

A wave of intense gratitude swept over me. All that we had done was justified; our life on Skilak Lake had produced this big dividend. I would never complain again of hardships in the wilderness.

But now I wondered whether we *should* go back to the wilderness. "Jack," I said, when it was nearly time for him to return, "we have nothing at home now that we couldn't leave for a year or two. Why don't the both of us work until the war's over?"

"I've thought of it," he admitted. "But I hate to leave the place—I think we should hold onto what we have there."

"We could probably pack things up so they would be safe until we returned," I answered. "We're needed very badly—there aren't half enough workers. And we could go back," I added, "when the war's over."

"I don't know," Jack said. "If we left, I'm afraid we'd never come back. Besides, don't you know what would happen as soon as we left the place? Bears would break the windows. Hunters would stop there, and probably some irresponsible Indian would burn the furniture because he was too lazy to cut wood. No, hon, it would never be the same to go back to."

My heart was torn by the picture his words produced. I couldn't stand to have that happen to our home that we had worked so hard for. I agreed with him completely.

"I've been doing a lot of thinking," Jack went on. "I found that when I had spent months without hearing another person speak, I was able to straighten things out in my mind better." I waited for him to go on and he did so with difficulty. "The only thing I'm afraid of is that you have lost confidence in me. Can you forgive me, hon?"

"We acted like a couple of mental cases, Jack," I answered humbly. "We both had a bad case of cabin fever—it was just a bad dream. I'll forgive you if you'll promise to forgive me."

Jack answered me only with a smile. We understood each other.

Jack's visit lasted two weeks. Our parting was not sad, for with Alec staying the winter, Jack could come spend Christmas with me. That was only two months away and after that, in two more months, January and February, my exile would be ended. I was more contented than since I had left home.

Our mail came by way of Seward, where I now received it and forwarded to Jack any letters that might interest him. The mail carrier delivered it to Cooper's Landing every two weeks.

Art's letters were very infrequent, and I was happy to see one from him in the mail. It meant that he was safe until very recently, I thought as I opened the envelope. A clipping fluttered to the floor. I picked it up, and the shocking headline danced before my eyes, "Clifford Currin reported war casualty."

"Oh, no," I whispered, "not Cliff. It can't be true." I tore open Art's short note. There were no details. Art simply stated that someone had sent him the newspaper clipping, and that he was sending it on to us.

The terrible waste and desolation of war was brought home to us. That dear, fine boy, who had said he could not bear to shoot a man, had met his death through a Japanese bullet on some island in the South Pacific.

I forwarded the clipping in turn to Andy, and with a sad

heart wrote Jack that Cliff would never come back to Skilak Lake.

One evening, as I walked along the dimmed-out street, a voice called my name. I could not see clearly, but I recognized the voice. My heart leaped in my throat. "Why, Alec!" I cried. "What are you doing here?"

Alec's head hung on his chest, and he mumbled so that I could not hear him. I could scarcely restrain myself from seizing and shaking him.

"When did you leave the lake?" I asked.

"As soon as Jack came back I went to Kenai," he answered, and added defensively, "I took good care of things there while he was gone."

"I am sure you did, Alec." But what was he doing in Seward? "Are you going back now?"

He did not answer me directly. "I expected to be gone only a short time, but then decided to go to Anchorage while I was away and get a release from the War Manpower Commission." That sounded strange to me. Alec had never bothered about a release before. But I forced myself to let him tell it in his own way. "At Anchorage they questioned me about not working. I was afraid they might take me in the Army. I asked if I *had* to work, and they told me I would get in trouble if I didn't get a job. They wouldn't give me a release. I asked if I could work in Seward and they said I could do that."

"And you have a job here now?" I asked.

"Yes," he answered. He had told the whole story.

With each halting sentence, my hopes had lingeringly died. I didn't believe a word of his story. He had no doubt become lonely and bored while waiting for Jack to come back, and he wanted to be with his own people.

I longed to give up my work and get a plane and go home at once. I could not bear to think of Jack there all alone through the long winter with no radio. I suffered through an agony of indecision. What finally made me decide to hold out was the knowledge that if I could talk to Jack he would say he was all right, that there was no reason for us to change our plans, and that I should stay until my contract year was completed. I knew he would be disappointed in me if I ran home now. But Christmas without him was an agony.

I resigned from my work, effective March 1st. On that day my exile would end and I would turn my face toward home. I did not know if I would go by plane or walk the trail through the snow. It depended upon whether I could get a plane to take me.

The time was drawing near. It got to be the end of February—four months since I had held in my hands one of those bulging envelopes. And then one day I snatched six all at once from the hands of the messenger. With trembling fingers I slit the envelopes. Then I read the last line—written only four days before: "It has been tough at times but now I think only of your coming."

Blindly I made my way to the privacy of the rest room, fighting for self-control. I read here and there, picking up bits, starting at the end and reading backward. Dates were meticulously noted. He dared not become confused as to the time.

Girls came and went, looking at me curiously. I went into a toilet booth and locked the door.

"A week ago," I read, "I was sitting in my pajamas and bathrobe, reading, when I suddenly heard voices. I thought, 'Hold onto yourself, old man. This is serious.' I hadn't the remotest idea they were real voices, but Flash barked and I opened the door. There were Andy and his new wife and Val." That explained how I had received the mail. It was the first I had heard of Andy's having married. It was still hard to believe.

Without a radio and with no communication from the outside world for four months, Jack had not known that the season for trapping beaver had been opened on the lake. Andy was camping at Egyptian Bay and trapping on the other side.

"The first thing I asked them was if the war was still on. I thought it must be for the bombers are still flying over."

My tears were from gratitude that he was safe. I actually *knew* that he was safe. When I had time to read it all, coherently and in order, there were many pathetic records.

Jack told of his joy over the mail that Andy had brought him—a whole sledful. They had snaked their boat down the shallow, ice-choked river in order to use it in their trapping, so they brought mail that had been accumulating at the Landing for months. It would have been far too much to back-pack. Andy had found our sled at the river cabin and brought all the mail that night. Among the letters was the one I had written about Cliff.

There was an account of shooting a large brown bear on the beach near the rootcellar. Jack was loading wood in the boat on the Neck. It was about 4:00 P.M., already quite dark, and snowing. He saw an animal across the bay and thought at first it was a moose. "When I saw it was a big brownie, I knew it was very likely the one that attacked Unk. He mustn't get away. I sat down on the boat, got a good rest, and let him have it. He kept going although I knew I had hit him. I shot again and missed; again, and hit him. I knew he wouldn't go far, but it was getting very dark—too dangerous to go after a wounded brown bear in the darkness.

"Dec. 8—Clear and calm. I took another look for the bear. I followed his trail to the woods; saw no further signs and concluded he got to his den. I was sorry to have left a wounded animal, even a brown bear, to suffer. I turned back, and about fifty yards from the beach I found him—a big brownie. He may not have been as big as some but he looked huge to me. I came to the house and got a ruler. Here are some of the measurements: Height 4'7"; head 19" from tip of nose to ears; front paw 13" long and 7½" wide; skull

12½" wide. No wonder he looked like a moose when I saw him in the darkness. I saved some of the claws to show you —they were over four inches long." Tears blinded me. Jack with his careful measurements!

"Dec. 14—Still no ice on the lake. Sawed up and hauled over a spruce tree. The bay was very choppy and I followed the shore line but that was better than shovelling the trail and bringing the wood on the sled as we did last winter.

"Am sure that I have coyotes in the snares on the other side, but I can't take the chance of being caught away from home for three or four days. The wind blows and blows.

"Christmas Eve—Cleaned house. Made some Christmas fudge for Flash and myself. Wish I could be in Seward as we planned. Surely you have heard that Alec did not come back. I gave up looking for him after a while. It may be that someone has brought my mail to the river cabin, but I can't get it and it might as well be in Seward. My motor and boat are too small to depend on in this weather."

I hated the lake as I sobbed, "Couldn't you give him a chance? Why couldn't you?"

"Dec. 31—This has been the one day in many weeks that I could have made it to the river cabin and back. The water had been calm all day, and I would have gone but I had the meat to take care of. Finished butchering and initiated the new meat house—much better than hanging it behind the house.

"This is one night of the year when I long to be among people, lots of people. I wish I could be in Chicago walking along State Street with the holiday crowds. If Alec had come I would be in Seward with you. We would watch the old year out."

There were records of one hundred and thirty days. Not a day was missing. The first date was October 10, the last February 7.

CHAPTER 16

MARCH, 1944. I had been unable to get a plane to the lake, and for days I had been waiting eagerly at the Landing, held up by a heavy fall of late, wet snow. It thawed and settled with agonizing slowness and made travel over the trail to the river cabin impossible. Now at last it had reached a level which would allow passage over it on foot, and I was ready to set out for home.

Because of the weather I had not been able to keep my promise to return on March first, and each day's delay made the pain of absence all the greater. Jack's two-week visit had been months ago, and I had been away from the lake for over a year.

One of the men at the Landing had offered to go with me as a guide, and Charlie kindly gave us a ride to the beginning of the foot trail, saving a seven-mile walk. A year of office work had done nothing for my endurance; we tried to keep up a brisk pace so as to reach the river cabin before dark, but after a few miles I was flagging badly, floundering awkwardly through the snowdrifts after my long-legged companion.

I was kept going only by growing excitement and anticipation as we passed more and more familiar landmarks on the trail. My thoughts raced on ahead of my weary feet, each mile bringing me nearer home.

It was almost like old times. Andy was to meet me with his boat at the river cabin, and would ferry me across the lake. I was reminded of the first time he had taken me, six years ago, across Skilak Lake. What a lot of things had happened in those years! Jessie was dead; Cliff was dead; Andy had remarried. All of them had gone, leaving us alone on the lake. I knew that Jack and I had changed too—nothing was the same.

Tired as I was, I dragged myself down to the beach. I knelt down and drank deeply of the water from my hands. "Lake!" I whispered, "I've come back." I didn't care if it was cold and unconcerned. It was a familiar acquaintance, if not a friend, and Jack was waiting for me only a few miles across the water.

There was a note in the cabin from Andy. He had received my message and had been there twice—the last time only the day before. He promised to come often so that my wait would not be long.

I wiped soot from the chimney of the kerosene lamp, and when my guide brought in wood and made a fire I laid out the food I had brought in my packsack—a can of meat, some butter, a loaf of bread, and some candy bars.

Right after our simple supper I stretched out my bone-weary frame on a bunk, and covered myself with what appeared to be the cleanest of the blankets and my coat. My guide began snoring almost at once, but I did not really want to sleep and be unaware of where I was. Contentment filled my consciousness. It would be but a little while now until I would be there. Jack was waiting for me only a few miles across the water.

My thoughts were calm and clear. After my long absence it would be like starting again, but we had learned much.

The war had handicapped us but everyone said it would soon be over. In Seward there was a noticeable slackening of tension in the Army.

When the fighting was over the world would become normal and the boys would come back. At least I knew Art would if he survived. Others would come in time. Life would never be soft but we would not have to ignorantly trust in the unknown. We had been tried and *knew* that we could make it.

I thought of the times when Jack and I had succumbed to the frustrations of our restricted closeness in such a bewildering way and tried to hurt each other. But now I saw our mutual love was lying there under the debris like a vein of gold, surviving the acid tests, untouched in its purity. We would not falter again.

My guide snored on but I enjoyed arranging my thoughts in an orderly fashion. We would be more patient and not try to go too fast. We would enjoy each day and not work grimly and too hard to enjoy the birds and flowers in summer and the peace of the frozen winter.

Jack had learned to be self-reliant, and he loved this life just as I did. As for me, I would give myself in preparation for my seed business when the war was ended; I would be well prepared next time. I thought of the comfortable, beautiful home we would have there by the water, living close to nature in our beloved Alaska. This rugged land called to my inner being and I answered with gladness.

I lost consciousness only after the window had become gray with the morning light.

For breakfast my guide and I had oatmeal that I found in a bag hanging from a rafter and several cups of strong coffee.

Light snow was falling. "The trail will be bad if we have any more snow," he remarked nervously.

"Why don't you start back this morning?" I suggested.

"You don't have to stay with me. I don't mind in the least waiting here alone until Andy comes."

"Oh, I couldn't do that," he said. "You might have trouble by yourself." He obviously didn't relish the prospect, however, of getting snowed in at the lake.

An hour later the snow continued to fall. "If you expect to make it today," I said, "I think you should be starting. Don't worry about me. Andy will be here soon."

"Well," he admitted, "I'd sure hate to have to plow through three feet of snow."

"I wish you would go ahead. You can't depend on the weather at this time of year." He needed no further urging and left with evident relief.

I was quite glad to be alone. When he had gone there was only restful silence. I was relaxed now and my sleep was sweet.

In late afternoon I went for a walk to look for dry driftwood for the stove. Various trappers had been staying at the river cabin that winter, and there was no supply of wood by the stove as there had always been when Andy lived on the lake. The trappers were newcomers that war and the beaver season had brought into the country, and they did not understand the unwritten law that any visitor should replace wood that he had burned.

It did not snow much after all, and it was not cold, but dark clouds hung low. The kerosene burned out in the lamp, and for a while I sat with the stove door open so that I could have the light from the fire. I was warm and comfortable. Surely Andy will come tomorrow, I thought as I drifted off to sleep.

I awoke with the sun shining through the little window. It was a beautiful, calm spring day and the lake was covered with diamonds winking in the sun when I went for water.

All morning I walked the beach. I could hear the gulls screaming from the rocky islands where they would soon lay their eggs and hatch their babies. Toward noon there came a dull throb over the water. The sound was so faint that it could scarcely be called a sound, but I knew that it was Andy's motor. In a short while my eyes picked up the speck on the water. It grew bigger and bigger and the hum grew louder. Two figures in the boat waved, and I waved both arms in reply.

Andy was smiling happily when he shut off the motor and the boat grated on the gravel. I knew he was glad to be the one to take me home; he knew how much it meant to me.

A girl with long straight hair hanging below her waist stepped from the boat, and Andy introduced her as Carol. This was his new wife.

I suddenly felt overcome. "Oh, Andy, I'm so glad to see you!" I hoped they did not mind my foolish tears.

"Are you all right, Mrs. Sharples?" he asked anxiously.

"Oh, yes. I'm just so glad."

"I ran down toward Dawson Bay to see about the ice before I came," he said. "The whole Point's surrounded with ice. We'll have to land on the beach and walk. Will you mind?"

"Heavens, no! I would love it. When shall we start, Andy?"

"Right this minute," he answered, smiling at my eagerness.

The girl didn't speak a word after we shook hands, and stuck shyly to Andy. She was a head taller than I but she seemed little more than a child. I could not think of her as Mrs. Anderson—there could never be another Mrs. Anderson.

I begrudged the time it took for Andy to shove the boat off the beach. When he started the motor we could not talk above the noise. It did not seem possible that there could be ice anywhere in the lake on that almost summery afternoon. I felt glad it was spring when I was coming home —the loveliest time of the year.

Soon Andy pointed silently at a dark line jutting out into

the water from the shore. That was the ice—the Point was surrounded by it. I could see what appeared to be a channel through it that almost reached the shore.

"Could we follow that opening, Andy?" I asked, "and land on the ice? Then we would have only a little way to go."

"'Fraid not. The ice is soft and I couldn't pull the boat up on it." He pointed to a spot well down the beach. "We'll land there where I can pull the boat up on the gravel. We'll have to walk a ways. I'm sorry."

"I haven't forgotten how to walk, Andy," I answered, laughing.

When Andy tied the boat securely, we started walking toward home. It was perhaps a mile. I walked fast, ahead of the others. The very rocks and trees were familiar.

I saw a tiny puff of smoke far ahead. I thought it must be from Jack's pipe, but I could not see him yet. Then I saw him, sitting on a log. Why doesn't he come to meet us? I asked myself as I ran, terror choking me. There's something wrong! Then I laughed to myself. He was only waiting to see if Flash knew me; he didn't realize how he had frightened me. Then Flash was jumping on me, but I did not stop to speak to her.

Before I reached Jack I could see his haggard features, his sunken eyes. There really was something wrong! Oh, God, why did I leave him there alone?

He got up slowly and came a few steps to meet me. Then he dropped on his knees at my feet. I knelt and put my arms around him. "What is it, Jack?" I sobbed. "Are you hurt? Are you sick?"

"It isn't me," he muttered. "I'm all right. I . . ." he seemed unable to go on.

"Tell me, darling—tell me what happened. I don't care what it was if you're all right."

"God, it was awful!" Jack whispered, his weight sagging against me.

"I must know, Jack," I begged. "Tell me what happened."

"The house . . ." Jack shuddered convulsively, his hands over his face. "The house . . ." Finally with a mighty effort, he got it out. "The house burned."

"Burned?" I repeated after him stupidly. "There isn't any house any more?"

Andy and Carol had arrived and were standing near. Andy had heard enough to understand and asked no questions until Jack had recovered somewhat. Jack seemed to gain strength from our presence, and we all walked across the neck.

"Sit here on this log," Andy said, his voice full of compassion. "I'll go back and tie up my boat better. I may be quite a little while as I'll have to make a fire to signal Val that we won't be back tonight. Then I'll take you to the Island." He turned back with long strides, the girl trotting at his heels.

Jack sat down on an old driftlog and I chose a hummock of dry grass. I had not given any attention to Flash, but she came and sat on my feet, leaning back against my knees as she always had done.

"Tell me how it happened, honey," I urged.

Jack rested his elbows on his knees, with his head in his hands. He leaned on his arms and began to talk slowly and painfully. "I know it was March fifteenth," he said. It was the day I thought you might come. What day is this?"

"This is March eighteenth. Was it three days ago?"

"I guess so—I can't remember. It happened about three o'clock in the afternoon. I had made a fire in the heating stove and was sawing wood not far away, but my back was turned to the house. I remembered afterward that Flash came and whined—it was her feeding time, and I thought she was hungry."

"You didn't hear anything?"

"Not a crackle of flames or noise of any kind. When I

looked around, smoke was pouring out between all the logs and the whole inside of the cabin was on fire. "It must have caught first in the paper on the ceiling."

"And the water pails were in the rear of the room, and the lake was far away," I said, remembering that the stove was just inside the door, the only door there was.

"The green birch I've been burning makes creosote collect in the stovepipe," he said, and added dully, "It was always dangerous."

"What did you do?" I asked.

"My first thought was of the gasoline in five-gallon cans stacked under the eaves. I took time to move it. You see—" he struggled to swallow and then went on "—I still thought I could put the fire out. But by that time I could only reach inside the door and get my rifle. I reached through the flames and brought out an armful of coats from the rod near the door, but it was already so hot they were charred and burning, so I threw them back into the fire. I could see my can of tobacco on top of the bookcase and I broke the window and got it—it has helped me to be able to smoke. There was nothing more I could do, so I stood—" he stopped before the painful memory, "—and watched it burn."

I sat by him on the log and put my arms around him. "Jack, Jack, nothing else matters since you're safe." But he was not listening.

"I kept shutting my eyes, expecting when I opened them to find that it was dream. It was amazing how quickly it burned itself out. Night was coming and I had to have shelter of some kind. I could have gone to the Island but I was afraid you might come while I was away." He dropped his head in his hands and groaned. "What a homecoming for you!"

"I don't care about that, Jack," I said, trying desperately to think of something to comfort him.

"I wasn't even wearing a coat," he went on. "It was warm and springlike in the daytime but very cold at night.

Then I remembered the stove in the chicken house. It was very dark when I brought it and set it up in the tent. I made a fire and Flash and I stayed there; I sat on a box until morning."

"My dear, my dear!"

"I decided to leave before day and run over to the Island and get some blankets and a coat. I had a pencil in my pocket, so I made some signs and put one at the boat landing, one on the beach where you would come if you crossed the Neck, and one on the smooth beach at the end of the road where you would land if you came by plane."

"What were the signs for?"

"So you wouldn't think I had been burned in the fire when you found I wasn't there."

"No, Jack, you couldn't let me think that." When I saw the signs later, they twisted my heart.

"I ran all the way to the Island across the ice and all the way back. I took this coat and some blankets and some cereal and canned milk. But I couldn't swallow, so I haven't eaten since. I suppose that's why I feel so weak." His head drooped again. "Your furniture and all the things you loved so much! . . ." He choked.

"Don't worry," I said soothingly. "I loved them, but after all, the furniture was out of place here. Right now I don't seem to care about anything but that you're all right."

The sun had dropped behind the mountain and it was growing cold. At first I thought, I won't go up and look at it; I'm numb now and I don't want to come alive. Then I decided, I'll have to see it sometime; I'll look at it now while I *can't* feel. So Jack and I, with our arms around each other, walked across the ice in the bay and walked up the incline, along the trail.

We stood looking down at the heap of ashes, with pieces of metal and broken crockery visible here and there. The house had burned cleanly and there were no unburned remnants. Where the greenhouse had been was a hole half filled with melted glass.

"I can only think of what might have happened," I said, as we clung together. "It could have come in the night when you were sleeping in the attic; you could have been overcome by the smoke while you slept." I began to cry for the first time.

"That wouldn't have happened, hon."

"No. It could have happened in just that way. The only reason it didn't is that we're not asked to bear more than we are able." I stopped and struggled with the tightness in my throat. "If I had come back and found just ashes—and you gone!"

"That didn't happen, hon. Don't imagine things."

We were both silent for a while. Then I went on, "We'll build again; I'll carry one end of every log. We're pioneers! They always have trouble, but they go on . . ."

Jack's hand closed on my fingers and he gave them a little squeeze, but he turned away from me and looked out across the lake. "No, hon. I came to the conclusion, while I was waiting for you to come and couldn't sleep, that I wouldn't build another house."

"But, Jack, you won't always be alone. I know Cliff isn't coming back." My voice broke and I fought back the tears. "But Art will come. Someone will come."

"We should not depend on other people, hon. It never works. We would never have come here if we had known we would be alone. We must face the fact that we may always be alone. You know the government is soon going to make this into a game reserve and stop all homesteading. Only those who have proved up can stay."

"But we have demonstrated that we can make it alone, Jack," I answered falteringly. I was bewildered at the change in him after he had been so determined when we talked in Seward.

"I know, my darling, and that's a satisfaction to me. But we would be starting again from scratch and we can see clearer now. We must judge if the hard work is worthwhile, and we must think of the future when I will not be able to carry a pack on my back." He spoke with sad seriousness. "It isn't defeat; we would just be sensible. The fire has decided it for us."

At that moment Andy and Carol were coming up the trail through the evening dusk, and Jack and I broke off our conversation.

The others stood looking at the ashes with us. Carol came and put her arm around my shoulders. "I liked you the minute I saw you," she said shyly. I was deeply touched. Some instinct made her express her sympathy in this way instead of by saying she was sorry my home had burned.

The ice in the direction of the Island was still good, and we walked straight across instead of following the beach. Andy led the way, testing as we went. Jack stumbled occasionally as he walked by my side; he was half-dead with fatigue.

As we neared the Island in the gloom, we came to a wide expanse of water. It swept along the shore of the Island and appeared to continue on down the lake. We found we could not reach the Island over the ice after all.

"Your boat's on the beach, isn't it?" Andy asked Jack. "You must wait here and I'll go back and get it to take us across."

"Sure, the sled's on the beach too," Jack answered, as if he had wakened out of sleep. "I'll go with you."

"No, no. I think you should go back to the beach, but you must stay with your wife. Make a fire and wait for us." Already on his way, he repeated, "We won't be long."

It was only a short walk to the shore. We made a fire and huddled beside it, waiting. We did not talk now, and I tried not to think.

Hours seemed to pass before we could hear the scrape of runners on the ice. Andy left the boat at the edge of the ice and dragged the sled to the beach. A pale moon was now shining.

As we all got in the boat Jack picked up the oars, but Andy quietly took them from him. I concentrated on the way the dim moonlight gleamed on the wet oars, as Andy lifted them rhythmically.

We landed on the beach below the house. The gate was closed with a piece of wire that Andy had some trouble undoing. With his flashlight he led the way to the house along the flagstone walk, where patches of snow still remained in the shade of the shrubs on each side.

"There's dry wood," Andy said, as he unlocked the door. "We'll soon have a fire."

The damp, musty smell of a deserted house smote us. Andy's flashlight wandered about the room and when it found a green glass candlestick holding the stub of a candle, he lighted a match. He brought a kerosene lamp from the living room, and the light revealed the familiar kitchen with the palm trees.

The present faded away and I saw those who had lived in this house as I had seen them when they welcomed me the first day I came. I saw Andy wearing his red bandanna. Jessie's bulk filled the doorway and one hand fingered her skirt, as she smiled brilliantly through precisely reddened lips. An adolescent Val stood shyly in the background. Cliff was there too, standing in a corner apart from the others, his hands in his pockets. He looked as he did when I talked to him about Unk and the little geese, his expression serious and gentle, his hair springing up in twin cowlicks. They were all there, as they always would be as long as the house should stand.

"You make the fire, Jack," Andy directed, "and I'll go up to the rootcellar; there're some cans of food there."

When the fire was crackling, Jack took the pail and went to the beach for water. I looked in the cupboards—I was actually hungry. Mice had left their trails all over the shelves. I found a tin half full of coffee and a glass canister containing rice. How wonderful to find so much!

Just then Andy and Carol returned. "Here's canned moose meat and milk," Andy reported.

"And I found sugar in a covered jar that the mice have

missed," I said. "We'll have rice, with sugar and milk, for dessert."

Dishes and silver were just as Jessie had left them and I set the table. The aroma of coffee filled the air and drove out the musty smell. I carefully lifted the hardened fat off the meat and heated it in a frying pan before adding the meat to brown.

We were all hungry, and Jack ate ravenously. Andy opened a second can of moose meat so that Flash could have some.

No one knew what time it was, but there was a feeling that it was near morning. "My grandfather's watch was burned," Jack said suddenly. No one commented, but the announcement brought back a sense of tragedy which settled all around us.

Andy brought some bedding and spread it around the stove on chairs. "It'll probably feel damp," he said. He also filled a hot water bottle from the teakettle and offered it to me. "You'll need this too."

The bedding was still clammy, in spite of the hot water bottle, when we went to bed. I no longer shrank from sleeping in Jessie's bed. Poor Jessie! I was very, very tired.

Jack by my side, wearing grotesque long woolen underwear, murmured drowsily, "I had a terrific headache all the time until you came, and then it went away." His arms around me relaxed almost at once.

I was grateful for the hot water bottle, for my vitality seemed to have been drained from me, and there was no warmth in my body. It was good to have Jack there, so close and real and safe. It was good to rest, but I felt as if I never wanted to sleep again. There were tiny rustlings and sighs through the house as if it were disturbed at our being there. Flash stirred in a dream from the rug beside the bed and yelped softly.

At last I was alone and could think. There was one point that was clear and sharply focused: our life on Skilak

Lake was ended. There was no opposition in me once I knew what Jack wanted. He was always more realistic than I, and now he was the first to see that it was best for us to go. This was a man's world, where women were secondary. The work must be done by man's brawn; for all his strength and energy, Jack was past fifty, city bred and slight of build.

I wished that I had asked Jack more about his plans. But, of course, we would go back to Seward—that would be the logical thing to do. It would be a friendly place to go to, and good jobs would be waiting for us.

I still had not recovered from the suddenness of it. It was as if I had inadvertently stepped backward over the edge of a precipice. As I reached out for something fixed to hold onto, my thoughts turned to the reasons why our life here in the wilderness had meant so much to me, but already the reasons were receding into the past. There would always be interesting adventure ahead for those who look for it. The future held unlimited possibilities for Jack and me so long as we were together. He was here by my side now—safe! Never again would I be separated from him and live with the agony of constant fear for his safety. Henceforth we would meet every danger together.

But during the solitary months that he had spent alone Jack must have finished his work and learned the lesson that he had come to Skilak Lake to learn. With no one else to depend on, he found he could depend on himself.

I might have had doubts now if Jack had been able to drag a few things from the flames, but the destruction was complete. Nothing of our home was left—nothing at all! I thought of our possessions that had been destroyed, and a sense of crushing loss came to me; but I was now able to face their loss squarely. It had been easy to bring them down the river, but even if we had saved some of our things we could not have conquered the current and taken them away. We would have had to abandon them, or stay there and take care of them.

If we had been faced with the problem of what to do with our possessions, I would not have had the courage to make the decision. I might have weakly decided to stay because we were tied to things that could not be moved. But this was not part of the plan that fate had worked out for us. Our life on Skilak was not meant to be permanent. I saw more clearly at each turn of the wheel that it was right for us to leave. Even as I grieved for my lost treasures, I rejoiced to be free of them.

We awoke next morning greatly refreshed. Most of the ice had gone out while we slept and the lake was clear almost to the Point.

Andy lent Jack a razor, and when he had shaved, I cut his hair. "You're a sight, Jack," I said, as I snipped. "You could have cut your own hair; I used to cut mine." Below the bald top of his head his hair was thick and hung in a tangle to his shoulders. "You don't know how it shocked me to see you looking like this."

Jack grinned sheepishly. "I thought it would be a good joke if I looked like Rip Van Winkle when you came, but I can see now that it wasn't such a bright idea." He admired himself in the mirror. "I feel like a new person."

"What can I do for you?" Andy asked.

"You've done so much already I hate to ask," Jack answered. "There is one thing. My motor isn't working well, and I wouldn't like to start across the lake with it. Could you take us to the river cabin?"

"Sure. Are you leaving? You'd be welcome to stay here until you get another house built. I could bring some of the other fellows from the Landing, and we could soon put up a good cabin for you."

Jack's voice was very firm as he answered, "No, Andy. Thanks, but we've decided to leave the lake."

"Oh, I'm sorry!" Andy looked astonished. "I don't blame

you for feeling that way now, but I hope you'll change your minds later."

"I don't think so, Andy," Jack replied. "We think we really should move on."

Jack turned to me. "I would like to go back to the place just once." He then said to Andy, "There's a quantity of gasoline that I'd be glad for you to have. There isn't much else—the wheelbarrow, my axes and saws, the outboard motor and boat. I'll leave them there for you to pick up later. I'm glad for you to have them."

"Yes, Andy," I agreed. "I'm glad too."

"Do you mind going back, hon?" Jack asked. "I think we should try to clean the place up some. We can drag a lot of the junk out on the lake to sink when the ice goes out."

"Oh, yes, I'll go, Jack. I'll go and finish with it. If I'm afraid to look at it again I'll only take the fear with me.

Jack hauled away in the wheelbarrow all the debris we could move and dumped it on the ice far out in the bay. This probably would not be important to anyone else, but it was a satisfaction to me, and I was glad Jack had thought of it. We also carried off a pile of blackened tin cans that had the ends blown out. It was moose meat that Jack had canned all by himself so that we would have it to use through the summer.

I stood leaning against the scorched bole of a birch tree and gazed into the ashes. Here and there I could see bits of things I recognized. Those funny-looking curled wires were part of an innerspring mattress. I turned my head until my lips rested against the smooth white bark. The swollen leaf buds would never open; the tree was already dying of its burns.

We had arranged to meet Andy at a point on the beach opposite Egyptian Bay. It was as if we were starting off on a hike as we had done so many times before, Jack carrying his rifle on his shoulder, and Flash eager to be going. I looked back once as we walked away, but there was nothing to see. The place where the house had stood melted into the landscape.

Next morning at the river cabin we were up very early. It was scarcely daylight when we were ready to take the trail.

Jack emptied the water pail and turned it upside down. He made some shavings with his jack-knife as Andy always did. The next one who came to the cabin might need a fire quickly.

My own work was finished so I ran down to the beach. It was a gray, cold morning, with a threat of snow, but it would not amount to much so late in the season. With my hand on Flash's head I stood gazing over the water, listening to a low, moaning roar which came from the direction of the glacier. The lake frowned darkly, expectant of the wind. Soon the white horses would rise up and begin their wild galloping.

I heard Jack's whistle and, calling Flash, hurried to overtake him on the trail. His head was high, and he strode along purposefully. Jack carried a light pack and his rifle, and I had no burden at all. We were free.